THE COLLIER'S RANT

CROOM HELM SOCIAL HISTORY SERIES
General Editors:
Professor J.F.C. Harrison and Stephen Yeo
University of Sussex

CLASS AND RELIGION IN THE LATE VICTORIAN CITY
Hugh McLeod

THE INDUSTRIAL MUSE
Martha Vicinus

CHRISTIAN SOCIALISM AND CO-OPERATION IN VICTORIAN ENGLAND
Philip N. Backstrom

CONQUEST OF MIND
David de Giustino

THE ORIGINS OF BRITISH INDUSTRIAL RELATIONS
Keith Burgess

RELIGION AND VOLUNTARY ORGANISATIONS IN CRISIS
Stephen Yeo

CHOLERA 1832
R.J. Morris

THE COLLIER'S RANT

SONG AND CULTURE IN THE INDUSTRIAL VILLAGE

ROBERT COLLS

CROOM HELM LONDON

ROWMAN AND LITTLEFIELD
Totowa, New Jersey

Croom Helm, 2-10 St John's Road, London SW11

ISBN 0–85664–253–3

First published in the United States 1977
by ROWMAN AND LITTLEFIELD, Totowa, N.J.

Library of Congress Cataloging in Publication Data

Colls, Robert
The collier's rant.

1. Coal-miners – England – Tyne Valley,
2. Tyne Valley – Social conditions. I. Title.
HD8039.M62G736 1977 301.44'42 76–54154
ISBN 0–87471–941–0

Printed in Great Britain by Biddles Ltd, Guildford, Surrey

CONTENTS

ACKNOWLEDGEMENTS

This is my first book and on reflection there is a whole education of friends and teachers whom I want to thank for its making. The best teachers are friends and the best friends are invariably teachers and the following people are important as both. Charles Constable, Jim Blance and Gordon Blair at (what was) South Shields Grammar-Technical School I have to thank as first guides in the ideology of intelligence. Stephen and Eileen Yeo at Sussex University I have to thank as inspiring teachers and friends. Gwyn Williams, who originally suggested the book, showed me what history could be, and Dick Ellis showed me what society might be – and I am grateful to both of them. I am similarly grateful to my grandfather and uncle who have both shown me other (pitmen's) realities of history and society.

I have to thank Beryl Lawson for typing my original drafts into order and the Social Science Research Council for funding research of which this book represents one part. This book was written fourteen floors above the Tyne but its research was far and wide and I have to thank the staff of all the offices, institutes, and libraries which I visited for their help and efficiency. Professors Williams and J. F. C. Harrison, and Stephen Yeo were scrupulous readers of the text but its standing faults are mine.

Finally, my wife Rosie contributed to the making of this work in a way more than a mere Acknowledgement could say.

Woodford Green, Essex, 1977 R.M.C.

FOR MY PARENTS

THE COLLIER'S RANT

As me and my marrow was ganning to wark,
We met with the devil, it was in the dark;
I up with my pick, it being in the neit,
I knock'd off his horns, likewise his club feet.
        Follow the horses, Johnny my lad Oh!
        Follow them through, my canny lad Oh!
        Follow the horses, Johnny my lad Oh!
        Oh lad ly away, canny lad Oh!

As me and my marrow was putting the tram,
The lowe it went out, and my marrow went wrang;
You would have laugh'd had you seen the gam,
The deil gat my marrow, but I gat the tram,
        Follow the horses . . .

Oh! marrow, Oh! marrow, what dost thou think?
I've broken my bottle, and spilt a' my drink;
I lost a' my shin-splints among the great stanes,
Draw me t' the shaft, it's time to gan hame.
        Follow the horses . . .

Oh! marrow, Oh! marrow, where hast thou been?
Driving the drift from the low seam,
Driving the drift from the low seam:
Had up the lowe, lad, deil stop out thy een!
        Follow the horses . . .

Oh! marrow, Oh! marrow, this is wor pay week,
We'll get penny loaves and drink to our beek;
And we'll fill up our bumper and round it shall go,
Follow the horses, Johnny lad Oh!
        Follow the horses . . .

There is my horse, and there is my tram;
Twee horns full of greese will make her to gang;
There is my hoggars, likewise my half shoon,

And smash my heart, marrow, my putting's a' done.
Follow the horses, Johnny my lad Oh!
Follow them through, my canny lad Oh!
Follow the horses, Johnny my lad Oh!
Oh lad ly away, canny lad Oh!

(Published in Joseph Ritson's
The Northumberland Garland
in 1793, the song is much older than that,
though its exact date is unknown.)

PREFACE

This is an essay and rough at the edges, rather than a well-rounded thesis. It is meant to be exploratory and provocative; hopefully its blend of labour and social history will enrich both subjects.

Material

The song material for this essay was discovered, in the main, at Newcastle Central Library. The library has a substantial deposit of Tyneside songs from the nineteenth century, including original publications in book form, and bound collections of miscellaneous 'chapbooks', the contemporary paperback: cheap and commercial, romance and drama, laughter and tears, usually published for the plebeian market. Also it may be noted that the expensive hardbacks were often little more than edited volumes of chapbooks, representing a national debt of plagiarism, perhaps 'beautified' with some noble stanzas thrown in for the more respectable clientele. The Bob Cranky songs help us form a crucial thesis for the argument of the essay. Frank Graham, the Newcastle publishers, made the work easier by their reprints of John Bell's 1812 *Rhymes of Northern Bards* (1971) and Thomas Allan's 1891 *Tyneside Songs* (1972).

All the other evidences of cultural expression were found in libraries and record offices and other places far and wide during three years of research financed by the Social Science Research Council.

Objective.

When I came across the songs, I was beset with the theoretical problems involved in the writing of a thesis on the Durham colliery community in the nineteenth century. The crucial difficulty was the old one of class consciousness and the historian. On the one hand, there was dissatisfaction with what one may call the 'empirical' tradition in social history: many times reading not unlike a police statement, there is an unbending adherence to facts, albeit those facts at the historian's disposal. Here, a spurious objectivity is the scholar's pride; class consciousness comes and goes as the evidence dictates – and when it comes, it comes in the predictable shape of working-class political or trade union activity; when it goes, it goes when that activity subsides, and evidence founders. There seems an unwillingness to try beyond formal categories of evidence in a subject which needs it and demands it. Moreover, I usually had no sense of the context in which this activity was happening, felt in no way the texture of the seaman's or the pitman's life, could not smell the cauldron of coal, iron and steam from which Tyneside was forged and in which the action was situated. Thus sensuously deprived I read such history almost in a state of suspended disbelief where the actor flitted like a ghost: yes, that was a fact, but I did not feel it connected to any flesh and blood if it was to be an *historical* fact.

It is both the strength and the weakness of the empirical historian's approach to society that he tends to judge its elements independently. The strength is those symbols of Individualism and Tolerance, part reflected in a self-styled 'value neutral' sociology. The weakness is that society is atomised; it is seen as possessing essentially institutions, ultimately individual persons, of *original* character: perhaps affecting each other, perhaps not; there for comparison and relative criticism, but not seen in fusion and change.

So much for my dissatisfaction with 'empiricist' history: I wanted to go beyond conventional evidence and sources of fact, and, rather than dissecting society and pickling the parts, I wanted as far as possible to leave it a living, organic whole.

But, on the other hand, neither was there satisfaction to be found with 'left' or marxist-oriented history. The flag of true class consciousness is raised high, the actors of history approach it in varying degrees and are judged accordingly; often, those who could not see the flag are neglected or dismissed. True, relief was found with Edward Thompson's talk of the historian's task of imaginatively reconstructing the worker's experience, but generally speaking it seemed that the greater weight of 'left' history lumbered into a theoretical morass marked by Lukacs' distinction between 'psychological' and 'ascribed' class consciousness. Too often the concepts were used, not in vigorous and creative relationship with the historical evidence, but as ideological catch-phrases which had universal meaning and instant application. Apart from fashioning facile history, which was bad enough, I felt that this kind of approach systematically exploited the men, women, and children who had laboured and lived the past.

The ideological struggle within the 'standard of living debate' amongst historians is famous. A general impression of the worker's lot up to around 1850 from the 'pessimist' school is one of confusion and deprivation. It is here that the Bob Cranky songs shed their light. On reading the songs of Tyneside working people for this period, the sentiments are far from confusion and wretchedness: on the contrary, they are jaunty to the point of arrogance. Troubled as I was with the kind of problems outlined above, I felt these songs had revealed themselves at just the right moment – could there here be a chink of light for my difficulties?

So encouraged, I approached the song and more general cultural evidence gladly but the complexities involved in using it soon became apparent; suffice to say that interest deepened as did complication, and here is the result.

Personal

It would be dishonest of me not to admit that in the writing Robert Colls was invoked as well as Robert Cranky, and that the academic objective was only one manifestation of a *personal* quandary. To explain: I was born in South Shields, a shipbuilding, mining and engineering port at the mouth of the River Tyne. My father works in the shipyards and we lived in Eglesfield Road, one row in those groves of Tyneside 'flats' which jut away from the river upstream through Jarrow, Hebburn, Wallsend and Byker to Newcastle on the north bank and Gateshead on the south. I half imagined all of England lived something like this, until, in the sixth form, I read *The Uses of Literacy*, and in 1967 I went to Sussex University. Amidst bourgeois Sussex, the self concept of being working class came upon me for the first time. I had never before had this sense of being different, and I cannot say that I enjoyed the pleasure. But history had assumed a new importance; it now became a means of understanding myself and my roots.

Alan Plâter's *Close the Coal House Door* checked this new significance I had attached to history. I first saw the play in 1969 and was elated: the mining folk of my region celebrated as heroes! difficult and stubborn no doubt, but nevertheless unsung heroes with an epic history. I saw the play again in 1972, after my researches had begun, and was partly embarrassed. This time, I felt it did not celebrate a history so much as a mythology; that it presented to the audience an image which was self-congratulatory; that their enjoyment, and my enjoyment, and my motive to understand history all basked in the same self-indulgence. This was a painful moment: regional identity, class consciousness and the historian's role suddenly split away in different directions – where once they had been combined, they now stood repelled and wary of each other.

And with good reason. When the elements are combined, history can be varnished by a sense of the past which blends region and class into a mythical 'Geordieism'. This 'Geordieism' has truly known hard times, but with humour and togetherness has won through. Out of the past struggle has emerged an heroic sensibility made in our own image: to be proud of it is to be proud of ourselves. This pride can approach bitterness, and in the North East it consistently votes Labour, but it fails to carry its impetus beyond mere *reactions*. It fails to do this because the self-image which created it is locked in the past, it is about what we have been and what we have done, rather than what we are and what we will do. To enjoy it is natural, but merely to enjoy it is self-indulgent. The self-indulgence cheats us and history, but it also implies a condescension which cheats others. Liverpool or South Wales might push us close, but what about those poor Suburban Serfs (conveniently placed south of Hatfield) who have no 'language', who had no childhood, who – for goodness' sake – have no history! Not that the condescension is always wilful: first flat vowel dropped and the Serfs know a Geordie ('or are you Welsh?') for what he is – a 'character' with an enormous capacity for beer who might start to sing at any minute. This recognition of 'type' can be reciprocal: given his self-image, Geordie might need no encouragement to live up to it. Now, if we can accept a self-image today, then perhaps those before us could have accepted one then?

Moreover, the myth behind the image holds truth but not reality; the active image can thus refract the reality it lives in, and, if so, the historian's role takes on a new dimension. This new dimension must take serious account of the myth and the image and their capacity for positively changing reality. As we shall see, in order to accommodate his new dimension the historian must not only look to previously unconventional sources of evidence, but also stress a more *total* appreciation of empirical data in context. This realisation informs the whole of the essay.

But Bob Cranky has not been invoked to purge myth and image from history. The historian's notion of the past comes to him on so many levels of thought, feeling and experience that a purging of personal sense and conviction would kill what is human in a discipline which is *about* human sense and conviction. In the past itself, the role of myth and image bears a complex relation to reality. It can intercept the divide between the 'realities' of social relationship and influence their nature. Therefore, Bob Cranky is invoked for two reasons: firstly to underline the content of myth and image in history; and secondly to publicly exercise the creative tensions implicit in making sense of 'a past' which comes to one as a very complicated and self-contradictory challenge indeed.

One more point needs to be made. A. L. Lloyd and David Harker are the experts in Tyneside singing. Their respective works have been invaluable to me, but the use and presentation of the songs here is chronically that of an historian with all the apologies such an admission entails. For instance, I know there is a tendency to view the songs rather coldly, as mere expressions of evidence rather than things to be enjoyed – however, I do hope that an historian's view on the caches I did work at will prove useful, incursive and conflicting as it sometimes is.

Though an historian's view, this is not a history but an essay, and is not strictly chronological. The main period involved is the nineteenth century, though there are excursions both before and after those hundred years, cultural phenomena being no devotee of the time categories of the historian's card index boxes!

Felling, Co. of Tyne & Wear, 1974 R.M.C.

1 SONGS AS THESIS FOR THE MINER IN HISTORY

Second half of eighteenth century; three men produce nationally known and accredited song collections:

Reliques of Ancient English Poetry, *1765, by Bishop Percy*
Gammer Gurton's Garland, *1783, by Joseph Ritson*
Bishoprick Garland, *1784, by Joseph Ritson*
The Northumberland Garland, *1793, by Joseph Ritson*
Minstrelsy of the Scottish Border, *1802, by Walter Scott*

1790s: A growing interest in the 'manners' of the Common People. Also, Newcastle is the chief provincial centre for the publishing and printing of chapbooks and broadsides, and in 1804 and 1806 two publishers – David Bass of Newcastle and John Marshall of Gateshead – produce timely collections of local song: Bass' Newcastle Songster; or, Tyne Minstrel, *and Marshall's* The Northern Minstrel.

1812: Rhymes of Northern Bards *edited and published by John Bell of Newcastle (1783-1864): '. . . an early and vitally important collection, for its editor attempted to come to terms with a culture in which he lived . . .' (David Harker).*

1813: First meeting of Newcastle Society of Antiquaries at Turk's Head Inn. Founded after a suggestion by John Bell.

1840s onwards: The pub concert develops into music hall and a new arena of working-class life and culture emerges.

1870s: Beginnings of a national revival in antiquarian interest based in the regions.

1882: Northumberland Minstrelsy *edited and published by Newcastle Society of Antiquaries: '. . . for all its plausibility and smoothness, cannot possibly be held to be representative of any area culture, being, as it is, an "idyllic" amalgam of otherwise unconnected material . . .' (David Harker).*

1907: Publication of English Folk Song. Some Conclusions *by Cecil Sharp. Mr Sharp records the death of an English rural tradition and attempts to give 'true' folk song some definition.*

I. Dimensions of Social History

Oh, the collier lad is a canny lad,
An' he's aalwes of good cheor,
An' he knaas how to wark, an' he knaas how to shork,
An' he knaas how te sup good beor.

This is the boast. I have heard it sung in folk clubs from Tees to Tyne and many is the Geordie who, if not exactly a 'collier lad', has felt common identity, perhaps pride, on coming from such a swashbuckling heritage.

But how true was it of the miner? This is the essential question that this essay, making various approaches and spying from various angles will try to answer. It needs to be answered, because existing histories of the miner have failed to answer it, and that failure has made for a one-dimensional history where the actual thoughts of the men it purports to write about are ignored. Histories of trade unions abound, but because they are institutional histories the men in them are confined, forgetting that the institution had only as much scope and life as its members cared to breathe into it. In such histories, society implodes towards the institution, rather than the institution exploding out from society, from which it finds its life and colour.

If there is a general inadequacy in history in catching the working man, it seems there has also been breakdown in fiction. Raymond Williams presents us with a depressing trail of wreckage: Mrs Gaskell, in *Mary Barton*, moves towards the Manchester working class with a knowledgeable sympathy in 1848, but ultimately recoils at the point of violence. With *North and South* in 1855 imaginative sympathy has shrivelled and we are left cold attitude. Dickens, Disraeli, Kingsley and especially George Eliot all have persuasive insight, but in the end the stage is set for a miming of middle-class fears, rather than a dramatisation of working-class lives.[1]

For the novelist, Raymond Williams explains reasons for breakdown in empathy as he sees them. For the historian the prime apology must be the admission that in existing formal sources of evidence Everyman's voice is not raised very loud or long. However, in spite of source difficulties, the main problem has been *cultural* rather than technical. For example, in 1942 Sir Richard A. S. Redmayne described the Durham mining village of Hetton le Hole as he remembered it in the 1890s:

> . . . the discomfort and inconvenience of the dwellings . . . a lack of adequate water supply, one outside tap shared between several householders, communal ash bins close to the cottage doors, bad roads and a dreary outlook – for pit heaps dotted here and there, with their monotonous regularity of outline and colour, cannot be said to have other than a depressing effect on the landscape. There was also an entire absence of buildings of any comeliness – the church of drab yellow brick, or an edifice of wood and corrugated iron, the Methodist Chapel, perhaps a little more impressive, though also frequently of the same drab colour.[2]

This kind of description of Durham colliery communities as a genre begins around the 1830s and gathers pace during the century coincident with the middle-class reforming conscience. Redmayne was writing and remembering for his own purposes and the scene was undoubtedly true in his eyes. Such descriptive pieces are the stuff of social history; the historian gathers them in and can present a well-researched portrayal of the mining village and go on to infer what life there must have been like. The more sympathetic the historian the more likely he will inveigh against such monstrous conditions in which the Durham miner had to live: the back-to-backs, the outside tap, the primitive toilet facilities, the overcrowded cottage, the want of amenities of every kind.

In one dimension all this, whilst valid, is not entirely true. The outside toilet, a brick sentry-box with the wide throne of a 'netty' seat, was unhygienic and no fun on a winter's night, but of a summer's afternoon what delights it held for children! A makeshift puppet show with the door wide open and a curtain across the front? A shop counter or a fort? A reporter like Redmayne was surely a man of conscience, but he was also a colliery manager and an outsider. To him the buildings of Hetton were an array of ugliness in such a way that they could not be to the miner and his family. George Parkinson,[3] an ex-miner writing in 1912, admits the simplicity, *not* the ugliness of his Wesleyan chapel; a chapel that for him was a place of Sunday evening warmth and light, sharp drama split by emotion, chorus after chorus from a full congregation. It was the colour inside the doors that the outsider like Redmayne was not to know, or understand.

The mining village *as a place to live in* was of another dimension to itself as a place to study. Village life can only in the most facile sense be understood by assessing the number of indoor taps per pit row. Areas of community life were literally invisible to the nineteenth-century outside observer. To know them demanded an intimacy with the community itself: a wall or a back yard or a gable end were more than architectural facets, they might have held significance as meeting places for that community. The colliery village as a place to live meant a network of meeting places: Sunday mornings at the 'Colliery Inn' corner; summer evenings squatted along the gable end; regular, arms-folded chats in the sanctity of the back yard when the men were at work and toddlers were at your feet. The working-class territorial imperative, 'next-door', 'our street', 'wor toon', was rarely visible to the outside eye, it could only assume shape and form when that eye was tutored by a cultural rapport; without it, significant aspects of the miner's village were as ghosts to be walked through.

Cultural problems of this sort have in themselves produced technical problems of evidence for the social historian.[4] But this is no reason either to ignore the dimension or surrender the battle, the battle for a people-based labour history which sees the worker not as merely part of a block but with thoughts and feelings about himself that matter, not only to him but to history.

It is in this context that popular song and verse are neglected as a source for social historians. Though often ostensibly fictitious, and forever heavily biased, they can tell us much about the miner's aspirations and self-image.[5] The intricacies of the 'folk song debate' are an obvious issue in using such evidence and will be dealt with later, but initially two problems present themselves and raise a provision. The first problem involves the temptation to construct a pedigree working-class culture, latent within bourgeois capitalism and opposed to it. This temptation is seductiveness itself to the social historian of working-class institutions: these songs are of the class for the class, these songs are not – now then, what is the difference and what does it tell us? A theme like this would be crude, ignoring the inter-related wholeness of society, and missing crucial syntheses, points that I hope will become apparent as the essay progresses. The second problem initially presenting itself is a similarly easy temptation to take too seriously the words of the songs. To assume that the singers and the company believed every word would be fatal to the task in hand, and yet the conceptual difficulties in sorting this one out would be enormous.

This essay is not a piece of phenomenology, it is endeavouring to talk about men's prejudices, sentiments, mentalities, often only half-articulated, rather than about well-thought-out political, religious or moral positions. For some, they may have been brought to a nicety, for others, not so. Those 'sections' of the colliery community I am to talk about, say Methodists at one extreme and drunks at the other, are defined in a model polarity for clarity rather than accuracy. The essay's case, and its whole handling of myth, image and reality rest on this provision. The polarities refer to rough values, not to conceptually-sifted thought patterns. There will have been people at the centre of the two spheres (with more in common than they ever guessed!), people drifting to the margins, people shuffling between the two, people in limbo, others existing around other spheres not as yet discovered or simply inexplicable to the historian. With such a provision in mind, the songs of the pit community can be seen as firstly holding significance in their own right, uninterpreted, as much a part of the pitman's daily experience as the wage he hewed, the ale he drank. And secondly, as reflective of other aspects of his life, facts of existing, thoughts on living – at best an unconscious natural record of Everyman's reaction to the world around him, sung with no eye on posterity, to suit no one but himself and his 'marras'.

II. Popularity and Purity: the 'Folksong Debate'

The necessary provision made, and statement of faith declared, it only remains now to look into the Folksong Debate. This is an essay in history and it would be foolhardy to be drawn too far: however, much of the song material comes to us from various wings of that debate, and as history must be historical about itself, a summary of it should be made.

What is folksong? It was the Rev. Baring-Gould, Lucy Broadwood, Cecil Sharp (one is tempted to say the *Rev.* Cecil Sharp), and a number of other enthusiasts who first posed the problem around the turn of the century. They did more than this of course. Every Englishman is indebted to their patient collections and struggle for recognition, but they also insisted on an academic definition for folksong, thus launching a debate which is still with us.

Sharp had some peculiar notions of racial character and was strongly influenced by German writers, musicians and folklorists, especially Carl Engel who drew a smart distinction between *Volkslied*, 'national song', and *Volksthumliches*, 'popular song'. In a series of articles for the *Musical Times* for 1878, Sharp took the *Volkslied* concept for England, called it 'folksong' and began his operation to remove it from popular song which was diseased in all manner of ways, the main infection being a contamination of print. Sharp's hygiene test of pure folk song was oral transmission: evolving communally it is improvised, changed and chosen, continually complete, continually in creation, the product of a people's intuitive discrimination devoid of conscious writing: 'Folk music . . . is the product of a race and reflects feelings and tastes that are communal rather than personal.'[6]

And these broad lines of definition stuck. As late as 1954 the International Folk Music Council defined its work in a similar vein. Opposition was swelling however and found its champion in systematic form with A. L. Lloyd in 1967.[7] Lloyd views the quest for pedigree purity as 'a vain preoccupation',[8] challenges many of the myths surrounding acknowledged rural thoroughbreds, and generally sees the Sharpian concept with a ready historical eye as too clinical for the discipline.

Certainly, for our purposes at least, the Sharpian concepts are unsuitable. They are too limiting to help us in revealing the miner and his culture at a particular time, but, as will be seen later, concepts of this type need to be watched for they have influenced previous selectivity and sifted much useful evidence. Our purposes demand a thoroughgoing popularity; not so much to consider how a song originated, but who sang it, who listened to it and why?[9]

So, with popularity as the watchword, let us turn to the songs of our Newcastle Collection. The idea of some songs being significant in their own right is relatively easy to pursue for ancient local verse and doggerel. This verse is usually easily identifiable if its source was a serious antiquarian who would preface his discoveries with the required information. John Bell[10] and Sir Cuthbert Sharp[11] pioneered the collection of this anonymous verse for the North East during the first half of the nineteenth century. Cuthbert Sharp, for instance, acknowledges his gratitude to Ritson and Bell and defines his aim as 'to collect a few of those scattered traditions which are fast fading from the memory, and sinking rapidly into oblivion'.[12] This material is, however, a minority form and, originally stemming from an oral tradition, it tells the social historian little, being often obscure in origin and nonsensical in meaning. Doggerel does not usually inform, it merely is, standing relevant as a fragment of expression, a daily cliché.

Most of the songs and verses are not so much embedded inside the culture, but *about* it: how true a reflection are they? For whom were they written? Did they manage to explode into popularity outside that fixed group? And, ultimately, how much can they tell us of the men who sang and listened to them? The best way to penetrate these questions is to look at the North East's two most important nineteenth-century song publications: John Bell's of 1812 and Newcastle Society of Antiquaries' of 1882.[13]

The publication of the Society of Antiquaries' collection in 1882 came at a period when Northumberland and Durham were witnessing a broad revival of antiquarian interest, an interest simultaneous with the surge of town hall provincial pride, and parallel with similar 'nationalistic' tendencies in Scotland, Ireland and Wales. So many Memorials, Sketches, Notes, Features, Chronicles, 'Bygones . . .', Rambles, Reminiscences and nostalgic lectures seem to have filled the bookshops, newspapers, institutes and market stalls of the day. Previous pioneers like Bell and Cuthbert Sharp had also been interested in the dying ways of their own day, but had avoided a glib fascination for quaintness, a fascination which became love-sick for a mythical past – the warm, sickly gush which was the stamp of the revival. Now to these sober revivalists, parsons, schoolmasters and businessmen, genuine authenticity of 'true' folklore was known only to them. They were men stuffed with opinion, from God to Gladstone, but they were also Romantics, and when the twain did meet the result was disastrous. The Romantic trades myths, his choice of evidence is arbitrary and so is his history. The opinionated man knows he is right because he is really a crusader. Both strains were blended in the Society of Antiquaries' 1882 *Northumberland Minstrelsy*.

David Harker[14] has looked in detail at which songs were omitted from the *Minstrelsy*, a work which drew heavily, though ungraciously, on John Bell's 1812 collection. 'Footy' Again the Wall', a pitman's free sexual invite, was too ribald:

> The wife went down the Moor Lonnin,
> And let her basket fa';
> For when she gat to the Moor Yate,
> Play'd footy again the wa' . . .
>
> Young Cuddy is a bonny lad,
> And Robin's tall and sma';
> But if you come to wour town end
> They'll footy again the wa'.

'I Went to Black Heddon' and 'There was Five Wives at Acomb'

My Eppie I trow,
My Eppie I trow,
And I cannot get home to
My Eppie I trow.

were drinking ditties, and hardly the kind of thing to encourage amongst the chaps in a period when temperance had become respectable. 'Little Billy' and 'The Little Priest of Felton' were anti-clerical snipes, a split in the consensus of estates Jubilee England looked for, and anyway far too unprofound!

The little priest of Felton,
The little priest of Felton,
He kill'd a mouse within his house,
And ne'er a one to help him . . .

and little Billy (wretched boy), he finds the parson in bed with his mother! – surely a stiff shock for the upright middle-class Nonconformist of the day. For 'The Sandgate Girl's Lamentation', Harker can proffer no suggestion why this song was omitted, but perhaps her keelman-husband's cruelty clashed with the editor's vision of the Historical Working Man, especially at a time when the worker was being encouraged to spend more time with his wife in cosy fireside bliss than at the pothouse:

I thought to marry a parson,
To hear me say my prayers;
But I have married a keelman,
And he kicks me down the stairs.

He's an ugly body, a bubbly body, (Chorus)
An ill-far'd, ugly loon;
And I have married a keelman,
And my good days are done.

'The Ploughman', 'Walker Pits', 'The Collier's Rant', 'The Waggoner', it is argued, were too trade and class conscious to get past the editor of the Society's selection board, Thomas Bruce, an ambitious schoolmaster who had hopes of Liberalism and prudery for the new working-class electorate. These were not the only songs omitted, but they were each outstanding and authentic pieces of local verse and were known to be such: Cuthbert Sharp had prefaced 'The Collier's Rant' as 'a true pit song, which few singers can do justice to':[15] and John Bell had prefaced 'Footy Again the Wall' as 'a song much sung some Years ago, by the Pitmen about Long Benton'.[16] With omission these songs were lucky, Harker noting that every song taken from John Bell's 1812 collection was in some way treated to 'beautifying', 'standardising', and in 'making phonetic', 'Ma Canny Hinny' alone suffered twenty-nine alterations at the hands of the editorial board.

So much for the *Minstrelsy,* what then of John Bell's 1812 *Rhymes of Northern Bards*? In contrast to the intuitive and predisposed concepts of 1882 Harker makes a case for a more honest approach to collection at the turn of the century. The Rhymes he rates highly, given that Newcastle was a major chapbook centre, and that Bell – at his Newcastle quayside shop, fronting on to a bustling Hogarthian world of the city's most plebeian district – was in a perfect position to collect. Another striking contrast to 1882 is that Bell was publishing to sell and not preserve, had edited by popularity and not to satisfy a Romantic's dream.

For a social history we seem near our quarry: it would seem fair to conclude that Bell's selective methods will offer us a reflection of working-class life. But just at the moment we seem ready to make claim Harker denies us.

Whilst agreeing to leave the 1882 revivalists lolling in their pageant past and on the superiority of the Bell collection, Harker warns us that Bell's material was neither *from* working people, nor, crucially, was most of it *for* them. His arguments point a warning first at the rash of contrived 'dialect' songs appearing after 1806 which could never be popular with working people, ' . . . it would not be working people themselves who would need their language written down . . .';[17] and secondly he warns that the content of many of the songs would have been grossly unsuitable. Echoing Cecil Sharp, the argument is that songs which mocked the working class would never be their own; similarly for subject matter centred around ' . . . disembodied mistresses, patriotic hurrah songs, anti Tory satire . . .'.[18] Gently dismissing Bell's 1812 collection, the crux of Harker's thesis is that it was not until the 1830s and 1840s and the music hall tradition of Bobby Nunn and Ed Corvan that 'a spokesman in song' finally appeared for the Tyneside working class: 'It seems to me that if we are genuinely interested in the culture of working people, then it is this group of traditions that we should be directing our attention, on Tyneside.'[19]

If Harker is right, then the two most celebrated North East song publications, Bell's of 1812 and the Society of Antiquaries' of 1882 are unsuitable to our purposes of finding songs which were honestly popular and honestly reflective of working-class life and labour. Moreover, if such material does not emerge until the 1830s then we should expect to find distinctions in the idea of social relationship expressed between those songs of the early century and those of mid-century; between those of Bell and company's chapbooks, and those of the pub concert and music hall stage. We should especially expect to find significant changes in the 'dialect tradition', in the cartoon mockery of working people, and in the subject matter of 'patriotic hurrah songs'.

That such changes were not found will be seen in the next chapter's consideration of the songs themselves. And in that fact, the songs yield their prize to our social history, their insight into the pitman's consciousness.

2 BOB CRANKY THESIS: 1814

The Revolutionary and Napoleonic Wars with France had two relevant effects on North East society. Firstly, from 1791-1815 the region had a major cycle of capital investment which was led by the coal trade with reverberations throughout the local economy. Moreover, for much of the war the pitmen enjoyed some prosperity and the respect of a strong bargaining position. Secondly, the keelmen and seamen of Tyne and Wear as well as being important to the 'home effort' for coal, were also important to the 'war effort' in manning the ships of the Royal Navy. Both occupations had a tradition of effective labour organisation which was tested as war brought them into a context of inflationary prices, technological innovation, the impress service and bad naval conditions.

The post-war years 1815-20 saw profound national discontent. Mass unemployment and rising prices were accompanied by increasing Radical alarm and government repression. Manchester set the nation's mood, which the North East shared. Sporadic labour disputes amongst miners, ironworkers, keelmen and seamen had punctuated the radical agitation of Newcastle's 'Political Protestants' since 1815. The Political Protestants reached their highest influence in Autumn 1819, when, in the aftermath of Peterloo, labour and political unrest appeared to fuse. Working-class militancy had faded by December, to be dimly revived by Queen Caroline's popular claim in 1820, and to fade again in the relative stability of the 1820s.

Up to 1850 North East patterns of demography, output and investment pointed to the future, but it was not until after 1850 that the region's shift to industrial capitalism as the dominant system of life and labour was completed. By the 1880s the current mould of North East imagery had set: the heavy industries – iron and steel, coal, engineering, shipbuilding, chemicals; the big names – Bolckow Vaughn, W. G. Armstrong, Swan and Parson, Bowes-Lyon, United Alkali, Palmers; and the slatey terraced suburbs, with their landscape proletariat.

I. The Early Period Songs

To the uninitiated the printed songs about North East folk of the early nineteenth century appear as a rich store of authentic material for the social historian. As one reads on however, much of the style and content, as Harker warned, becomes familiar as a *conscious* form of writing. Suspicions are aroused with writers like Gibson:

> Roll on thy way, thrice happy Tyne!
> Commerce and Riches still are thine[1]

who could write songs of the flowing Tyne in grandiose Romantic fashion as well as songs of the humorous escapades of Tyneside 'characters' in rugged dialect. For the historian concerned with vivid insight it is a disappointment indeed to discover the dialect type to be as stylised as cheap Wordsworthian imitations of a Goddess Tyne.

Dialect

The obvious pose for dialect song was to write it in Tyneside slang and use all the correct sayings of the area: 'Smash!' is an exclamation used so much as to be almost the symbol of contrivance. William Mitford's 1816 'XYZ at the Races':

> Smash! Jemmy let us buss, we'll off
> An see Newcassel Races:
> Set Dick the Trapper for some syep,
> We'll suin wesh a' wor faces.[2]

'Marras', 'hinneys', 'man' are friends, some occupational trades terms are used, the rest is a racey Tyneside-Scottish:

> When aw pat on maw blue coat that shines so,
> Me jacket wi' posies se fine, se,
> Maw sark sic sma' threed, man,
> Maw pig tail se greet man!
> Od smash! what a buck was Bob Cranky.[3]

And just to show not educated men are we, 'dictionary' words are not only mis-spelt to catch a Tyneside tang, but they are also misconstrued. Selkirk's 1814 'Bob Cranky's Leumination Neet' celebrates victory in cock-eyed style:

> . . . Aw seed croons myad o' lamps blue an' reed,
> Whilk aw wad no like put on mi heed!
> 'G. P. R.' aw seed nex,

For oor Geordy Prince Rex; –
Nyan spelt it se weel as Bob Cranky.[4]

Neither it seems could our Everyman Crankys spell kaleidoscope, for in William Mitford's 1827 song the instrument predictably becomes a 'skellyscope'. But the funniest misconstruction is Robert Gilchrist's 'The Amphitrite' of 1824. This song concerns a bunch of keelmen, daft lads every one, who are, of course, unable to remember the name of the ship they must load, 'The Amphitrite'. At first they think it was 'The Empty Kite', then 'The Appetite', finally finding the ship after wasting a whole day punting the river for shipnames that did not exist. The song cleverly puns the dialect meaning of 'kite', a belly. After a long and riotous day:

Then into the huddock, weel tir'd they all gat,
An' of Empty Kite, *Appetite,* lang they did chat,
When the Skipper discovered (mair wise than a king),
Tho' not the syem word, they were much the syem thing.[5]

Cartoon

The second aspect of these early century songs is that the working man is seen as a peculiarity, and the brunt of it falls on the two most conspicuous social groups of the area, the keelmen and the miners. So conspicuous in fact that as characterisations they were interchangeable:

My bonny keel laddie, my canny keel laddie,	The bonny pit laddie, the canny pit laddie
My bonny keel laddie for me O!	The bonny pit laddie for me O!
He sits in his keel as black as the deil,	He sits in his hole as black as a coal,
And he brings the white money to me O.	And brings the white siller to me, O!

Both are bumpkins and 'reet charactors'; loyal, ignorant and generally drunk:

Of a pitman we'll sing
Who works for the king
Jovial, good natur'd, and civil . . .

they stagger their way from pub to race meeting, brawl to pantomime, in and out of love and work, endlessly offering up their salty observations on all things from Bonaparte to black pudding. A kind of Social Fool, they are not always so foolish and their words not always in jest. Bob Cranky's comment could sustain a serious theme. His 'Leumination Neet' sees him off to Newcastle to enjoy the sights, but they do not dazzle his eyes from the fact of high prices:

> Aw tel'd her what news aw had hard, man,
> That shuggar was sixpence a pund, man,
> An' good beef at a groat: –
> Then oor Nan, clear'd her throat,
> An' shooted out, 'Plenty for Cranky!'

But ' 'Twas a' lees', there was Peace but not Plenty. Cranky may not be 'se clever', but he knows his worth:

> Then agyan, what a sheym an a' sin!
> Te the Pit dinner nyan ax'd me in:
> Yet aw work like a Turk,
> Baith wi' pick, knife, and fork, –
> An' whese mair a Pittite nor Cranky?
>
> Or what cou'd ye a' de without me,
> When cau'd ice an' snow cum aboot ye?
> Then sair ye wad shiver,
> For a' ye're se cliver,
> An' lang for the pick o' Bob Cranky.

Cranky-ism was also invoked for disputes with the industry. A broadside of 1829, 'Great News for Pitmen', accuses 'an eminent Coal Viewer' of deliberately deceiving the recent House of Lords committee on the Coal Trade. The viewer is clearly John Buddle – indeed an eminent figure in the industry – and the broadside quotes chapter and verse of his contradictory evidence to the committee. The inevitable song follows the argument and with great good humour Mr Buddle is called a liar and a cheat: 'If it was not for the better Spirit of their Wives, as the Pitmen assert, they would sink under it – they commonly cheer them with a Local Song':

> Pluck up yur Pluck,
> Ye'll be Shure of Good Luck

Tell the Warld this honest Remark, Joe;
Ye'll give hard Wark for Breade,
Yur Family to feed,
And y only ax Breade for hard Wark, Joe.

When y can get that,
Then aw'll tell ye what,
Aw'll tell ye what Pitmen shud de, Joe;
They shud every hour
Pray for wur great Viewer,
Wur Viewer that NEVER tells lees Joe.

John Shield's 'Bob Cranky's Adieu', 'On going with the Volunteer Association, from Gateshead to Newcastle, on permanent Duty', shows Cranky's potential seriousness in the pay of the Establishment. But Henry Robson's 'The Colliers Pay Week' is more typical and tells of Benwell's pitmen on their fortnightly pay spree to Newcastle; the married men take their families and shop, the bachelor lads go in a gang and drink:

. . . Those married jog on with their *hinnies*,
Their canny bairns go by their side;
The daughters keep teazing their minnies
For new cloths to keep up their pride . . .

The young men, full blithsome and jolly,
March forward, all decently clad;
Some lilting up, *Cut-and-dry, Dolly,*
Some singing, *The Bonny Pit Lad* . . .

The drinking goes on all day until the gang, now more flushed than jolly, end up at a Quayside pub in the evening for a dance; soon a fight breaks out with some Willington young bloods intent on the same partners. The song has an exciting mood. You can see the sensual preening of the dance, hear the crack of heels:

. . . The damsel displays all her graces,
The collier exerts all his power,
They caper in circling paces,
And *set* at each end of the floor:
He jumps, and his heels knack and rattle,

At turns of the music so sweet
He makes such a thundering brattle,
The floor seems afraid of his feet.

John Leonard's 1813 'Winlaton Hopping' and the anonymous 'Wreckenton Hiring', from the 1820s, are in the same uproarious tradition, the wild extravaganza in a haze of baccy and beer:

. . . The fiddler's elbow wagged a' neet,
He thought he wad dropt off his seat,
For deil a bit they'd let him eat,
They were sae keen o' dancing, O:
Some had to strip their coats for heat,
And sharts and shifts were wet wi' sweet;
They crammed their guts for want o' meat,
Wi' gingerbreed and scranchim, O.[6]

Invariably the songs are humorous comic cuts and their heroes caricatures; the keelman is generally more roguish but bonny, the pitman a lovable oaf. Thomas Thompson's version of 'Weel May the Keel Row', greatest of traditional Tyneside songs, reflects this well: handsome, athletic, brave,

Whe's like my Johnny,
Sae leish, sae blithe, sae bonny,
He's foremost 'mang the mony
Keel lads o' Coaly Tyne . . .

A selection of titles, all before 1826, tells us enough: 'The Pitman's Courtship', 'The Pitman's Museum', 'The Pitman's Ramble', 'The Pitman's Dream', 'Bob Cranky's 'Size Sunday', 'Bob Cranky's Complaint', 'The Collier's Keek at the Nation', 'Bob Cranky's Adieu', 'The Pitman's Revenge Against Bonaparte', and even his dog gets into the act with Mitford's 1816 'Cappy, or the Pitman's Dog'. There are many more . . .

Because these men are caricatures the essence of the fun is not really to do with black pudding or body snatching or Bonaparte or whatever they deem to be cheeky about – but is directed inward, at them, and only partly by them; no matter what the subject, what they are about to say will be funny because they are clowns. A good example of this is Thomas Marshall's 1829 'Tars and Skippers'; in it, a group of sailors and a group of keelmen (with pitmen, it could be any combination of the three) separately contrive to protect dead comrades from the 'body-snatchers', horror-men of the time who would unearth corpses for sale to surgeons for anatomical research. In a graveyard scene, keelmen and seamen stumble into each other in the darkness, each mistaking the other for the dreaded 'Resurrectionists':

> . . . The tars, now alarm'd, they prepared for attack –
> Ower a styen byeth the skippers now fell on their back;
> O Lord! exclaim'd Jacky, we cannot lie here,
> Or we'll byeth be tyen off by resurrectioners, aw fear! . . .
>
> A signal for action – the tars gave a cough,
> To the skippers' amazement, a pistol went off –
> The skippers byeth drunk, now sober did feel,
> To get out o' their way, they byeth tuik to heel . . .[7]

Patriotism

A bowdlerised dialect, a cartooning of pitmen and keelmen, and the third ingredient of these early century songs is patriotism. It is a brittle, local patriotism, predictably mixed at the time with a wartime jingoism. These songs are, I suppose, broadly 'political', but Tory fanfares or Radical agitation, the appeal remains one of *true* patriotism. This transcendent appeal of true patriotism will require an explanation diverting us from the songs.

The peculiar evolution of the English state attached preponderant importance to the rule of law: the Magna Carta and the Bill of Rights had legendary significance. The framework of the English state as our early nineteenth-century Tynesiders knew it had been secured by the end of the seventeenth century, but in the political revolutions that had gone before it, the nation had been subjected to an unprecedented political education. The apologetic taken by the ruling class for the state out of this political whirlpool was a mingling of traditional mores about what it meant to be a Freeborn Englishman, and the civil rights and property individualism of Thomas Hobbes and John Locke. Without making any case for an intelligent consensus, these notions remained, until, under a growing pace of economic and social change in the late eighteenth century, catalysed by European Revolution and ultimately, war, there was class identification, and in the end, dislocation. The effect was an explosion of the nation's political philosophy into a thousand bits: of Englishmen's freedoms under a 'constitutional' Alfred the Great; of seventeenth-century doctrines on the sacro-sanctity of property; of the newer revolutionary theories of the political economists – Adam Smith at their head; and of the contrasting syntheses of Paine and Burke. Broadly speaking, political stock was taken in *bon accord* with class interests. There was contradiction in the process but by the end of the War in 1815 and in the depression thereafter, the three main contending parties, the radical middle classes, the inchoate working classes and the aristocratic establishment, could all advocate their apologetic in the traditional language of the rights of Englishmen under the law – *true* patriotism. It might be small farmers in Wales suffering enclosure or turnpike, or Yorkshire frame knitters suffering encroachments of machinery, or Durham miners suffering the incursions of a changing economy, but when they did protest, they did so in reference to the erosion of their 'rights' by 'unconstitutional' unlawful intrusion on them as Freeborn Englishmen whose Birthright was Liberty. There may have been Paineite, Owenite or Methodist rhetoric in descant to it, but that was the major theme – and remained so well into Chartism. Those 'rights', looked back to as practised in some Eden before the Fall (and who Satan was depended on who you were and where you lived), may have been mythology, but when believed and acted upon they immediately became real.

Such invoking of 'real' justice in opposition to stray justice, such rallying of traditional law for disruptive, *un*lawful acts can be seen in the Tyne seamen's strike of 1793. Capt. Peter Rothes, as impress officer for Newcastle, reported to the Admiralty on January 30 that the local magistrates were incapable of controlling the seamen's ceaseless parading and counter-marching, their speechifying against the wages and conditions whilst in His Majesty's service. And yet the seamen were loyal patriots; a petition of theirs declared that:

> . . . not being desirous to increase the Evils and Burdens which War always brings upon a Nation, and of which we have always borne, and are still willing to bear, the greatest share we are not so absurd as to desire that we should have the same Wages in time of War . . .

The seamen were 'still willing to bear' because they still nursed hope in their 'rights' of redress – Patriots and Redressers they lived:

> . . . under a constitution which we admire and venerate, and which has been the boast and glory of Britons in every part of the World; we are shock'd to observe, that though we are certainly neither less useful, industrious, or loyal, than any other part of the Community,

we alone are deprived of the Rights of personal protection.[8]

To return to our Newcastle songs: there appears to have been a wave of 'patriotism' during the 1790s, and another in the agitations of 1816-20. Bell's collection devotes over twenty pages to patriotic songs, little more than boasting doggerel, inaugurated with the impact of the Volunteers and lingering up to publication in 1812. Much of their philosophy calls on Englishmen with special freedoms to lay bare their arm and defend them from foreign despots. If it was God-given to be an Englishman, what a bonus to be a Tynesider! 'The Patriot Volunteers: or, Loyalty Display'd' is a superb example of this sentiment, written on the formation of the Newcastle corps of Volunteers in 1795:

> There is not in the world's terraqueous round,
> A better king or constitution found,
> Than Lov'd Britannia's sea girt Realms can claim,
> As rich in Blessings, as renown'd in Fame;
> Her laws, and Social Liberty, design'd,
> To perfect happiness, and dignify mankind.
>
> These to preserve, through each succeeding Age,
> Our Patriot Volunteers with zeal engage.
> Behold them brilliant on the shores of Tyne,
> Newcastle Heroes Gateshead Heroes join!
> All free-born Sons, they Freedom's Rights defend,
> And each to each secures a steady Friend! . . .

With a collaborator's sense of flattery, the pitmen are toasted in a song celebrating the opening of Jarrow Colliery in 1803. The worthy miners could always be relied upon to keep Britain Great:

> . . . These brave lads around us, their tools will lay down,
> And fight for their country, their king, and his crown!
> But the Frenchmen destroy'd, or drove back to the main,
> They'll take up the Pick-axe and shovel again.
>
> . . . Your glasses now fill to the lord of the mine,
> And drink him long life in a goblet of wine:
> On this joyous day let no bosom be sad,
> But bumper it round to 'the bonny pit lad'.

And if the bonny lad should fail us then there is his social twin, the keel lad. A song in Praise of the Keelmen Volunteers' sung to the rousing tune of White Cockade swells with more vainglory:

> . . . With spirits heroic and sublime,
> Our lads are brought up on the Tyne;
> They will our foes with sorrow fill,
> When once they sail from Newcastle:
> Where bullets fly and cannons roar,
> They'll sweep the seas from shore to shore;
> And all the world their wonders tell:
> Huzza, Keel Lads of Newcastle!

Nationalist patriotic songs of the period also remind us that the Volunteers were deliberately dazzling as a 'spectacular, attractive and continuous public demonstration of "loyalty" ',[9] the Establishment armed. In 'The Patriot Volunteers' the Freeborn myths are used for a crude jingoism, and there is much praise for coming out, showing your manly loyalties:

> Whilst snarling Disaffection slinks away,
> These HEARTS OF GOLD true loyalty display.

Moreover, that loyalty is summoned on grounds of a national covenant. Those who would not join the Heavenly Host and chose to slink away on their bellies are cast either as 'Ferocious Monsters', agitators and scoundrels everyone! or as naive prodigal sons, duped by others:

> . . . We have at home, alas! some secret foes,
> Which, well as Frenchmen, valour must oppose.
> Though savage TERRORISTS their Schemes pursue,
> And still mislead a blind ungrateful Crew . . .

Songs such as John Shield's 'Bob Cranky's Adieu' well show the colourful dash of the Volunteers, and the impact it made; the pitman compares his working clothes to the swaggering uniform 'A sougering to Newcassel' has provided for him:

> . . . It's but for yen and twenty days,
> The foulk's een aw'll dazzle, –
> Prood, swagg'ring i' my fine reed claes:

Odds heft! my pit claes – dist thou hear?
Are waurse o' wear;
Mind cloot them weel, when aw's away;
An' a posie gown
Aw'll buy thee soon,
An thou's drink thy tea – aye, twice a-day,
When aw come frae Newcassel.

That the Volunteers were a symbol of true patriotism is illustrated in the fact that the songs of opposition inveighed against them on the same moral basis as songs in their support: those qualities of manliness, a big-hearted boldness, a sonsy independence. John Shield's 'Blackett's Field' romped in the irony that a force so keen on martial display were forced to drill indoors to, as Bell tells us, 'prevent the crowd interfering with the evolutions of the corps':

For pity's sake, then, Ridley!
Thy *turnkeys* straight *discharge*,
And let thy armed Patriots
Again be drill'd *at large*:
So shall my Sunday afternoons,
In *gazing*, joyous flee,
When the brave Association Lads
Ar'n't under lock and key!

'Burdon's Address to His Cavalry'[10] cynically reviewed the bravery of the local militia involved with Britain's own fighting Tars, then unemployed and protesting in the Tyne seamen's strike of 1815:

. . . Now's the time, ye sons of Mars,
You've to conquer British tars . . .

But my lads, be not alarm'd,
You've to fight with men unarm'd,
Who in multitudes have swarm'd.
We will make them flee.
Come, then, my noble sons of Tyne,
And let your valour nobly shine;
There at last has come a time
To show your bravery.

And by 1819, Peterloo fuelling the flames and the district in the midst of a radical revival, the local Yeomanry are founded in the December and are derisively nicknamed 'noodles'. With them it is all pomp and no circumstance; they have no one to fight, but cut a fine figure of sham manhood:

> What a pity they cannot get medals to buy
> It greatly would add to their grandeur:
> 'There's Waterloo soldiers!' the strangers would cry,
> And think Archy was great Alexander.[11]

But to be anti-militia was not the same as being unpatriotic. Many lines jeer the unquestioning discipline and peacetime spuriousness of army life but also swear loyalty to George and Constitution against foreign threat. In 'Coaly Tyne'[12] it is precisely those graces which saved us from overseas tyrants which are called upon to defend us from domestic ones. This song captures the whole spectrum: proud Englishmen, prouder Tynesiders and a muscular (true) patriotism. It accepts the need for an army when fighting France, but declares its constitutional redundancy when defending Tyranny at home:

> With courage bold, and hearts so true,
> Form'd in the British line;
> With Wellington, at Waterloo,
> Hard fought the sons of Tyne.
>
> When peace, who would be Volunteers?
> Or Hero Dandies fine?
> Or sham Hussars or Tirailleurs? –
> Disgrace to coaly Tyne.
>
> Or who would be a Tyrant's Guard,
> Or shield a libertine?
> Let Tyrants meet their due reward,
> Ye sons of coaly Tyne.

The analysis is typical with its eighteenth-century baggage of absolute 'goods' and 'bads' to be defended and attacked whether or not in accord with social realities – and there is no comparison between Napoleonic, Bourbon or Hanoverian tyrannies – but the writer is groping towards an understanding of the army's domestic role.

The songs of 1816-20 in the Newcastle collection are mainly radical and more 'political', but remain in continuity with earlier themes: generally centred around reformist ditties, the extension of franchise, and the Queen Caroline royal soap opera, radicalism still appeals in the manly voice of a Tyneside upbringing and national patriotism. John Marshall's 1816 publication of 'The Gateshead Cabinet, being a small collection of songs by T.V.R.', and selling in chapbook form at 3d was obviously intended for radicals. Businessmen and bankers are the subject of innuendo – reminding us that long before working men achieved political franchise they could, in certain urban areas, exhibit a degree of influence in strikes or at elections by discriminating between retailers on the customary Saturday night shopping expedition. As well as songs of economic franchise, the Tyne seamen's strike of 1815 is supported as a debt of popular gratitude to our distinguished Tars, 'The corner stones they should protect that tars may get their right'; and Cobbett is toasted as too clever by half for his enemies in the Government. Also included as rhymes for radicals are, significantly, strictures on the demon drink, and notice of William of Orange's victory at the Boyne as a day in Liberty's calendar:

> When he landed he wrote, saying,
> I want not to reign,
> Give the people their rights, and
> I'll go back again.

A chapbook of 1820, 'The Wreath of Freedom or Patriot's Song Book, being a collection of songs in favour of Public Liberty', says it all in its title. Against Sidmouth's infamous Acts curbing civil liberties, the collection is a 'wreath', a snub to the traditional title, a 'garland'; and, as a 'Patriot's Song Book' we are reminded of that broader mentality of patriotism alluded to earlier. The sentiments of 'Dear Freedom' are classical *philosophe*, anglicised with Paine and made musical with Burns:

> We dare na meet, we dare na speak,
> We dare na sing, nor a' that;
> Our dearest rights we dare na' seek –
> We'll se them swing for a' that.

'Ça Ira' sings of:

Tom Paine, a true Englishman high in renown,
Shows that plunder's the system of mitre and crown . . .

whilst another tells Burke to 'be off!' and take his hacks with him. The songs are full of Reason, Truth, Virtue, Justice, Equality, Liberty and Knowledge. Philosophy, in right *praxis* fashion is espied 'arming', Britannia once suckled Liberty's breast but has since lost Her nipple, Goddesses are smiling sympathy everywhere freedom is dared, and such sweet smiles are a tocsin to arms. 'The Progress of Liberty' confirms that particularly English loyalty to a Constitution.

. . . a structure sublime
Cemented with true British blood
Tho' besmeared with the rust of all conquering Time
Still its plans and proportions are good.

To Burke the very excellence of the English Constitution rested in its age and gradualness founded in balance through custom. This song, however, echoes the ringing temperament of Paine; he is as impetuous as impatient, there is not much reverence for the past, it makes only rust, let us steel ourselves and look to now. Other songs in the collection include the famous 'God Save the Rights of Man', and 'Rule Britannia', 'On which thy darling sons are slaves'. And even emigration, no freedom-ride in the 1820s, is cast within the romantic precedent of the Mayflower.

The Writers

Just as a postscript before looking at the songs of the later period, it is as well to consider what sort of men wrote these and like verses. Writers in the vein we have styled 'patriotic' tend to be more obscure for obvious reasons, though we have quoted from John Shield ('Bob Cranky's Adieu', 'Blackett's Field') and James Morrison ('Burdon's Address to his Cavalry', 'Newcastle Noodles'). Of these two radical patriots, Shield owned a Newcastle wholesale and grocery business, and Morrison was a journeyman painter. Another well-known radical, John Leonard, famed more for his 'Winlaton Hopping', was a Gateshead joiner possibly with private means. The 1891 edition of Allan's *Tyneside Songs* lists John Shield, John Selkirk, Thomas Thompson and Henry Robson as the area's exponents of dialect song during the early century. Although local men, they were not of the Tyneside *sans culotterie* of whom, and partly for whom, they wrote:

Selkirk was a clerk and failed merchant, Thompson was a successful timber merchant (he died of pneumonia after trying to save his stock from a flooded Tyne in 1816), and Robson was a respectable printer. Of other writers we have quoted, William Mitford ('XYZ at the Newcastle Races', '1814') was a shoemaker turned publican, and Robert Gilchrist ('The Amphitrite') a businessman-sailmaker. And such seems to be the mark of our early nineteenth-century bards; small businessmen, successful merchants, shopkeepers, publicans and artisans, the poorest probably being the occasional Quayside clerk or schoolmaster.

II. The Later Period Songs

A printed dialect, cartoon imagery and a ready patriotism; these are the trends in subject matter we have found in the songs of early century. What of those songs which came with the advent of music hall and its immediate predecessor, the pub-cum-singing room? With an emergent working-class self-awareness we might expect the songs of the 1840s to the 1860s to express a change in subject matter, at once more truly reflective of working-class life and expressive of a different approach to the idea of social relationship. Some of this does occur, but in the main the content more than resembles the earlier styles. The major exponents of early music hall, Bobby Nunn and Edward Corvan with George Ridley and Joe Wilson following, were more proletarian in their origin than their predecessors, class lines becoming more intransigent. Usually they had suffered disablement or were consumptive, but they were nonetheless professionals in a way that those before were not. And yet we find them writing in much the same style with many of the same mannerisms of the same cartoon types and misadventures as those who had written twenty to thirty years previously.

Dialect

Nearly all of their most popular songs are in Geordie slang, if anything, more overdone than previously. As in Corvan's 'Asstrilly; or the Pitman's Farewell':[13]

> Greet men may de a vast, man, but wor fine times thor past,
> man;
> Gosh! aw waddent leave wor canny toon, but aw's forc'd te
> gan away:
> So aw'll myek ne mair emoshun, but cross the salt sea oshun,

Where aw've a kind o' noshun when aw howk aw'll get gud
pay.

Difficult spellings are still beyond us: Newcastle Polytechnic becomes a woman, 'Polly Technic' 'Wiv a' her wonders in her train'; and Paganini the violinist becomes Baggy Nanny, a fiddler:[14]

An ootlandish chep seun appear'd on the stage,
An' cut as odd capers as wor maister's flonkey,
He skipp'd and he fiddled as if in a rage –
If he had but a tail he might pass for a monkey!
Deil smash a gud teun could this bowdykite play –
His fiddle wad hardly e'en please my aud granny, –
So aw seun joined maw marrows, and toddled away,
And wish'd a gud neet te the greet Baggy Nanny.

In a spoken section of another of Corvan's emigration songs, 'Asstrilly's Goold Fields; or Tommy Carr's Letter', Corvan would actually make burlesque of Keelman Carr's word difficulties. Carr is wilfully ignorant, a letter from him is dated, 'Melbourne, Octember, aw mean Septober the 35th 18 hundred en eggs en bacon', and reads:

Afore thou opens this letter excuse maw bad spellin': pens is varry bad here, en hoo can a body spell wiv a PHEMWHTN (pen). [Marcy (aside), what a lot o' letters he has for spellin' pen. What a *scholla̅r* he's turned, he must gan tiv a neet *skeul* through the day: aw shuddent wonder . . .]

The letter ends 'from yor Confectionate Brother' and we are in no doubt that the pit-keel character is as daft a lad as ever.

Cartoon

So keelmen are still in cartoon, and there is still free exchange with pitmen. Scores of songs continue to record their chaotic excursions and home-spun opinion. Corvan's 'The Kipper'd Herrin' begins:

'Boot pitmen an' keelmen thou's heard some queer jokes,
What wi' blunders, mistyeks, an' thor queer funny spokes,
For when we get a drop o' beer we're a' full o' glee;
Lads! we myek mony a blunder when we get on the spree.

– this spree involved poisoning a pit mate greedy with his herrings!:

> He tuik fower greet big uns yen neet doon the pit,
> An' he waddent let yen doon belaw tyest a bit;
> So a pennorth o' Jalup we put iv his bottle,
> An', lads! hoo we laffed iz it went doon his throttle.

Corvan really seemed to enjoy this kind of Bumpkin-on-a-frolic writing: 'Tommy Carr's Adventures in Astrilly' is the further exploits of our Tyneside Barry Mackenzie; 'The Greet Bull-Dog o' Shields' has two likely lads off to spend a week's wages; 'The Fishermen Hung the Money O!' is based upon the story of Hartlepool fishermen who were said to have hung a monkey as a French spy after a shipwreck during the Napoleonic Wars:

> They tried ivery means to myek him speak,
> They tortor'd the Monkey tiv he loud did squeak;
> Says yen that's French, says anuther its Greek,
> For the Fishermen then gat drunkey, O! . . .

and the 'Stage-Struck Keelman', in title alone, might stand as a parody for this whole cartooning style. Other songs like this and worthy of mention are William Dawson's 'The Pitman's Ticker and the Wag at the Wa' ' and 'The Pitman's Visit to Stephenson's Monument', and Corvan's 'The Jolly Keelman; or Tyneside forever'. George Ridley might have written the greatest of them all, the thunderous 'Blaydon Races', a song that seems to invite 'two black eyes and a broken nose', but Corvan's real rival in this genre is Bobby Nunn. Nunn's 'The Pitman and the Blackin' ', 'The Sandgate Lass on the Ropery Banks', 'Jocker, The Fiery Clock Fyece' – 'As aw cam staggerin' through the street' – are all superb examples, and in his 'The Keelman's Reasons for Attending Church' our jolly keeler's apologetics are predictably not pious!

> Aw just gan there te see the preest,
> An' hear the bonny organ;
> Aw'd suener hev a haggish feast,
> Or drink wi' skipper Morgan.
> Te tell the truth what myeks me gan,
> Wor maistor he's religious,
> He'll think that aw's a godly man,
> *An' mebbies raise me wages!*

And lastly J. P. Robson's 'The Use An' The Abuse; or the Pitmen An' the Preachers' must be included because of its pugnacious combination of mockery with shrewdness. The pitman is still there with all of his eccentricity, true, he likes to 'weeten his whussel', but that by no means stops him lending many a wise word – ignorant as he may be – on the subject of alcohol and teetotalism. His analogies are simple, 'Becaws a man's hung, mun we myek ne mair twine?'; his education is experience of life itself:

> Teeto'lers may jaw 'boot the drink as they will,
> An preach till they're black i' the muzzle;
> Maw feyther an' muther byeth lik'd a gud gill,
> An ther son, tee, maun wheeten his whussel.
> Gud yell has duen mair for te warm a man's breest,
> When Misfortin' hes cum wiv his hammer,
> Then a thoosan' dry sarmins frae ranterfied preest,
> That gets paid for his lees an' his yammer.

The cartoon can still turn Social Fool when the occasion demands it.

Patriotism

Chest-beating patriotism also remains, but by now there are no foreign tyrannies to fight, and class struggle has lost its flash and smoke to go underground. The result was that the expression of that patriotism changed. Songs are still written for the occasional industrial dispute, which is to be expected with a predominantly working-class audience, and famous are Corvan's two songs in support of the Tyne seamen's strike of 1851. Similarly Corvan wrote songs of protest like 'The Toon Improvement Bill', 'The Soop Kitchin' and 'The Rise in Coals', but they are essentially mild. The harshest he gets is in the latter, 'They ken hoo te swindel poor folks . . .', and his 'The Queen Has Sent A Letter', commemorative of the Hartley Colliery mass burial of 200 in 1862, is a simpering protest indeed. The change in the patriotism of the old radical kind is that it has lost its political edge. Patriotism has by now become more a trivial local jingoism than a social clarion call: the men of Tyneside are no longer scaring the French at Trafalgar and Waterloo except in retrospect,[15] instead they are now belittling the Cockneys with feats of strength and science.

Just how the Cockneys became the new clan enemy is difficult to conceive, but it is not surprising that an area which had experienced massive economic expansion over a relatively short time should develop strong feelings of regional pride. The new provincialism was grafted on to a tradition – as early as 1824 William Oliver's 'The Newcastle Millers' taunted London Boxers:

> The fancy lads that thou can boast wad tyek an 'oor ti tell,
> Let Cockneys tawk o' Moulsey Hurst, we'll crack iv Barlow Fell.
> Jim B - - n hez up te Lunnin gyen, ti show them hoo ti hit an' parry;
> But still we've bits iv blud at hyem, that for a croon wad box Aud Harry.

But by the later period songs are recording the Tyne's superiority over 'Lunnin' in all things from policemen to architecture, as in Nunn's 'St Nicholas' Church':

> Of a' the churches in our land
> Let them be e'er se braw,
> St Nicholas' of Newcassel toon
> Completely bangs them a'.

Robert Emery's 'surrealist' titled 'The Wizard of the North; or, The Mystic Policemen' tells of John Elliot, a Newcastle tailor turned policeman who found promotion in London. Londoners are again the target but Americans also find themselves in the fray and are cuffed for good measure:

> The Cockneyfied runners of Bow Street may pine,
> To think they're eclips'd by a son of the Tyne;
> Let them bluster like Yankees, but little we care,
> For wor Journeyman Tailor can make them all stare.

Thomas Thompson's early 'Canny Newcastle' appeared in John Bell's 1812 *Rhymes*. It is one of the first and certainly the definitive Tyneside piece of finger-at-the-nose provincialism: you may boast of London's golden splendours but how can they compare with fresh-faced Newcastle? By 1840 we have John Morrison's 'Canny Sheels' and regional jingoism gone mad. Shields, we are told, now jostles Newcastle to be conqueror of the Cockneys; Thompson had laughed at the Monument – Newcastle had shot towers grander! Morrison laughs at the Shot Tower – Shields has her lighthouse!:

They hev a bit place where they myek a few shot,
    Lunnun's Column tiv it's like a nine-pin;
And St Nicholas' compar'd wi' St Paul's an' what not,
    Wey its a yuven compar'd tiv a limekiln.
If their Shot Tower sae hee was placed on wor Sand End,
    'Side wor Light House to scraffle to glory;
Their journey to heaven wad suen hev an end,
    For by gox they'd ne'er reach the first story.

That the Shields of the time was a dirty and overcrowded sprawl along the riverbank serves to remind that the song was written for droll laughs, that the humour was self-mocking.

By the 1860s the patriotism of fearlessness in battle had been replaced by skill in sport. Victorian athleticism emerging, no one was more celebrated in the area than Bob Chambers, a puddler from Hawk's iron works, who was accredited as world rowing champion. He had a remarkable record contest, winning 89 out of 101 races, for six years holding the championship of the Thames, tantamount to national honours, and in 1863 defending that title from an Australian, Richard Green, to be acclaimed world champion. George Ridley's song, 'Chambers', in name alone invokes the solitary bearing of legend: a true Victorian Hero, he is honest and gives of his best:

Tyek Bob all in all, as Shakespere says,
    We'll ne'er see his like agyen,
He waddant de an unjust thing
    To hurt poor working men;
Win if he can, it is his plan,
    So get yor money on,
For whenivor he shows he always goes
    The whole hog or none.

The anonymously written (1863) 'Bob Chambers' portrays those envious Londoners as supporting the Australian challenger rather than our own Hammer of the Thames. After a bad start Chambers pulled away to win by a quarter of a mile:

The start was myed, away they went,
    Byeth strove wi' might and main,
But Greeny, lad, had little chance,
    For Bob began te gain;

And as he pulled his famous stroke,
The Cockneys a' luk'd queer,
But uz Tynesiders cheered him on,
An' shooted far near –

Sentiments of this kind did not stop at Chambers, they begin to appear as a common form of ode to local sporting stars. 'Honest Bob' was congratulated with music hall zest; Joseph Allison, a Weardale leadminer and hero of the flourishing Cumberland Wrestling circus in the 1860s, was celebrated in death with a Tennysonian balefulness:

Allison's dead, Allison's dead.
Around the dread words quickly flew,
The spirit of the valiant dalesman's fled,
The greatest wrestler it ever knew[16]

But it is Ned Corvan who takes the whole image of regional patriotism – out of athleticism by heroism – and brings it down to earth. His 'Wor Tyneside Champions' choruses Chambers' prowess but at the same time extends it into the hearts and muscles of all our men. Rowers like Harry Clasper and Chambers emanate from our river keelmen and the implication is that there are many more where they came from! There are runners and quoits champions galore, and

When pay-week comes, wor collier lads for the toon they a' repair,
Then ower the moor, an' roond the coorse, ye'll fynd them boolin' there . . .

Saint, wor famis champion, with his bold eye keen and clear,
Like leetnin' sends oot mighty thraws, the best o' men scarce near . . .

The beauty of this song is that whilst our national champions are hailed, our local ones are acknowledged, and both are transcended by the traditions, sports and customs of the ordinary men and women of the area that bred them.

Another aspect of such regional pride, more subtle and less braying, lies in the type of song which romances the place as full of spirit. In them the area's eccentrics – Blind Willy, Captain Starkey, Black Pudden Betty, Bugle-Nosed Jack, Cull Billy, Cuckoo Jack – all of them strange, some of them alcoholic, or lunatic, are lauded as madcaps and sages. They set the crazy scene; they lend Tyneside a rich rum flavour; they animate its innate spirit.

John Bell's 1812 collection has none of this. Though published when the town's greatest 'characters' were alive and kicking there are only two references to the most celebrated of them all, the ale house fiddler, Blind Willie. Robson's 'The Colliers' Pay Week' has a verse with a straight reference to Willie 'sat scraping' in a pub of call – this was a matter of fact and there was no felt need to romanticise it; and Thompson's 'Canny Newcassel' (a song of provincial boast, remember), resists any temptation to put Willie in a hall of fame. The only other song to a town 'character' in Bell's collection is John Shield's 'Cull, alias Silly Billy'. William Scott, or Cull Billy, lived in the lower part of Newcastle with his mother. Both were dwarfs and lived in poverty. It is pertinent to remember, in view of Billy's later celebration, that Shield's song about him originally appeared in the *Newcastle Chronicle* of August 1802 as a cry for human treatment of this, our Tyneside hero-to-be:

> Oft have they [the boys of the town] followed him around the street, beating and hooting him, as boys hunt a cat or dog; and yet no notice was taken of this, until one, more compassionate than the rest, stept forward and interceded for him . . .
>
> 'Whence those *cries*, my soul that harrow?
> Whence those *yells*, that wound my ear?
> 'Tis the hapless child of sorrow!
> 'Tis poor Billy's plaint I hear.
> Now, in *tatter'd* plight I see him,
> Teazing crowds around him press;
> Ah! will none from insult free him?
> None his injuries redress?

After 1812, the date of Bell's publication, there were vast economic and social changes astir. Disparate efforts to reform the culture, and ultimately the character of working people, followed in the wake of the 1815 peace. Moral stability, political order, work discipline, were codes preached and practised by men as different as Primitive Methodist pitmen and New Poor Law 'feelosofers'. This cultural revolution will be looked at more closely later, but for our purposes in this section, the period after 1815 saw a drive for respectability, for a cultural accommodation by working people of the new industrial and political order. The old 'picaresque hedonism' of traditional popular culture was under continuing attack, and such a cleavage was driven that the distinctions of respectability and unrespectability are the underlying propositions of the nineteenth-century English working class. And it was in this atmosphere of distinction, split and comparison, that characters of the Old could be increasingly distinguished as eccentric. Not that every working pitman before the cultural revolution lived the life of a Blind Willie with his daily quayside round of music and drink – far from it; but in the new atmosphere such men were taken as symbols of what was disappearing, and the more it disappeared the more could it be unreal, unreal and precious.

The business seems to have begun in earnest with Robert Gilchrist in the 1820s. His 1829 'Bold Archy Drownded' laments the death in 1828 of Archibald Henderson, a river strong man and simpleton. All the characters of the day are there to comment – Bullrug, Golightly's Will, Nelley Marchy, Cull Billy, Blind Willie and Captain Starkey, though Starkey had been dead for six years! His 'The Lamentation on the Death of Captain Starkey' complements the affair with a tribute:

His gam is up, his pipe is out, an' fairly laid his craw –
His fame 'ill blaw about, just like coal dust at Shiney Raw.

Gilchrist's 'Blind Willie's Singing' speaks for itself, and his 'A Voyage to Lunnin' sets them all squarely where they belong:

Farewell, Tyne Brig and cannie Kee,
  Where aw've seen monny a shangy –
Blind Willey, *Captain Starkey* tee –
  Bold Archy and great *Hangy*.
Farewell *Shoe Ties, Jack Tate, Whin Bon,*
  Cull Billy, and *Jack Cummin*,
And *Judy*, *Jen Baloo* aw'll sob
  Your praises a' at Lunnin

Thomas Marshall's 1829 'Blind Willie v. Billy Scott' is not content to leave the stars in array: Marshall instead pits them against each other and feathers are let to fly!

'Blind man, come, don't be so mulish,

If I'm silly, no doubt I'm not right;
You for to say that I'm foolish!
Thank God! I'm endued with my sight!'
'But, Cull Billy, what browt ye here now?
Nebody can say that it 's reet.
Gan away, or aw'll blind ye wi beer now,
For cummin te myek gam o' maw seet!'

'You stand on a groundless foundation,
What else can such as you think?
You indulge yourself in dissipation,
You are both blind and stupid with drink!'
Willie sat an' heard Cull Billy pratting,
Quite heedless tiv a' the abuse:
His hand on his knee he kept clapping –
'Cull Billy's cum fra the madhoose!'

However, it is William Oliver's 'The Newcassel Props' that best typifies these patriotic songs of the 1820s. Oliver sorrows over the deaths of known eccentrics and sees in it the crumbling of a town:

Oh, waes me, wor canny toon, it canna stand it lang –
The props are tumblin one by one, the beeldin seun mun gan . . .
'But cheear up lads, an' dinna droop', Blind Willie is still alive!

This tradition appears to have continued with those writers and singers of the concert music halls in the later period. Bobby Nunn wrote an obituary song for 'canny aud Blind Willie' and his 'Luckey's Dream' is for Cull Billy. As in Gilchrist's 'Bold Archy Drownded', the cortège is an illustrious one:

But Hangy luickt above them a',
He is see sma' and lang, man;
And Bobby Knox, the Dogbank ox,
Was sobbin' i' the thrang, man.
And Coiner, wi' his swill and shull,
Was squeakin' like a bairn, man.
And Knack-knee'd Mack, that drucken fyul,
Like a monkey he did gairn, man.

Whilst lesser writers like Robert Emery could still prattle about the old stars long after their deaths (like 'Mally and the Prophet' from the 1840s), writers like Nunn, Corvan and Ridley kept the tradition up to a contemporary pitch by inventing new romances. Nunn wrote of Bella Roy, a well-known drunk and street vendor, and Corvan in 1860 commemorated 'The Death o' Cuckoo Jack'. Cuckoo Jack Wilson was a waterman with an expert knowledge of the Tyne, which before the instigation of the Tyne Improvement Commission in 1850 was shallow and sanded in parts. His role was that of semi-official scavenger of the river, hiring his knowledge of its straits and his range of hooks, grapples, nets and tridents to those who needed them. A quick-tempered skinflint, Corvan acknowledges his 'character' with an elegy:

> In wor celebrated metropolis o' the north, Newcastle-upon-
> Tyne,
> A scullorsman leev'd, ca'd Cuckoo Jack, a genus o' the grapplin
> line . . .

and even Jack's son, scamp of the quay, had his own salute in another song:

> Bowld Sandy Bowes – young Cuckoo Jack,
> They shout as suen's ye torn yor back,
> 'How! where are ye gawn o' Sunday?'[17]

George Ridley's 'Johnny Luik-Up!' was of John Higgins, Newcastle town crier during the 1860s and 1870s with barking voice and bell:

> Noo aw propose when Johnny dies
> That they tyek oot one of his eyes,
> An' put it inte cock-eyed Tom that sells the pies,
> Then we'll niver loss seet o' Johnny.

and similarly Ridley's 'John Spencer' was of a man who (most of the time) delighted in being doorman for travelling exhibitions. Finally, Joshua Bagnall's 'Cuddy Willy's Deeth' of 1847 must be mentioned before we too slip into the Romantic ghetto of 'characterful' Newcastle. 'Cuddy Willy' was one William Maclachlan, a ragged simpleton beggar who contrived to play his home-made fiddle (a piece of wood and some lengths of string), from pub to pub. Maclachlan died in 1847 after being treated to as much brandy as he could pour down his throat in one evening. Bagnall's final verse is like any other of these songs and appears to forget that for amusement the man had been treated to his own death:

> But iverything cums tiv an end,
> An' so did bonny Will, man:
> Ne mair happy days he'll spend:
> He noo is lyin' still, man.
> He nivver did ne body harm,
> For a' he was se silly;
> The toon seems noo te want a charm
> Since it lost poor Cuddy Willy!

By the 1880s and 1890s provincial pride of the *Northern Minstrelsy* revival kind, alluded to in Chapter 1, continued to rejoice in the area's eccentrics of yore. But by now there is a difference. The 'characters' are sanitised; they seem to have lost their grotesque disabilities, their work-house backgrounds, their rags, for a new suit of jester's clothes; and they were always 'of before', in the old good old bad days. *The Monthly Chronicle of North Country Lore and Legend* for 1888 tells us of Blind Willie's '. . . sonsy, contented, sightless face' and the article begins, 'In the early years of the present century Newcastle was possessed of a motley group of eccentric characters whose peculiarities . . . afforded fruitful themes for the lyrical effusions of the local bards'.[18] An article on Cuckoo Jack puts them a generation away and stresses their harmless individuality:

> During the last generation, Newcastle, and the waterside district in particular, was wonderfully prolific in 'characters'. Most of these were well known by popular nicknames . . . Some of these individuals were merely 'eccentrics', with peculiar, and, generally, harmless characteristics, that caused them to be well known and sometimes notorious. Others, again, displayed special powers of mind or body, along with certain distinguishing whimsicalities, by which they gradually attained a popularity more or less remarkable and worthy of admiration.[19]

In fact, if it is 'distinguishing whimsicalities' that are in vogue, then the eccentrics are only rivalled in the *Chronicle* by the pitmen. In a special section on North Country Wit and Humour the pitman is repeatedly cast as both the object and the subject of situation jokes. Typical jokes are A Pitman's Appetite, The Pitman in a Fix, The Miner and the

Oratorio, A Pitman's Wife, and The Pitman and His Bulldog.

> A pitman was amusing himself with his young bulldog, when it seized him by the calf of the leg, and held on. The owner yelled, but on a friend offering to choke the brute off, his master, with an eye to the future of the animal, shouted, 'Divvent touch him, divvent chowk him off; let the beggar tyaste blood!'

Anecdotes like this are worthy of a Bob Cranky 80 years previously. The eccentrics and their songs started off as an aspect of regional jingoism, but they also fuse into the cartoon type for pitmen and keelmen, which runs through the length of nineteenth-century Tyneside singing. The eccentrics came to staff a second lumpen-column to the pitmen and keelmen. They, like the pitmen type, are seen as lending the area its flavour, and with the area eager for such tokens in a flush of local identity, they are hailed from the grave to be used as simultaneous characters, romanced in all manner of situations until it is impossible to know fact from fiction.

We can now appreciate that alongside the more sedate activities of the North East's mid and late Victorian Revivalists, its romantic parsons, businessmen and schoolmasters, the music hall brought its own chorus of regional pride. The Grainger, the Oxford and the Victoria can hardly be considered as contributors to regional antiquarianism, but instead stomped out – in dialect, cartoon and local patriotism – their own mythology of what it was to be a Geordie. This creature was increasingly unreal and by the 1880s was surely an anachronism. Cloth caps, quoits, whippets and brown ale chauvinism might have been nearer the mark for the late century, but that is our anachronism! Instead this Geordie increasingly looked to a Newcastle of the earlier period, full of character and animated cockiness, and as such, complemented in class liaison the Revivalist scholars of the town's middle class.

Chapter 1 ended on the speculation that the age of the plebeian pub concert and music hall would render important class-based distinctions in song from that of early century: distinctions, for example, in the dialect type, in the caricature mockery of working people, and in the idea of patriotism. We looked forward into the century for song we could identify as more thoroughly working class, but the truth is that its stars who tramped the boards largely remained within the tradition.

III. Bob Cranky Vindicated

How then do we view these songs as historical evidence? We begin by accepting thematic persistence, that the tone and sentiment of the works remains the same. Through the period of Bell and into the music hall a strong regional patriotism exists though there are shifts in style and, most importantly, the pitman remains an oft hilarious but always a canny lad. By the late century the canny lad atmosphere had frozen into a cliché and in some ways was not so likeable: an example of this is a pit poem by John Rowell Waller in *The Monthly Chronicle* of 1891. Waller ransacked just about every character cliché there was. The central figures are Geordie and Nan, straight out of Thomas Wilson's 1826 'The Pitman's Pay'. Geordie is a good worker who likes a pint and has been in many an accident but has always come up smiling; he is equally superb at bowling, buckstick, dancing, 'An' quoits – man', and is proud owner of the best greyhound in the north, a 'banty' cock and marvellous pigeons. Geordie is sixty-four years old and still going strong . . . age cannot tire myth. Secondly we remember that nearly all of the songs were written for entertainment. This is vital because it introduces a relationship between the song and its listeners. We cannot but conclude that they were sung because they were acceptable to the audience, and the principle of popularity for our purposes is incorruptible. If we accept this then we must infer that the miners, keelmen, seamen and other working groups of Tyneside must have actively enjoyed their role as celebrities, found, in fact, a self-celebration in their attested notoriety.

There is historical evidence that points towards this collective egotism. That the miner was a singer has been well established by all researches. Mrs Montague, a colliery owner in the Tyne Vale at Denton in 1775, was both entranced and relieved by the singing of her miners. She wrote to a friend of her 'black friends':

> I used to give my colliery people a feast when I came hither, but as the good souls (men and women) are very apt to get drunk, and when drunk, very joyful and sing, and dance, and holloo, and whoop, I dare not on this *occasion* [her husband had just died] trust their discretion to behave with proper gravity . . . I cannot yet reconcile myself to seeing my fellow-creatures descend into the dark regions of the earth: tho' to my great comfort, I hear them singing in the pits . . .[20]

In the 1850s an observer of the colliery districts could regret that although the miner's 'library' was scrappy to non-existent, often little more than the Bible and a few dog-eared tracts, 'it is a curious fact, indeed, that in England, the poor man's library frequently consists of a dream-book and a song-book'.[21]

But it seems that the North Eastern miner was more than a singer, he was an inveterate composer as well. Tommy Armstrong was 'the pitman's poet', a position of respect in the late nineteenth century coalfield. Armstrong wrote reflectively of the pit community, but certainly he was influenced by the music hall: the brand name of 'holy daftness' is there, as is the self-mockery, as is the interspersing of verses with comic asides directly to the audience. The responsibilities of pitman's poet were typically put by Tommy, 'When ye're the pitman's poet and looked up to for it, wey, if a disaster or a strike goas by wi'oot a sang fre ye they say: "What's wi Tommy Armstrong? Has someone druv a spigot in him an' let oot aal the inspiration?" '[22] So prolific were such men that challenge matches were arranged in pubs for the title of pitman's bard, when songs were made on the spot from random subjects suggested by the audience. In harmony with this singing culture is the miner's mania for rhymes and nicknames. In 1952 an eighty-year-old ex-pitman from West Stanley, Co. Durham, remembered:

> Making rhymes and songs used to run through the pit like a fever. Some of 'em seemed to go daft thinking up verses. Even us young lads used to answer back in rhyme. The men would get down, take a little walk, see what the last shift had done. The man who'd been working in your place had always left his smell behind him, and we'd even make a rhyme on that. One would say, 'Whe's been hewin' in maa place in the 'oors sin Aa've bin gan? Aa reckon it was aad Basher wi's lavender hair-oil on.'[23]

The first miners' MP, Thomas Burt, tells of his uncle Peter Burt, who for years was famous at his colliery in Northumberland for a particularly barbed verse he had made on a company official during the 1840s. On a lower level to the rhyming tradition, but still instructive, is the miner's art of nicknaming. A writer in 1942 looked back on his experience of Durham colliery life at the turn of the century: '... conferring nicknames on their companions on account of some peculiarity or characteristic, so that the surname often sinks into the soubriquet', reached for him the height of an art form.[24] These nicknames could be funny or vicious but are probably best when obscure. An unpopular deputy could find himself called 'The White Rat', a miner could be called 'Ducks' for no apparent reason – Seaham Colliery is called the 'Nicky Nack' for a million, equally definitive reasons. Redmayne remembers that in the 1890s *kaylobjay* in one Durham village was the nickname for a dandy. This stemmed from the presence of French prisoners of war in the area during the Napoleonic Wars – ample warning of what can happen to *quel objet* when translated by 'pitmatic'.

In the light of rhymes and nicknames it seems a fair hypothesis that the coalfield bard had no monopoly over the making of verse. It was instead an inherited and communal thing, symbolised in him. Certainly, that community seemed enchanted by folklore and myth, almost exclusively centred in occupational terms, and this is usual of conservative industries, especially mining, throughout Europe.[25] But what is clear is that the North East miner had his own tinge of instinctiveness, his own singing democracy founded in an enthusiasm to make music about mere scraps of daily life, a style which can be contrasted very well with the choir traditions of Welsh colliers. What is also clear is that the miner's self-celebration in song had a trait of humour that was consciously self-mocking. This should be easy enough to understand if one remembers how miners spent seven hours of every day. There was, and is, something punishing about the pit, a struggle against the earth, and in which the dangers of accident are too real to be realistically contemplated. In such conditions the only sane reaction is to swear and laugh. The swearing is loud, the laughter is self-inflicting; without it the miner would not be a miner for long. We have seen from the songs this element of caricature, and though few were written by miners, it seems natural that they should laugh with them. David Douglass, himself a miner from Wardley, Co. Durham, has written on this curious self-mockery, and in its drollness, its use of exaggeration to win a laugh; what he has written rings true:

> Sometimes a whole team of men will be the centre of a joke for years. 'Wi wadn't pay ye Mullergate men in washers or brass buttons.' A whole team of caunchmen might be met with a chorus of 'Crunch, tinkle, tinkle, tinkle' (supposedly the noise of a few small lumps of stone coming off their shovels), or a lazy individual 'Throw some breed aboot an' set the hens on scrattin' and thi'd shift mer stones than him.'
>
> Ah met some funny fellers when working doon below
> But Tony is the slowest man yid ever want ta know.
> He can shovel with one hand, with the other have a blow,

And shift more stone with hes hanky.[26]

(a song of Wardley Colliery)

This trait is a precondition of popularity for many of the songs, and reminds us that popular song is not necessarily reflective of reality in a simplistic way – the self-mockery was not masochistic. Popularity guarantees acceptance, not factual accuracy; and after that we must be prepared for a refraction of reality through those who accept the song's reflection of it.

It could be argued that because the North Eastern miner lived in social and geographical isolation he may have been somehow outside the fun that was made of him. It would, however, seem that this social 'isolation'; or at least sense of isolation, only reinforces the theory of self-celebration. Leifchild, in his report to the 1842 Children's Employment Commission on collieries for North Durham and Northumberland stresses that the pitman often displayed a feeling of being special in belonging to a hereditary closed shop, that, whilst it often missed the facts of the matter, was at least true in the miner's own estimation of himself and his community. Every observer of the colliery communities in the first half of the nineteenth century and well after, makes the immediate homage to the pitman as 'a peculiar race'. The 1842 reports cast him as physically, as well as 'mentally', peculiar; a local topography for 1856 says they are' . . . in every sense a peculiar race, and strange indeed is their manner of life';[27] Mackenzie in 1825 remarked that 'as the colliers form a distinct body of men, and seldom associate with others, they entertain strong feelings of attachment' and reckoned ' . . . that by an acquaintance with one of them a tolerably correct judgement may be found of the whole body' so knitted was their complete cultural sense.[28] The Newcastle Religious Tract Society in 1817 talked of the pitmen as it might talk of the pygmies 50 years later: 'Were there not numbers of persons in the neighbouring collieries yet inwrapt in moral darkness, as profound and opake, as if they had been reared in a heathen or pagan country?'[29] And Leifchild was so confused with them at first that he considered asking for an interpreter![30] As in the songs, this distinctive sense of the miner was paralleled by that of the keelman, who belong to '. . . an unmistakable body, and, like the pitmen, they have their songs, their odd stories, and their oddities . . .'[31] Also, as in the songs, their respective oddities, even appearances, were virtually interchangeable: in the summer of 1795, a Newcastle Volunteer called Thomas Purvis quarrelled with some pitmen in a beer tent while still in the blue tunic and red cape uniform of the force. With a curse, 'Here's the damn'd Newcastle Bugger of a Volunteer we'll do for him now', the hapless Purvis was beaten by the pitmen on his way home. They obviously knew who he was, but justice was confused by Purvis' uncertainty of who they were; throughout his deposition to the magistrates he refers to 'the said Pitmen or Keelman'! Similarly, in an 1812 letter to the Coal Trade Committee, William Potter referred to the need 'to civilise such eccentric mortals as pitmen and Keelman'.[32]

Not only was the collier and the keelman's collective ego-awareness a matter of words, they had also proved it in action. An alliance of keelmen and miners (worse still with the seamen) was the spectre that haunted their worshipful mayors and corporations of Newcastle throughout the eighteenth and well into the nineteenth centuries. The miners proved themselves the customary shock troops of English *taxation populaire*, and if the nineteenth century was to see a changed format with the passive strike, all the old intransigence remained, as did the notoriety: Lord Howick, debating the Pensioner's Arming Bill in an 1844 Parliamentary wrangle, claimed 'That the pensioners [ex-servicemen] ought to be well fed and clad, for it was quite possible they might come into conflict with strong athletic bodies of working men, for instance the Colliers!'[33]

If a cultural isolation aids our thesis, the notion of a geographical one is not defensible. Most mining villages were isolated but not remote. Industrial needs demanded efficient and direct transportation to the rivers, the Tyne to begin with and then the Wear and Tees, resulting in a crisscrossed network of waggon ways and later railways. The rivers themselves were also used. These means were freely, if uncomfortably, availed of by miners and their families on fortnightly shopping sprees into Newcastle and Sunderland markets. Newcastle was the pitman's Mecca where there was much more to do than shop. The miners were also famous lovers of the calendar of race meetings, fairs and wakes, high days in the popular culture of the time. Neither should we forget that capacity of nineteenth-century workers for walking. Miners' union mass meetings during the 1840s gathered anything up to 25,000 men and boys, at one spot, from all over the two counties, and such mobility was not peculiar to miners. If the villages were not remote, some of them were not even isolated. There was mining all along the banks of the Tyne up to Newcastle, and the miners of, say, St Hilda's Colliery at South Shields, were in no sense an isolated group. Shields was primarily a sea town, expanding and cosmopolitan, whose miners could never have been removed from their popular image as it was sung in the pot houses, fairs and concerts of the port.

To argue that the pitmen were a class apart in no way solves the difficulties of comprehending this strange phenomenon of a self-celebration that bordered on mockery, whose humour was integral to the dialect, whose dialect stood for a cheeky patriotism that meant much more than nationalism, or even provincialism. But there should be no need to search round it. The refracted images of the verse may have been zany and exaggerated, like fairground mirrors to make one laugh, but it suited its subject. The pitman, it seems, revelled in his caricature, and it is here that we can take our prize from the songs, our insight into the pitman's consciousness.

3 CULTURAL REVOLUTION

PART ONE: THE WORKING-CLASS CHARACTER

The industrialisation of the nation relied heavily on North East coal, and from 1800-41 output rose from 3m to 8m tons. (It would rise to a peak of 56.4m tons by 1911, but it was in the initial period that the impact of change was greatest.) The North East was the home of the modern railway, and it was there in particular that the railway investment 'mania' of the 1830s to 1840s was most closely connected to renewed enterprise in coal: between 1829 and 1843 the number of collieries more than doubled from 73 to 155. Coalface technology changed little so the trebling of output during the first half century was met by a trebling of colliers: from about 11,000 in 1792 to 32,800 by 1844.

But the process of industrialisation represented more than increases in tonnage and manpower. At first, industrial capitalism was a precarious force which threatened social stability with the impact of its economic and social encroachment. In an 'age of iron' the old cohesive juices of society were drying up in a blast of political economy and religious evangelicalism. New classes were being made as power shifted, and innovation replaced tradition as scale displaced community. The mood of a rural society was going just as surely as its people and its share of gross national product. As the craftsman lost his price and found his wage, then so did the collier lad lose his celebration and find his 'character'.

Only some pitmen accepted the Bob Cranky caricature. The rumbustuous 'canny' collier was not for all; some hated it and fought it all their lives. In 1842 one hewer, in the pits since he was nine years old, told the commissioners that many of his fellows were 'desperately wicked', almost heathen in their drinking and debauchery.[1] He was a Methodist Sunday School teacher. In March 1844 at Chester le Street in Co. Durham ' . . . resides a certain Collier, who used to play an instrument in the colliery band', who had left the flamboyant sinning of secular music on his joining the Methodists, for which he was promptly sacked from the company.[2] Not long before a Methodist miner had been sacked from his lay preaching because a brother believer had seen him playing quoits in a pub and directly reported the sin.[3]

The changes in the balance of economy and class power witnessed by the nineteenth century brought in their wake a cultural revolution. This revolution was spearheaded in the mining communities of Northumberland and Durham by the Methodists, Wesleyan and Primitive, who had the effect of splitting those communities into two groups. It is this process of cultural revolution, both crude in its effect and subtle in its chemistry, that this chapter will deal with.

I. Wilson and Chicken

The old order changeth . . . all the old patterns of social relationship, all the old expectations of social behaviour, were in dislocation. In verse, even self-conscious efforts to portray the miner as he was can be seen as soaked in the tempo and mood, thought and conventions of their age. The two most popularised of these are Edward Chicken's 'The Colliers' Wedding', first published in 1720 and in its fifth edition by 1778; and Thomas Wilson's 1826 'The Pitman's Pay', a real North Eastern favourite for the century. It is hoped that these two poems will illustrate the changes current.

Chicken immediately defines his purpose:

> I sing not of great Caesar's might,
> How brave he led his men to fight . . .
>
> I choose to sing, in strains much lower,
> Of collier lads, unsung before;[4]

This is immediately complemented by Wilson's opening lines:

> I sing not here of warriors bold,
> Of battles lost or victories won . . .
>
> I sing the pitmen's plagues and cares,
> Their labour's hard and lowly lot,
>
> Their homely joys and humble fares,
> Their pay-night o'er a foaming pot.[5]

Both poets were serious in their intention to write about the life and labour of the pitmen. Chicken's poem is a classic in accuracy and record: John Brand uses it as supportive evidence for nine separate aspects of weddings in his authoritative *Observations on the Popular Antiquities of Great Britain* (1777).[6] And in a letter of introduction to 'The Pitman's Pay', Wilson said, 'The following verses form part of an humble attempt to describe the manners and habits of the pitmen of this populous and important district. Nothing of this kind has appeared to my knowledge since the days of 'The Collier's Wedding' . . .'[7] And yet they are so very different. Chicken, a respectable schoolmaster and vestry clerk of Newgate Street in Newcastle, writes without shame or moral. His poem is a romp; ribald and saucy, it shocked the patriarchs of Victorian propriety. There is no guardedness about drink, the collier rarely graced a church, but Chicken is never sanctimonious:

> . . . rested on the *Sabbath* Day
> From ev'ry Thing but Drink and Play.
>
> . . . And thus the COLLIERS and their WIVES,
> Lived drunken, honest, working Lives.

The stages to the wedding are rapid, the courting is untutored: Tommy sees the lass from Benwell dancing at a hopping, and pounces:

> And all the young unmarried Fry
> Did strive each other to outvy;
> And wou'd on Hopping-days be drest
> Genteel and in their very best.
>
> . . . Then seiz'd her Hand, and being strong,
> He lugg'd the willing Maid along.

In rough style the collier declares his love and sets about proving it:

> Thus Country Squires and merry Blades
> Hug fresh unopen'd Chamber-maids;
> Will kiss them till their Breath blow short,
> To make them eager of the Sport.
>
> 'I faint, O! – Tommy cut my Lace,
> And throw my Apron o'er my Face . . .'
> . . . When those within can hold no longer,
> Because the Enemy is stronger,
> Make signal that they do surrender.

Jenny's mother is next sought for permission to marry; they find her spinning, and she is no pillar of respectability.

> An Earthern Pot with humming Beer,
> Stood on a Table very near;
> For she would funk, smoke, fart, and drink,
> And sometimes raise a hellish stink.

> [she] . . . reeled to Tom with her consent,
> And spew'd her Liquor as she went.

The wedding itself is a gala of flowers and games. The whole village is invited and follow the couple, who ride on horses, to the church. The girls avail themselves of the opportunity of romance and dress buxomly, beribboned with flowers. Two lads lead Jenny, two girls Tommy, and the crowd ' . . . mad with Joy, like Bedlam follow'. Finding the church closed, little reverence is shown:

> Knock, swear and rattle at the Gate,
> And vow to break the Beadle's pate;
> And call his Wife a Bitch and Whore,
> They will be in, or break the Door.

Entry is gained and there is a mad scramble over the pews to cluster around the bride and groom at the altar. After the ceremony, Jenny is sacrificed like a pig in a poke in a ritual of male dominance:

> Whole troops of COLLIERS swarm around,
> And seize poor Jenny on the Ground;
> Put up their Hands to loose her Garters,
> And work for Pluck about her Quarters;
> Till Ribbons from her legs are torn,
> And round the Church in Triumph borne.

The traditional 'kail' is then galloped for, and the following feast is greedily innocent of etiquette or 'manners':

> Impatient for the Want of Meat
> They feak, and cannot keep their Seat;
> Play with the Plates, drum on the Table,
> And fast as long as they are able . . .

Some eat the Bread, some lick the Salt
Some drink, and other some find fault . . .

Swift to the smoking Beef they fly;
Some cut their Passage through a Pye:
Out streams the Gravy on the Cloth;
Some burn their Tongue with scalding broth . . .

'Now Geese, Cocks, Hens, their Fury feel
Extended Jaws devour the Veal.

Dancing is inaugurated by the groom. It is physical and uninhibited; with knees bent and petticoats lifted,

The Pipes scream out her favourite Jig,
Then knack'd her Thumbs and stood her Trig;
Then cock'd her Belly up a little,
Then wet her fingers with her Spittle;
So off she goes; the Collier Lad
Sprung from the Floor, and danc'd like mad:
They sweep each Corner of the Room,
And all stand clear where e'er they come.

Propelled on strong ale, the dancing continues all night till the weaker brethren

. . . reel and rub their drowsy Eyes;
Dead drunk some tumble on the Floor,
And swim in what they drank before.

The order of the day ends in procession to the bedroom where the couple are put to bed by their female guests: Jenny is first laid out 'Her Neck and Breasts are both display'd / And every Charm in Order laid'; followed by Tommy whose protests are in vain 'for that's the law':

Young Tommy cock'd, and Jenny spread,
So here I leave them both in Bed.

Wilson's 'Pitman's Pay', in contrast, walks with a measured tread. The poem cannot describe without comment, and the subjects are serious;

industrial disputes, technology, work, village life. Some of Wilson's observations must rank amongst the finest dialect poetry ever written. Here he describes how owners would deliberately get their men drunk in order to sign their yearly work contract, the Bond:

> Just like wor masters when we're bun,
> If men and lads be verra scant,
> They wheedle us wi' yell [ale] and fun,
> And coax us into what they want.
>
> But myek yor mark, then snuffs and sneers,
> Suin stop yor gob and lay yor braggin';
> When yence yor feet are i' the geers,
> 'Ma soul they keep yor painches waggin!

Though more serious, yet Wilson is without that strait-laced primness which characterised so much later moralising for the working class. There is no prejudice against drink; going to work is not yet an ethical responsibility:

> A *cuckoo morning* gives a lad,
> He values not his plagues a cherry!
> A *backe* or *knowe* myeks hewers glad –
> A *gaudy day* myeks a' hands merry.[8]

and Wilson still likes a rip-roaring party. In fact he laments the fading away of celebrations on the generous scale of Chicken's 'Wedding'. As an example he quotes the current trend in christenings; in his youth at the turn of the century they would be a day long affair, lots of guests, 'grey hens [beer jugs] uncorking', and 'Substantials that wad bide some cuttin':

> But christenin's now are suiner duin,
> By far than what they used to be
> Folks were not axed for efternuin,
> Te get blawn out wi' blashy tea.

Thomas Wilson was no moraliser, but like almost every other observer of the pitmen in his day, he was sensitive to changing them. He is a gentle writer, ever sympathetic to the collier, and too catholic in his tastes to be a bigot, and yet because he is all these things he wants some character reform. To do this he presents two contrasting pictures of home life, for the responsibility of rescuing the men from excesses at the pub he rests squarely on their wives. One pitman suffers from being married to a woman who is a slut, a spendthrift and a shrew:

> But this is a' of little use,
> For what aw dee is never reet;
> She's like a'larm-bell i' the house,
> ding-donging at me day and neet.
>
> She's just a gannin' heap o' muck,
> Where durts of a' description muster
> For dishclout [dishcloth] serves her apron nuik,
> As well as snotter clout and duster!
>
> She chalks up scores at a' the shops
> Wherever we've a twel' month staid;
> And when we flit, the land lord stops,
> Ma sticks till a' the rent be paid.

Needless to say this pitman is reluctant to leave the pub's careless pleasures! In contrast is set the domestic bliss of Nanny and Neddy. Nan comes to the pub and with gentle persuasion coaxes her husband out: 'Ma Nan – ma bairns – ma happy hyem/Set ower hard labor's bitter pill', and no wonder!

> Aw'll tyek thee hyem a pot o' beer,
> A nice clean pipe and baccy te –
> Thou knaws aw like to hae thee near –
> Come, hinny, come; gan hyem wi' me.

The pathetic touch is added by Ned having a worrying cough, which, we are led to believe, may prove fatal. Wilson ends by trying to make the reader envious for the fireside chair of domestic science:

> Here then, we'll leave this happy pair
> Their 'home affairs' to con and settle;
> Their 'ways and means', with frugal care,
> For marketing next day to ettle.

By the late nineteenth century Wilson's portrait of the miner is accepted by bourgeois antiquarians as a fair estimation, though they are quick to add that it was written before 'improvement' institutions such as teetotalism had begun their great work – *The Monthly Chronicle* even prints two pictures of the pitman's pay day: one, in Wilson's time, a sorry sight of tap room debauchery; the other, an 1890 version, of a respectable queue of home-loving family men. Chicken's picture on the other hand:

> . . . is not very pleasant reading. It bears strong traces of the impurities that characterized a preceding age . . . If the little coarseness that remains can be tolerated, the reader will obtain from Chicken's masterpiece an interesting account of customs that fortunately have fallen into disuse, and of manners that, happily, have passed away.[9]

As the passage correctly implies, it was not Edward Chicken who had changed but the age in which he lived, 'Our forefathers, apparently, saw nothing amiss in the poem. They enjoyed the coarse humour of it . . .' And, significantly, it was not until the 1820s, with moral sensibilities sharpening, that 'A modern version' of Chicken's work was published. In 1829, T. and J. Hodgson published the poem rigorously edited by William Cail 'toned down to suit ears polite'.

II. Scrutiny

An 1802 description of colliers at Warden Row, near Sunderland was given by a clergyman tourer; ' . . . we here saw a decency in persons and habitations, and a decorum and civility in manners and behaviour, that one seldom meets with in more refined societies of men . . .'[10] By 1825, the birth-pains of the new industrial society having been suffered, the psychology and manners of working men are increasingly the subject of class concern – and Eneas Mackenzie feels it necessary to play the apologist. His descriptions of the area's fairs and hirings are not exactly those of Chicken's, and yet his age denies him Chicken's shamelessness:

> At these country dances practices prevail which would shock the delicacy of more refined society. The youth usually sits with his arm around his girl's waist; and if the room be much crowded, the young women not unfrequently sit upon the knees of their partners. Towards the close of the entertainment, the fiddler, at the end of every dance, gives a shrill shreak with his instrument, which is understood

> to say, 'kiss her'; . . . Were a youth to neglect the performance of this established ceremony, his mistress would consider herself affronted . . .[11]

Also, 'these dancing parties often exhibit scenes very indelicate and unpleasant to the peaceable spectator',[12] with virility at stake and drink encouraging the virility. Midnight courting, connived at by the girl's parents, is no less shameless, but fathers 'have no notion of denying those under their care that indulgence which they themselves and their ancestors have practiced with impunity before them'.[13]

By the 1830s such descriptions of the pitman as the Reverend Warner's of 1802 above, become increasingly impossible. There are too many axes to grind: reformers of all sorts would lay claim to their own benevolent influences, and whilst admitting there was still a lot to be done in ameliorating the miner's morals, stood aghast at the awful savagery that existed (around 1802!) before they came. In 1802 Reverend Warner was admiring the people and deprecating the industrialism. By the 1830s and 1840s observers were admiring the industrialism and deprecating the people. The whole tone of the pitman's traditional way of life and labour was under attack. By the 1860s the mining community has become subject for a species of primitive, popular 'social anthropology'. In various reports and investigations the *scrutiny* remains moral, but it has also become 'scientific':

> This washing process is done very effectually. A large wooden tub of hot water is placed before the fire, and the man then sits down on a small stool, with one leg on each side of the tub, and being supplied with a piece of soap, he begins by washing his hands, arms, and chest; head, neck, and face follow, and he ends with the lower extremities, one after the other.[14]

Late nineteenth-century antiquarians are forced back to 1840 to find examples of the great hewing matches between local champions, like that between Joseph Rhodham and Robert Whitfield at Shield Row Colliery who began back to back in a narrow board and drove away from each other for a week of competition. Company discipline, regulated working and union restriction all made for the cultural extinction of men like John Temperley of Craghead who would hew his wage in two and a half hours – what took other men a shift of six hours. Coincident with this, the century saw a decline in the status of the collier from craftsman to labourer as the industry expanded, the number of colliers grew and relations with employers became more impersonal. The gala festivities that would accompany the opening of collieries for instance, roasted ox, plum pud and ale for all, with dancing and speeches, was dying out. Significantly the opening of Waldridge in 1831 saw the workmen eating in a field and the 'gentlemen' for dinner at 'The Lambton Arms' in Chester le Street. As early as 1825, in a union pamphlet the United Colliers were demanding wage parity with 'mechanics' and not the semi-skilled; and in respect of another occupation, the cordwainers, John Sykes' 1823 remarks, that their guild procession and festival coronation of their patron saint was a *'silly childish parade'* which he hoped 'is now laid dormant forever', are telling indeed.[15] The volatile temperament reflected in the madness of a hewing match similarly existed in the greedy *débauche* of the hoppings. If the Cranky songs of Chapter 2 are fictional fact-for-fact, they are right in atmosphere. Bourgeois economic rationale, with a sense of moral values in close attendance, found itself unable to cope with the spendthrift carelessness of a pitman who could buy beer and ribbons at the hopping and eat milk and oats for the rest of the week. We can imagine the stern features of an evangelical missionary in response to a popular culture of Sunday ' . . . dancing for ribbons, grinning for tobacco, women running for smocks, ass races, foot courses by men, with an odd whim of a man eating a cock alive, feathers, entrails, etc.' Cockfighting itself (an altogether fairer proposition), was inveighed against, along with many other of the miner's customary sports, by reformers as diverse as Jacobins and Methodists and liberal humanitarians. During the 1770s every *Newcastle Chronicle* carried at least six notices of forthcoming cockfights in the city: by 1887, so successful had been the new economy and its cultural revolution that the *Monthly Chronicle* featured it as quaint; not only were the pitmen fond, but in an age which obviously had different notions of social hierarchy, cockfighting ' . . . was then patronised by persons of the highest rank and stations, up, at all events, to the close of the last century, without any impeachment of their refinement or humanity'.[16]

On 24 August 1818, James Losh, a radical Newcastle barrister with substantial private means from coal and chemicals, had a visitor; Losh recorded in his diary:

> Tom Bigge left us to return home . . . he has also too great a fondness for what is called good society and a consequent contempt for all those persons and things which appear to him plebeian and common. This however seems to be the prevailing weakness of young

men in the present day and if not carried too far may be of service in protecting them against Indulgence in the grosser vices.[17]

The movement for change, change of the kind Edward Chicken and Thomas Wilson reflect, was inaugurated in the North East by a flowering middle-class consciousness at the end of the Napoleonic Wars. Tom Bigge illustrates how this consciousness was accompanied by a strutting moral rectitude. The nature of this rectitude and the battles it waged had some popular outlet in singing, and this is the subject of Part III.

III. Interpretation

At 6 a.m. on the morning of Thursday, 19 July 1821, the Castle cannons crashed out a royal salute, whereupon the Union Jack was hoisted, the river craft ran up their colours, and the church bells of Newcastle 'rung a merry peal'. The coronation of George IV was the occasion in a city bedecked for royal festivities; the Corporation had planned a day of celebration; by 3 o'clock in the afternoon it had a riot on its hands.

How that riot was interpreted, in song and report, will tell us much about changing attitudes to the Tyneside working classes.

At 9 a.m. there was a boat race for the working craft from Walker Quay to the bridge, cheered on by gathering crowds milling along the riverbanks. At 9.30 a.m. the Mayor and Corporation read a congratulatory address to the King, and George Foster was invested with the gold chain and medallion of office, where upon the whole party marched in procession to St Nicholas' for a coronation service. Whilst still in service things were warming up outside. A gang of women, carrying an effigy of Queen Caroline, paraded to cheers, and there were signs of boisterousness when the mail coaches, covered in ribbons and flags, clattered into the city. The Corporation, in honour of the day, had erected three beer and one wine pant, appropriately crowned and garlanded, at various places in the lower parts of the city, a maze of lanes and alleys steeply rising from the Quayside and teeming with people. Also they had ordered the roasting of two oxen to begin the day before, roast meat to be distributed to the crowds on the big day. On their return from church the Corporation drank the King's health and the pants immediately began to flow wine and ale.

Then there was tumult. Swarms struggled to be near the flow; at the Sandhill a sailor 'shinned' up the fountain and to great hurrahs tore away its crown and enthroned himself. At the Old Flesh Market the butchers were pelted from the stage with the very meat they had carved and thrown to the people, the stage and spit were demolished, the ox seized and dragged through the streets. The mail coaches were the next target; they were stoned, and when stoned enough there was always the gaudy target of the Yeomanry. Their commander ordered retreat, and he himself, the honourable Sir Thomas Burdon (knighted in action against the Tyne seamen in 1815, subject of James Morrison's scathing 'Burdon's Address to His Cavalry') 'narrowly escaped with the loss of his hat'. Another sailor (they were obviously superb climbers) clambered up the crane which had lowered the ox, and clapped up the inscription 'the Queen that Jack loves', to the inevitable cheers. The ox at the Spital was also dragged away, and, past masters of spectacle, the people of Tyneside made parade: 'The immense dripping pan, with its appropriate Brogdignagian ladle, were escorted about the streets in the same way as the carcases.' Having run dry, the pants were smashed, windows were broken and wildness increased until, mercifully for the Corporation, all was stifled by mid-afternoon with an exodus to the Town Moor for the races. By evening, momentum lost, all seems to have been quiet, for the city's bourgeoisie were free to make their own celebrations. The free burgesses and their families visited the theatre without charge, there was a ball in the Assembly Rooms, a dinner in Trinity House, and the usual distribution of money and treats to the hospitals, schools and gaol.[18]

Such are the facts; the reasons for the trouble are more obscure. A batch[19] of songs on the day appeared in 1822, price twopence. The songs list a number of causes and after that interpretation takes over as to which combination one chooses. The bourgeois radical line was that the people saw the affair as degrading – a cheap alcoholic bribe to laud and honour an unpopular king, the Queen Caroline affair still fresh; whilst the idea of butchers hacking roast flesh on a stage and throwing pieces to the people below, like so many baying dogs, needs no further explanation – it added insult to injury. It is certainly true that the meat was hurled back at its carvers, forcing them to beat a hasty if puzzled retreat from the platform. But apolitical explanations reckoned this was because the crowd was drunk, or because the meat was dirty, or burnt, or fatty, and make no mention of a trodden pride flowering in riot. The radical songs, however, do just this: 'Newcastle in An Uproar' talks of burnt and smouldering 'muck heaps' which 'smoked just like tinder':

> But the stuff they threw out put the folks in a fury

Both stones and brick-bats they snatched up in a rage;
And a radical troop, thus equipp'd in a hurry,
With vengeance bang'd carvers and beef off the stage.

Some songs attest the breaking of the pants to similar concepts of evolving pride, even denying the thought that any was drunk; others put this and the rioting down to general expressions against waste and royal opulence in a time of crisis.

Whatever the reasons, the radical authors clearly took their major objection as an insult to the people's dignity. Burke's nickname, 'swinish multitude', weighed heavy, and songs like 'The Newcastle Swineherd's Proclamation' clearly used the day as a retort to it. The Corporation are swineherds, the people are the swine (but not Gadarene they):

With cart grease basted, dredg'd with dust,
 The outsides burnt, the insides raw,
Next to some tit bit carrion, must
 Delight a hog's voracious maw . . .

And grunt, ye pigs, with savage joy,
 While stuffing full your craving maws . . .

Then, all ye lordly herds, laugh loud . . .

Next sagely argue o'er your wine,
 This crew, debas'd beyond compare,
In fact and reason are true swine,
 Unlike Corinthian Pillars fair.

But regeneration is at hand! The people refuse to grunt:

Blush ye great Rulers of the town,
Behold your nauseous loathsome boon!
See men, with manners more discreet,
Disgusted, spurn your beastly treat!
And know, all you who term us swine
That Reason rules the sons of Tyne.

The bourgeois radical vision of Liberated Man was similiar in its hope of sobriety, order and the capacity for reasonableness, to the schemes of any work-discipline prophet. Radical reformer and industrial entrepreneur alike had to reckon with the kind of popular behaviour another song describes at the scene of the free beer pants:

> The folk that were round it appear'd to be growling
> And fighting amongst it, like as many cats;
> While others I saw among mud and dirt rolling,
> And drinking the wine out of lousy old hats.

Newcastle's worthy burghers were probably quite innocently working within accepted coronation tradition, though it had been 60 years since the last and the nature of politics and protest had changed. Drinking habits had not however, and it comes as no surprise to find, as we do, temperance and radicalism working, and it seems singing, side by side during these crucial years of persuasion.

That not all radicals were as easily pleased as the songs, and that they too envisaged profound moral changes for the working classes may be seen by comparing three newspaper accounts of the celebrations. The *Tyne Mercury* wanted franchise and had a reputation for radicalism. It does not close its eyes to wine pant scenes:

> For what reason we could not discover, an individual seized the spout . . . and did not leave it till some time after his jacket and pantaloons had been literally torn from his body. When a considerable portion of what is called the *buff* was perceptible in the person of this persevering man, the flat of the hand and several of the pots and hats in the neighbourhood very soon changed from buff to red, but naked and exposed the fellow continued to exert himself, and clung to the spout as if he had been a part of it. We have heard he exhibited some indecencies, which we are not sorry we did not witness; but it should not be forgotten that the wine was most anxiously wrung from the tail of his shirt . . . Several seamen, pitmen, keelmen and others were at different times mounted on the roof of the pant . . .

Moral rectitude soon shows itself, when, in the tradition of English middle-class radicalism, the unseemly sides of upper and lower class life are lump(en)ed together as degenerate:

> Of the taste of port wine with Englishmen there are not many opinions, but of the smell, when plentifully incorporated with

> such sweaty and greasy doublets as the Sandhill afforded – fah! We shall think of it as long as ever we think of either George the Fourth or a bottle.

The *Mercury* calls in 'the spirit of the age' on its side in a plea for some moral propriety, some economic rationale:

> . . . we cannot but observe that, however, well meant, the ox roastings, beer swillings, and the like, both in this town and other places, have proceeded from a miscalculation of the spirit of the age. Though the oxen were received in this town in a manner in which we can never wish thinking Englishmen, or men of any kind to exhibit their contempt, there was a very general feeling amongst all classes that the money was improperly lavished on these beastly sights, and an immense number of orderly and well disposed persons, who were as loyal but not so noisy, as low in circumstance but not quite so low in conduct as those who thought they could only resent a disgusting display by increasing the disgust and adding to it destruction and tumult, would have been glad to have shared a better regulated bounty.[20]

In contrast to the *Mercury*, the *Newcastle Courant* was a Tory newspaper. Its account of the proceedings is quite different: there is no moral judgement; apart from one mention of a Caroline inscription there is no mention of radical possibilities; the full congratulatory speech to the King is reproduced, as is a meticulous description of the military manoeuvres. Everything trotted along in an atmosphere of 'jolly good fun', and the *Courant*'s reticence to rebuke is not only to do with defending the name of its King. The acts of sabotage are described, but there is almost an innocent's reluctance to reprimand:

> The mob afterwards pulled down the pump, tore up the pipes that conveyed the beer to it, and committed several other outrages, but still good humour was depicted in almost every countenance . . . The ale from the pant continued to run for a considerable time, but much of it was wasted in fun . . . The pelting of the meat and the demolition of the staging was solely due to culinary imperfections. The roasting spits promised a feast '. . . but from the unskillfulness of the cooks, the event was not equal to the expectation. The fires were . . . lighted too soon or were too violent . . . the outside appearance was not very inviting, being

> black and apparently burnt to a cinder . . .[21]

And finally, just to add balance, what was the interpretation of the city's other major newspaper, the *Newcastle Chronicle*? The *Chronicle* was Whig, gently reformist in its attitudes, and it carried a very cool summary of the proceedings. The report seems to agree with the *Courant* against the *Mercury* that there was no political motivation: amidst a scene of noisy but cheerful confusion, 'Great good humour seemed to prevail, the only object being to derive as much frolic and diversion from the passing scene as possible. No political feelings seemed to disturb their minds. The fountain was eventually, we understand, pulled down.'

But the *Chronicle* can be as little trusted as the others in its account of the Tyne's sons o' toil. The town Whigs, for obvious reasons if they were reformist, had been upset by the Corporation's recent sense of repressiveness after the radical outbursts of 1819. The *Chronicle* congratulates the Mayor for his new indulgence:

> It is gratifying to observe such a change of behaviour in those who possess power and jurisdiction over us, as we may hope with reason that it proceeds from a conviction, instilled by experience, that their fellow townsmen are too peaceably disposed to deserve to be treated with suspicion . . .[22]

Indeed, the paper's hardest language is on behalf of the oxen, who were exhibited 'with a degree of pomp and exultation which might have been allowable, perhaps, in an uncivilized barbarian'.

This comparatively minor incident (Newcastle being well used to riots of all shapes and sizes), shows us the degree of differences there was in period sensibilities to the working classes.[23] The *Mercury* hopes for better things and is disgusted; the *Courant* is content, and sees no change or cause for alarm in such a tiny incident from, after all, a lower order always potentially disgusting; the *Chronicle* wants freedom of speech for the £10 men who read it, so it plays down the whole affair.

IV. Changers

By 1831, I have no doubt, middle-class attitudes would have been less diverse. By then, the drive for cultural change amongst the 'lower orders' had gained momentum.

Newcastle alone had nineteen societies pushing for that change on religious grounds.[24] It is interesting to look at some of their work just to grasp the scale of the campaign. The Sunday School Union was probably the most powerful group; founded in 1816 primarily from fears of working-class discontent, it commanded 128 schools, 13,397 children, and 2,489 teachers. The Bible Society had been founded in 1809 and by 1829 had distributed some 20,000 Bibles and 18,000 Testaments; similarly the Newcastle Bible Association between 1813-17 had given out 1,191 Bibles and 886 Testaments; the Tyne Union Committee was doing the same work among 1,200 Tyne vessels. As well as the Religious Tract Society, founded in 1810 and circulating the propaganda of its London parent body, the Unitarians and Quakers both had tract societies, and the Wesleyan Lending Tract Society between 1825-28 had given out 5,000 tracts weekly by 160 volunteers. Societies for Catholic Religious Defence and for Promoting Christianity amongst the Jews (f. 1824) were also active. The Bethel Union Society had been founded in 1822 for the preaching and teaching of Dissent among the seamen, and for the benefit of all working people there were the various missions: the Missionary Society of London, the Baptist Missionary Society, the Church Missionary Society, the Continental Missionary Society, the *Ladies* Continental Society, the Moravian Missionary Society and the Methodist Missionary Society. The Town Mission of Newcastle upon Tyne and its Vicinity had been set up in 1829 with a cosmopolitan make-up of Evangelicals; it aimed not only at the conventional preaching, circulating, prayer and conversational plan of campaign, but also at systematic, regular visiting of households. Also founded in 1829 was the Society for Promoting Christian Knowledge in Newcastle upon Tyne and its immediate Vicinity: preaching the iron doctrines of King Calvin, the society soon won a reputation for vociferous action. If one adds to these peddling groups the work of the churches proper, and especially the bubbling Methodist offshoots – foremost among whom were the Primitive Methodists who had moved rapidly through the district in the early twenties and were entrenching in the late twenties – then the picture is a maelstrom of religious activity. Without doubting the personal sincerity of its adherents, it is important to remember that these labours strove for more than religious converts. For the nonconformists and Methodists especially, religious faith demanded social evidence. God's free grace was not sufficient to take on trust, the convert or the merely interested needed to show his salvation in his daily habits. What in fact these groups were doing was offering an alternative culture; standards of what became hallowed as 'respectability' were being forged. Traditional habits and values seldom fitted the new patterns; obsession with Jehovah was often only an introit for obsession with working-class character and morals; the former frolic of, say, a pitman's excursion as in 'The Colliers' Pay Week' in its impulse and spontaneity must be replaced by more sober standards. That Jehovah was sober then all well and good; later He also will become an extraordinarily able political economist.

For Tyneside the Jacobin scare of the 1790s and the intermittent bad harvests, especially the harvest of 1794-5, were reinforced by serious labour troubles. The seamen were in action against the impress in 1790, against voyage payments in 1792, against conditions of Royal Naval service in 1793. The keelmen of Tyne and Wear were on strike in 1793, the Tyne keelers again in 1794; 1803 saw another keel strike this time against the impress, and another in 1809 over inflationary prices. In 1793 various coalmines in the area were out, and 1795 even saw the customary passivity of the Dales leadminers broken. In 1810 the pitmen were striking against the Bond in a full scale action. Although there is little evidence to suggest any political complexion to these discontents, the keelmen, seamen and miners were in a position of industrial interdependence. A strike by one group created a bottleneck and affected the others. That all three could be out together was a constant headache to the authorities. The seamen did in fact send emissaries to the collieries on more than one occasion, and for a period in 1793 the Tyne was in a situation tantamount to a general strike. Traditional labour action on the river was not content with a withdrawal of labour. Protest usually took the form of *direct* confrontation and exercise of power: the seamen would seize the river and control daily sailings according to their demands, the keelmen would blockade the river or sabotage its facilities, whilst the pitmen were infamous for commando attacks on colliery machinery in times of trouble. In 1794 the Tyne keelmen had destroyed dock staithes threatening their employment; in 1793 500 seamen armed with cutlass and pistol had attacked the *Eleanor* at Shields in an attempt to rescue the impressed aboard; in 1795 all three groups had joined in an act of *taxation populaire* at Newcastle. After the War the area saw the more dangerous manifestation of a wave of strikes coincident with popular radicalism. The peace got off to an unruly start with an insurrection of Wear keelmen and the strike of Tyne seamen in 1815. The keelers rioted and broke up new staithes, bridge and spouting at Sunderland; the seamen, with arrogance, displayed superb organisation in their seizure of the river. 1816 saw sporadic trouble in the collieries, and miners were behind a grain riot at Sunderland in the October. In 1819 and 1822 the Tyne keelmen were in action again, and the emergence of the United Colliers Association in 1825 frightened the owners – their fears justified in the massive strikes of 1831 and 1832, interspersed only by a strike of seamen in July 1831. From 1817-19 the district experienced radical discords, reaching a post-Peterloo crescendo in 1819, the authorities seeing Jacobins everywhere.

But there was another factor, something which was to demand a more sophisticated level of social control than the Riot Act. The Hon. Captain Cochrane, with HMS *Hind*, had been sent to the river during the 1792 Tyne seamen's strike. On 20 November he reported to Henry Dundas at the Home Department in London that:

> Upon my arrival at Shields I found every thing on shore perfectly quiet the seamen every where behaving with the utmost degree of Civility and regularity except that they made a point to Board all the Ships that sail'd to satisfy themselves that the Crew had not broke through the General Agreement . . .[25]

A magistrate, writing to the Department on the very same day, came more quickly to the point. 'There has been thro' the whole of this affair, a degree of system and order unknown in former riots, so much so, as to make the Part the Magistrates had to act, embarrassing and difficult.'[26]

Throughout the first half of the nineteenth century, traditional, direct forms of working-class protest were to exist in uneasy alliance with the new tactics of trade unionism. The riot, in spite of the sense of purpose it often displayed, was relatively easy to deal with by carrot and stick, mercy and terror; the organised strike, conscious of the collective strength of *workers*, was much more difficult to cope with in the old style – '. . . make the Part the Magistrates had to act, embarrassing and difficult'. In 1854 James Mather was in a position to describe the phenomenon exactly. About the miners he said, 'The strikes as they have been conducted of late are not like the strikes of former times, but more like capital in deliberation.'[27]

A flexing middle-class initiative, a rumbling working-class discontent, sometimes in alliance, at other times in opposition, always feeding off each other in creation and recreation, produced, during and after the War, attempts at cultural integration. Amongst these attempts the religious groups listed above were only one; typically bourgeois in consciousness they began in a muddled fashion, disparate cliques in the face of political challenges – later their value as apostles of social control came to be recognised by industrial interests. Prominent among these interests were the coalowners as mining became more sophisticated and the miners more deliberate, and by mid-century it is possible to see in the colliery communities the drive for cultural integration and social control on a broad, openly-confessed scale.

PART TWO: THE METHODISTS

1791. *On the death of the movement's initiator, Reverend John Wesley (1703-91), there were about 80,000 Methodists in Britain. The period immediately following his death saw the final breaks with the Church of England, the growing political importance of the annual Conference, and the replacement of Wesley's autocratic leadership by a managing bureaucracy of professional ministers. Gradually, Methodism became less of a religious movement and more an organised denomination.*
1800-50. *Wesley and his preachers had always sought and had often won the affections of the poor, but the first half of the nineteenth century were years of unprecedented revival and growth. In 1801 there were 94,380 members, 825 meeting houses, and 165,000 seats; in 1851 there were 483,569 members, 11,000 meeting houses, and 2,194,298 seats. One historian has estimated that two million people were directly under a Methodist influence in 1851. (R. F. Wearmouth, op. cit., p. 16.)*

But the years of growth were also the years of secession and offshoot: Methodist New Connexion (1797), Band Room Methodists (1805), Primitive Methodists (1811), Bible Christians (1814), Tent Methodists (1820), Protestant Methodists (1829), Wesleyan Methodist Association (1836), Wesleyan Reform Union (1859). The Wesleyan Methodists were the original body and they remained the largest and most influential group. It was the Primitive Methodist group which emerged as the Wesleyans' major rivals. In 1851 there were 302,209 Wesleyan members, and the Primitives, with 106,074, were the second largest Methodist group. Between them, the Primitives and the Wesleyans came to dominate the religious life of the Nort East colliery communities, although in this case it was the Primitives who were the majority group. As the century progressed, Wesleyan-Primitive differences became more historical than real, and in terms of individual experiences the differences between them must always be interpreted rather than assumed. However, the original reasons for the break were solid enough.

Primitive Methodism was founded in Staffordshire in 1811 when two ex-Wesleyan groupings, Hugh Bourne's 'Camp Meeting Methodists' and William Clowes' 'Clowesites' united to form the 'Primitive Methodists'. Both groups had suffered expulsion from their Wesleyan Circuits for field preaching – the 'camp meeting' – an activity which the Wesleyan bureaucracy feared as dangerous to the public order and its own good. In an age of unrest, 'emotions' (and working-class emotions in particular), were to be calmed and not inflamed. The Primitives were always the most democratic and working class of the major Methodist groups, and, during the difficult years 1800-50 they grew quickly and explosively.

In 1820 Primitive Methodist preachers first crossed over from North Yorkshire into County Durham. By 1825 their societies were firmly established in Teesdale and Weardale and in the coalfield. The Primitive Methodists were Bob Cranky's major persecutors, and they were the predominant Cultural Revolutionaries of the colliery community.

I. Conversion

In 1879, Robert Grieves, a miner who had been converted in 1833 at East Cramlington to the Primitive Methodists, lay dying on his bed. Just before his final breath the chapel brethren visited him and bawled hymns and prayers around his bed. Grieves himself joined in the last two lines of 'Guide me, O Thou great Jehovah!' and demanded them over and over again, 'Songs of praises, songs of praises I will ever give to thee'.[28]

Grieves and Methodist miners like him had been giving up songs of praises all their lives; a poor death it was indeed that was not glorified in song. For Methodism was music: music spearheaded its mission; it marked out the good life and pointed out the bad; it sang out the dead and sang in the reborn. Singing in the chapel was as vital to the 'respectable' miner in clarifying his new self-image, in celebrating his self-significance, as it was to his 'unrespectable' neighbour in boasting 'Cranky' chorus in the tap room down the lane. Just as John Wesley had identified with religion a real or supposed experience, so did the songs of Methodism reflect that experience factor. William Crister, a Wallsend Wesleyan pitman famous for his preaching, would stalk penitents at their pews during choruses looking for signs of psychic struggle; with the music rocking, Crister would deliberately take on the emotion, '. . . he wept, he prayed, he rejoiced, and felt something of the struggling spirit . . .',[29] and try to infect others with it. Crister was doing what all Methodist preachers of the period were doing; he was poaching the penitent's psyche, bringing on an inner struggle, a realisation of sin which would erupt in crisis – a begging of forgiveness, salvation by hysteria. Brother Isaac Thompson, a Byker Hill Primitive, just a mile upriver from Crister, certainly knew how to poach the penitent. In 1825 he recalled how 'one woman who was very dressy' entered their lovefeast and sat, rather than kneeled, in the pew. Thompson's wife immediately kneeled before the woman and asked God 'to bring her down . . .': 'I went and kneeled behind her, and Brother W. Steel at her left hand, and Brother J. Robson and some of our friends from N. Shields Circuit on her right hand: and we prayed earnestly to God to convert her soul.' The dressy woman was 'down' shortly afterwards, feeling her sin and approaching contrition.

Conversion was the *experience* so necessary for the free-born Christian. Allowing for the violent leakage of Methodist membership through the volatile years up to the mid-century, it resulted in the convert transforming his self-image and therefore his habits. John Wilson, the great leader of the Durham Miners Association at the end of the century recalled how his conversion not only finished him with drinking and gambling, but fundamentally altered his whole concept of life, becoming a gift and a matter for stewardship. Characteristically, he marked this shift of consciousness by quoting a hymn and a text:

> In evil long I took delight,
> Unawed by shame or fear,
> Till a new object struck my sight
> And stopped my wild career.

'No one who saw Saul set out on his way to Damascus "breathing out threatenings and slaughterings" would have thought that he would be stopped in the manner he was.'[30] A century before, the very founder of the movement to which Wilson aligned himself, the Primitive Methodists, was similarly being haunted by his hedonistic self. Like Wilson, William Clowes, a highly-paid, skilled potter, felt nothing but melancholy after drunken evenings. If Wilson marked salvation with a hymn, Clowes was reminded of his Fall by a song:

> Before my conversion to God, the internal misery of which I was the victim was in many instances unsupportable . . . Sometimes in the night I have been agitated with terrible dreams, and, starting up, I have been afraid of looking out of my bed, supposing the room to be full of devils and damned spirits . . . Well I remember how conscience used to lash me when I used to sing this song [a drunkard's ballad] and with what power and force those words were occasionally applied to my soul: 'For all these things God will bring thee to Judgement.'[31]

And so this figure of Olde England, a prize dancer, bruiser, gambler and drinker, a man who had taken the 'King's shilling' from two recruiting sergeants for a drink, a man who delighted in his coat of yellow buttons, was 'lashed' by the words of a ditty and the words of God. The power of words and music on the consciousness was not lost on Clowes or the Primitive evangelists who followed him. Primitive Methodism was founded in rupture with the Wesleyans over the holding of camp meetings, all day affairs of hymns and preaching in the open field. The main cutting instrument of Primitive mission, the camp meeting was staffed by believers from the whole district and persecuted the sins of England; fairs, hoppings, race meetings were the venue for regular confrontations with the Devil. At other times, the camp meeting was held not only to win converts but to raise morale. But whatever its purpose, the itinerant evangelists who led them were aware of the manipulative power the meeting could give them. Atmosphere needed to be created; intended camps were always preceded by prayers for fine weather on the day. Obviously a drizzling field would dampen the best ardours; very rarely do the journals of the preachers or the magazines of the movement record 'movings' or conversions when the weather was unfavourable. Sometimes the weather could have only added to the atmosphere. Imagine a camp meeting during the remarkable Weardale revival of 1823: held at night against the looming blackness of a mountain side, the wind howling down the valley, the flickering lamps bobbing above shadowy faces, all listening to the charged language of exhortation, all singing hymns as the emotionally exhausted collapsed and the pitch of everyone rose with each sinking. The dales are wild enough in their natural state without such dramatic props; the atmosphere of such revivals must have been searing. The theology was battle raising, the hymns were martial, the preaching was led by men who saw the world as a fight. Hardship, struggle, exhaustion, blisters, were mere by-products of a world in sin: Christ was the way out and the way forward. The itinerant preachers saw themselves as religious shock troops, carrying out commando swoops on the key strongholds of Satan; the fair was an obvious one, but they would find most things as such. Here is an account of a camp meeting by Thomas Batty, 'the Apostle of Weardale'; a Yorkshireman and ex-seaman, Batty was one of the first Primitive Methodist preachers and he led the Weardale revival of 1823. The account is a good insight into how such men saw their work, though the last sentence carries a touch of farce, making Batty's intensity more preposterous than it already is – the Lord's kindled 'fire', almighty as it is, is susceptible to His mortal rain:

> The noble spirited troops from Shotley Bridge and Newlands made a fierce and glorious attack on the enemy, joined by many companies of brave, disciplined veterans from various quarters, headed by their officers (I mean class leaders). We commenced the action, or engagement, first by entreating our Almighty and Eternal Lord . . . We then took ourselves up to that powerful weapon – prayer . . . After this, 'the Sword of the Spirit, which is the Word of God' was drawn, and while it was wielding there seemed to be a moving . . . different companies were formed, and all opened a tremendous fire upon the enemy . . . However, we did not appear to advance much, or gain much ground here, and the rain came on, which caused us to retreat.[32]

This sort of meeting was deliberately trying to beat up a religious enthusiasm and hymns and prayers were employed in a process of self-manipulation; one must be careful as to time and place, but E.P. Thompson's phrase 'psychic masturbation' does not seem unsuitable. But songs were employed in a much more straightforward manner too. Primitive Methodism came to Murton, like everything else, with the colliery in 1839. It was literally brought with the hymnal: John Robson and Ralph Fenwick, pitmen of neighbouring Easington Lane, led a singing procession of converts into the village and sang till a crowd had gathered. Similarly Kelloe Colliery's revival of 1843 was induced after much planning, basic to which was open air singing and praying with meetings every night 'at which cries for mercy were heard, mingled with songs of thanksgiving'.[33]

The tenor of Methodist singing changed with the character of Methodism in the later nineteenth century. The age of 'mahogany

Methodism', fine varnished pews, ever grander chapels, pulpits and choir stalls more like a stage set than an exhorter's box was coincident with national prosperity and social stability. The battles of Kelloe, the campaigns in Weardale, the skirmishes with rural gentry and atheistical radicals became the subject for old generals' memoirs. Music became less an instrument of war, and more a form of social entertainment. Revivals remained of course, but the later music of Moody and Sankey is awash with cosy sentiment and easy faith, reflective of entrenched positions rather than impatient crusades. But it remains a fact that the Methodists loved their hymnal: the Primitives saw it democratically as *theirs*, and at the 1853 Conference they nearly split the Connexion over the introduction of a new hymnbook, lay sections accusing the professional ministry of springing it on them without enough consultation.[34] In worship and praise with music for tapping feet the Methodists sang out with gusto, expressing themselves as loudly and as significantly as those in chorus (if not harmony) down at the pub. The pub had its own styles and images which conversion would deliberately challenge and which chapel life and music would continuously refute. Methodism purported to offer an alternative personality and one facet of it was the concept of *Death.*

II. Death

Miners like Joseph Gardiner, converted in 1829 at the age of fourteen, 'delighted very much in singing, and was leader of the Percy Main Choir for some years'.[35] Many of the hymns he had spent his life singing, albeit joyfully, were songs of death. At the core of Primitive Methodism during the first half of the nineteenth century was the language of death; and all of the offshoots, whatever their other differences, were unanimous on Hell. Men were cast as possessing souls, a living, almost physical thing, somewhere in the body. One's soul was the very *quick* of one's life: one could insure it for eternity by coming to Jesus, one could fail to insure and be bound, everlastingly, to the flames of Hell. Methodists claimed revealed knowledge of the plan of human existence and Divine Will; accept their salvation and everlasting life was yours. But they could never be sure. The nearest they could get to knowing was at the deathbed of the believer. The result was a fixation with the experience of death: groups would cluster round a dying man to keep up his morale, and to satisfy their curiosity. The obituary column became one of the central features of Methodist magazines: interspersed with verses of hymns, the vital statistics of a man's life were recorded. Until late in the century there is usually no mention of his secular life or work or if there is, it stands incidental, usually as relevant to his previous state of sin. Under whose preaching, exactly when and where, was he converted into grace? Did he encounter any changes of heart, backslidings, torments or slackness during his religious life? Regular mention is given of his life before conversion – generally in the 'bold service of sin' style. All of this can be regarded as a dossier to the final act; the death scene is what really counts. The body is wracked but the concern is for the soul therein – how healthy is that? The dying are interrogated without fear or favour as close to the final moment as possible and their last whispers signify the ultimate proof: 'is Jesus precious?' 'is dying hard work?' 'are you safe in the Lord?' And if no whispers are forthcoming, a salute of the arm signifying victory at the moment will do. Flushed with relief would the deathbed group be on receipt of a happy death, of falling asleep in Jesus: Ralph Lonsdale, a Weardale leadminer died in 1849:

> Shortly our dying friend sung, with almost more than human voice and energy . . . The faith of the praying band rose to the throne of God and a stream of glory descended into every waiting soul.[36]

Lonsdale died crying 'Come Jesus!'; Robert Young, a Northumberland pitman was equally fortunate crying 'Come now, Jesus; I am waiting; I want to be fully thine',[37] as was John Robinson, another leadminer:

> He shouted with a loud voice, 'I want no other it is enough'. For two hours he struggled with death, and shouted the praises of God . . . He lifted up his hand for the last time, and said, 'It is all here' . . . The room was filled with the glory of God. His head dropped to one side. The last words that he uttered were 'Praise the Lord!'[38]

Sister Alice Proud was happy in death but it is only through another sister's dutifulness that we know: Alice had been converted at the age of fourteen in 1836, and 'A few minutes before she died, Sister Mary Ann Mills visited her, and while standing by her bed, she called for Jesus to come to take her happy spirit.' Brother Robert Grieves had been down the pit since the age of seven in 1823 and as the brethren sang, Robert showed a contrite heart and a native wit: 'He remarked that God's love was a river to swim in; but he had only been an ancle-deep plodger.'

During the period the area was flooded with Methodist tracts, little tales of conversion and piety dramatised around the bed of the dying. One such tract was *The Power of Divine Grace exemplified during the last illness of William Chapman*, printed at Darlington in 1844. The story is period cliche: a heavy drinker, braggart and blasphemer who collects the bounty of his life by dying at the age of thirty-one. He is saved however by the sheer persistence of local religious folk who ignore his first rebukes and relentlessly set about breaking the man down. He finally cracks: 'I shall not be here long; and if I die as I am, *it will be awful*, if the Bible be true.' He swears against drink, when he is no longer in a position to drink, with warnings for all, 'nine out of ten of the infidels cannot meet a sick bed and a dying hour with their principles', and with that dying hour there is the pathos of the righteous: to his converters, '. . . and then taking my hand, he said, while the tears filled his eyes, – "Bless you, bless you; I shall never forget you" '; to his mother, 'Dear mother, mind and attend your place of worship; do what you know to be right, and prepare to meet me in heaven'.

If Chapman's sins had been social, then Henry Black's were intellectual, and they demanded just as much repentance. Black, an apprentice surgeon, died in Sunderland at the age of twenty in 1841. His father was a staunch Primitive but Henry had read books 'calculated to bring religion into contempt and set at nought the sacred truths of Christianity'. Worried for the state of his soul (which presumably could be contaminated by the mind), Methodists from his father's chapel besieged his bed during a long illness until he succumbed in death, asking for Bunyan.[39]

The South Shields pitman class leader, Anthony Young, would always begin his classes with the verse 'O that without a lingering groan/I may the welcome word receive!' Killed in an explosion at Hetton Colliery in 1861, Young had his wish, but his words reveal that if he did not know it in concept, he knew it in fact, that Hell was the basis of a theological system demanding control. After the paroxysm of conversion had taken fire from the miner's belly, the chapel to which he belonged would exact that control in social measure. The pioneers of the cultural revolution in the colliery communities of Northumberland and Durham were the Methodists; they were the first to run up the flag of 'respectability'. Men were to be rescued from their own personalities and their own traditions, symbolised by the ale house; feeders and retrievers of sheep:

> It was soon known through the village that he had been converted. He attended chapel night after night whilst the services were being held. Knowing the temptations to which he would be subject from his old companions at the end of the week, a few thoughtful, good men arranged, without his knowledge, to keep him company during his vacant time on the Saturday night and Sunday. He attended three services at chapel on the Sunday, including Sunday school . . .[40]

Notice here the Primitive Methodist 1834 definition of 'crime': crime incites the *unruly* in a man, religion corrects it:

> During his youthful days he was notorious for drunkenness, and almost every other species of crime. One Lord's day, while playing at football he got his leg broken; by which afflictive dispensation he was led to reflect on his state as a sinner.[41]

III. Children

There is something humorous in the picture of the pensive (ex) footballer considering his ways! However, the fun disappears when one considers the nature of Methodism's attack on the children of the mining villages. Let us consider the early experience of the Newcastle Sunday School Union. In 1866 the Union, predominantly a Methodist enterprise, was celebrating its Jubilee Conference. Not without self-conceit, the worthies looked back on 50 years of triumph: the Union had been formed on the pious wish of George III that every child should be able to read the Bible, and, we are told, had known the sweet delight of making active and cultured minds. A 'nonconformist' Sunday School alliance, the Union began in 1816 with 36 schools and 3,000 scholars. Growing rapidly to 1818 with 8,000 scholars, the Union faltered and declined during the radical years 1818-20, and thereafter recovered to grow sporadically through the 1820s and fully to establish its position during the 1830s. Eight thousand Wesleyan scholars were seceded in 1836, yet in 1843 the Union still covered 111 schools, 10,415 scholars and 1,844 teachers. Although the Jubilee Conference echoed with tributes to Man's intellect as 'a precious gift', the historian of the movement, writing three years later, was much more candid on its origins – in 1816 the Union's founders realised the danger of reading Paine and Volney by 'the more intelligent of the working classes'. The Union took the view that since it was teaching reading skills it had the right to choose the literature, and with help from the Religious Tract Society distributed thousands of anti-deistical tracts: 'The infidel publications of the day were producing a ferment of discontent . . . Pending the formation of a Library Fund the committee did their utmost to promote the circulation of books and pamphlets suited to the times.'[42] By 1835 the Union had put out on Tyneside nearly two million such tracts. But its aims were broader than this. Walters dates 1780-1860 as the crucial years witnessing a burst of zeal unknown in the history of the Church. The Sunday Schools, Foreign Missions, Home Missions Bible, Tract and Book societies of these years he sees as saving us *as a nation* from 'the most fearful blasphemies' and sins of eighteenth-century society:

> In England especially the conditions of industry were verging towards a new system; the circumstances of the industrial classes necessarily followed in the same direction . . . A new age was produced, a new system of society, and the people needed to be trained for its requirements. Formerly when population was sparse and widely scattered, prudence and economy were not so needful . . . When little else was asked of man but mere brute effort, it was not so much out of keeping for him to have a brutish mind. But now population was no longer scanty, and the demands on human intelligence had become more numerous and peremptory. Education had become not merely a desideratum to the people, but a moral and physical necessity.[43]

Education was not now a matter of charity alone, but a duty if society was to function coherently. That it did function was a matter for self-congratulation by men such as Walters himself; the people were saved from themselves, though he sees them more as dismembered parts than as people: 'Their heads were to be needed as well as their hands. Their hearts also were required to enable them to appreciate and reciprocate the new relations into which they were destined to enter with their superiors and among themselves.' Thankfully, bodies like the Sunday School Union, he considers, had succeeded in creating the correct temperament for these 'new relations', *class* relations of worker and capitalist, founded on character: '. . . the eventful changes of the people during the last eighty years, on their progress . . . from low and sensual habits to sobriety and virtue, from tumultuous discontent to good order . . .'[44]

Central to the work of the Union had been the writings of Isaac

Watts. Watts' work came out of a harder seventeenth-century Dissenting tradition, but his First and Second Catechisms, and his Songs for Children had been the mainstay literature of the affiliated sunday schools through its career, and for pitmen like John Clark, converted at the age of fourteen in 1819, such songs had burned deep: he remembers committing 'to memory several of Dr Watts's hymns for children, and often felt devout and happy whilst reciting or singing them for his own edification or that of others'.[45] Songbooks such as Watts's *Songs, Divine and Moral for the Use of Children*[46] recognise no innocence in the child's personality, and will therefore not tolerate the excuse of age. Though called 'Divine and Moral', every song is moralistic, except that those divine claim a religious apologetic, those moral are rudely stated. Their main aim is to repress all childishness, all uninhibitedness in pupils: the child must be watchful because God is all-seeing and knowing, an omnipotent snoop – young masturbators are warned:

> Almighty God, thy piercing eye
> Strikes through the shades of night,
> And our most secret actions lie,
> All open to thy sight.

Repression and control must be ceaseless for Satan lives in all things child-like, whilst Jesus, the perfect child, a prodigy of pure goodness is the model of obedience:

> At twelve years old he talk'd with men,
> (The Jews all wond'ring stand),
> Yet he obeyed his mother then,
> And came at her command.

Total obedience was necessary if the child's moral self-image is to be created. There are songs against lying, quarrelling, fighting, swearing, idleness, mischief, 'evil company', disobedience, getting out of bed slowly, thieving and vanity – for youthful beauty fades with the rose and what then? Watts even threatens the child when he is playing games:

> Why should I love my sport so well,
> So constant at my play,
> And lose the thoughts of heaven and hell,
> And then forget to pray.

Work songs are there, to be as tireless and regular as the sun; and the scoffing of others is warned against, complete with a mean little woodcut of two black bears tearing limbs asunder:

> God quickly stopp'd their wicked breath,
> And sent two raging bears,
> That tore them limb from limb to death,
> With blood, and groans, and tears.

All the exuberance and careless vitality of children is dangerous, it is necessary to drain away the blood in them and make of them transcendent angels, angels with serious faces:

> If we had been ducks, we might dabble in mud;
> Or dogs, we might play till it ended in blood;
> So foul and fierce are their natures:
> But Thomas, and William, and such pretty names,
> Should be cleanly and harmless, as doves or as lambs
> Those lovely, sweet, innocent creatures.

Isaac Watts's concept of children came from a century and a theology which scarcely allowed the concept of childhood. The Methodist ideal child was old and faithful and came straight out of this tradition. The first Weardak society had been founded in 1749; in 1771 there was a revival and many of the converted were children:

> The chief instrument God has used among these is Jane Salkeld, a schoolmistress, a young woman that is a pattern to all that believe. A few of her children are, Phoebe Featherstone, nine and a half years old, a child of uncommon understanding; Hannah Watson, ten years old, full of faith and love; Aaron Ridson, not eleven years old, but wise and stayed as a man; Sarah Smith, eight and a half old, but as serious as a woman of fifty; Sarah Morris, fourteen years of age, is as a mother among them . . .

And for the 1830s, Reverend James Everett at Wallsend Colliery remembered one Sunday scholar commonly called 'The little Old Man' 'because of his stability, good sense, and sedative habits'. The Methodist ideal child, 'wise and stayed as a man', drew on an imagery and practised a personality that was little different from that of the adult.

The ultimate jurisdiction of course, was the existence of Hell. Watts' theology is as simple and lurid as Punch and Judy; the sunday school plays Policeman and God is the Executioner.[47] Vengeful and vindictive, death strikes at will; there is no way out for the sinner:

Why should I say, ' 'Tis yet too soon
  To seek for heaven, or think of death?'
A flow'r may fade before 'tis noon,
  And I this day may lose my breath . . .

'Tis dangerous to provoke a God!
  His power and vengeance none can tell;
One stroke of his almighty rod
  Shall send young sinners quick to hell.

As the final exactment, Watts demands gratitude. Firstly to Christ and salvation, redeeming from 'the slavish chains', then a gratitude to England, a Christian state, ' 'Tis to thy sovereign grace I owe/That I was born on British ground', and goodness knows what graveyard fantasies a young mind conjured on the lines:

Then if this Gospell I refuse
How shall I e'er lift up mine eyes?
For all the Gentiles and the Jews
Against me will in judgement rise.

Thirdly there is a gratitude incurred to the sunday school, because by it the pupil can know what 'a wretched slave to sin' he was, and that really he 'can do nothing well'. And finally, and most preposterously, the child owes gratitude and humility to the rich:

What though I be low and mean,
  I'll engage the rich to love me,
While I'm modest, neat, and clean
  And submit when they reprove me.

The Union was founded in 1816, and the early years were the years of revival, Winlaton in 1817 and Weardale in 1823 even witnessing children promoting their own hysteria. But they were also years of leakage in membership. Walters based his history on the reports of the Union, which appeared only spasmodically, but it is possible to see in them a neurosis over membership figures. By the 1830s, despite the serious Wesleyan secession of 1836, the obsession with numbers has calmed, the reports are now more concerned with institutional organisation and promotion. The Union has its aims, and the obligations of its scholars more clearly defined; it begins to get more organisationally trim: committees to encourage Bible Associations, select classes, serious singing, a rota of regular visitation and recruitment, annual festivals, library schemes and financial stability are all achieved. In 1833 the Juvenile Temperance Association with a mighty pledge was formed. This is the creation of a network, making more efficient, making more *continuous* the presentation of new self-images to children falling within its dynamic. The network makes mindful the duties, obligations, responsibilities, subscriptions and measures of achievement resting on the child – setting the snare which would hold some for a lifetime.

Intermittently, the results were remarkable. During the early period the reports put as much emphasis on outward discipline as inward peace, the word 'order' is used to nausea; the impact is greater because the land is virgin:

> The effects produced on this colliery [Killingworth, 1818] since the commencement of the Sunday School are remarkable . . . At that well known place of wickedness, the Crane [underground, at the colliery], where blasphemies of every description used to be heard, one of the lads is to be seen reading the Bible to those sitting around him in the most profound silence.[48]

Later, one can see a more sophisticated appreciation of disorder as a cultural phenomenon; the sunday school provides an alternative way of living, not just a crushing of the old. Of Prudhoe in 1833:

> Twenty years ago, at the time of the formation of our school, the Sabbath was generally spent, not only by the children, but by grown up persons, in field diversions, such as football, clubs, handballs etc. which often ended in quarrelling and fighting. We see little of this now . . .[49]

The 'crane' it seems, was tamed throughout the area: of Gateshead in 1820, 'Many of the boys who attend the school work in the pit. They have been brought from a state of the greatest rudeness to a mild and gentle behaviour'; of Weardale in 1828, 'the manners and habits of the children, which were rude and immoral, are now orderly and virtuous'; of Usworth in 1828, 'nearly all the boys work in the pits during the week, in consequence of which they have no other instruction than ours'; and of one of the many, at Westmoor in 1835, 'A little boy also, who is at work in the pit twelve hours daily, learned in one quarter, besides catechism and other tasks, 442 verses of the Bible!'[50] The successes were not solely industrial. In 1831 the Union could thank itself, with 15,000 pupils and 3,000 teachers, for presenting 'an opposing phalanx to the surging masses of the discontented, disloyal, and sceptical'. Similarly, the miners' strike of 1831, restrained and disciplined, was due in its caution to a religious education of the miners in their youth.

And yet, the efforts of the Sunday School Union, so accommodative to the new order fast emerging, were not the efforts of a concerted middle-class consciousness. In 1818 the Union taught 11,000 children for a paltry expenditure of £67 7s 1d. Throughout this period, its work so obviously crucial to the merchants, manufacturers and shipowners of Tyneside, the Union was forced into begging letters. They read not unlike the demands of a spent mistress upon her master:

> The owners of collieries are respectfully entreated to recollect how much they owe to this society. They cannot have forgotten the tumult among their men a few years ago. To what is it attributable that another such scene did not occur lately, when so many parts of the kingdom were agitated with the spirit of discontent, but to the diffusion of the light and knowledge of God? Those of you who knew the banks of the Tyne twenty years back can fully confirm . . . [etc.][51]

It was not until later, when threatened by trade unionism and long strikes, that the coalowners realised their vulnerability and took education seriously. Only in the 1850s do the coalowners grasp how manipulable children's characters might be and the wisdom of James Montgomery's sunday school hymn:

> Our time is all to-day, to-day,
> The same though changed; and while it flies,
> With still small voice the moments say,
> Today! today! be wise, be wise!

IV. Morals

If the advocates of sunday schools waged battle in trying to instil new songs and new virtues, the advocates of tract societies fought a rear-guard action in trying to destroy old songs and old values. A woolly sense of moral rearmament linked licentiousness with atheism, in-decency with Jacobinism, for of course the reactionary mind responded to both with equal horror and equal comprehension. In 1795 moves were afoot in Manchester to establish a tract society intended to counter the political by stamping out the obscene:

> . . . an antidote to the poison continually flowing through the channel of vulgar and licentious publications. These, by their cheapness, as well as by their being, unhappily, congenial to deprived taste obtain a mischievous popularity among the lower ranks. It is not the impure novel or romance which attracts the common labourer's ear, or defiles his cottage: but his gross and polluted phrases may often be traced to those profane and indecent songs, and penny papers, which are vended about our cities, towns and villages, by hawkers; of whom it is a low statement to say, that more than 20,000 are employed in this traffic.[52]

Suggested songs for hawking at markets, fairs and 'in the obscurer parts of a town' are the inevitable Watts' *Hymns for Children* and such sober-ing pieces as 'The Apprentice's Monitor, or Indentures in Verse, to be hung up in Shops', 'The Gin Shop, or a Peep at a Prison in verse', and 'The Roguish Miller, or Nothing got by Cheating, a True Ballad'. The Newcastle Religious Tract Society was founded and staffed in 1810 by the same men who formed the Sunday School Union six years after-wards – Messrs. Wawn, Fenwick, Brunting, Angas, Annandale and the Reverend Pengilly. Their aims were not unlike the Manchester proposals, only more overtly religious. Reverend Edwards reported in 1817: 'Previous to the origin of Tract Societies in this country, it would be recollected, to what an alarming extent lewd songs, silly tales, and all manner of low and vile publications were hawked about and sold among our poor . . .'[53] The society believed that the recent economic depression was the trumpet sounding for the Revelation of Divine Truth, that affliction was good for the soul and the Lord often uses it when he wants men to hear Him. But men cannot be as Joab was if they are deafened by obscenity and Jacobinism. To counter blasphemy was the same as countering sedition, for Christianity is the foundation of our state against anarchy and atheism. The naivety of their political perspective is suggested in that they reserve the strongest contempt for Voltaire, a witty old *philosophe*, and not for a man of revolutionary action, a Robespierre or a Marat. Their argument is, and, given their own efforts, had to be, that the power of the press is crucial: leaflets and not pikes brought the Revolution, tracts first demoralised the mind of France and only then could the 'people's axe' do its scything. Voltaire is an ogre, evil shines from his forehead, horror is his *plume* and it is a relief to be out of his company; ' "Ecraser l'infame" he shouted of Our Saviour! contemplating with malignant delight the success of his diabolical machinations.'[54] The 'hell inspired labours' of this Satan stalk Britain and France still, *Jacobinerie* will subvert by sapping our moral strength, beware!

In 1822 the Church of England is active in Northumberland and Durham extending the free library system successfully operated by the Society for Promoting Christian Knowledge. The system rests on the inflated proposition that 'Every Parishioner who can read is liable to have his mind poisoned by the Blasphemous Publications with which the press most infamously tempts the world'. Every parish church is to have a minimum of twelve volumes, theological apologetics and various duties, warnings, instructions, letters, addresses, exhortations and meditations for the Poor. But no flight of generosity this! There are strict conditions before the labourer can lay his grubby fingers on the tracts, particularly that the reading is for the whole family, and only to be done in winter' 'as those readings ought never to interfere with the necessary work of the summer'. Apathetic clergy, those who perhaps do not share the scaremongering of Durham's Cathedral cloisters, are warned within an inch of their souls:

> If it should so happen that any Parishioners had been perverted by any infidel publications, *for want of having the antidotes above-mentioned duly placed within their reach,* the officiating Minister of the Parish cannot be insensible of the fearful account which will be one day required of him, by reason of such neglect.[55]

Eneas Mackenzie in 1827 had confidently asserted that the Newcastle Religious Tract Society intended 'to drive foolish ballads, tales, and stories out of circulation',[56] and with a shade more political malice the various lending libraries that sprang up intended to do the same. Amongst the miners, efforts to do so redoubled with crisis, and yet by 1850 the political cast of these efforts (though not necessarily the cultural one) was judged to have failed. At Seaton Delaval Colliery it was admitted that only the self-taught élite had joined the library, 33 out of 850 colliers, and that more guidance was needed to their reading if the desired effect was to be won:

> . . . merely to read and write, left to themselves at the most critical period of their lives, without advice or guidance, very naturally seize upon such publications as afford excitement, either by the abuse of those above them, or by captivating theories that flatter the vanity of the ignorant, and promise ease and enjoyment by some new arrangements of society.[57]

In the same report, a respectable Wesleyan of Seaton Delaval speaks of the miners' dislike of such good literature as Chambers' Edinburgh Journal, and preference for a penny weekly (he refuses to pass the words over his lips, but it sounds like Harney or Jones) 'that speaks against everybody'. It is hardly surprising that those pitmen who could read preferred 'exciting' literature to that which was offered them. Under the circumstances, with one or two exceptions, one can imagine a miner doing all he could to avoid such reading matter. The principal volumes of Urpeth Colliery's lending library in 1847 were such startling pieces as *Abbott's Young Christian, Chambers' Miscellany, Mechanics Magazine, Susan Carter: A Colliery Tale* and *Life of Sir Isaac Newton.* Burns, Milton and Shakespeare were there and, we know, did lend sustenance to many a man, but these are honourable exceptions to the ceaseless round of *Backwoods of Canada* and *Rise & Progress of Religion in the Soul.*[58]

The kind of exciting literature so preferred was categorised in the report of 1851 as, 'Infidel and Chartist', 'Chartist Only', and 'Hostile to our present Institutions and of an immoral tendency'. Newcastle's chief seller of periodicals and papers for that year sold 3,976 copies pf such matter, to only 888 classified as 'Religious and Moral. Containing useful information'.[59] At various times local authorities and members of the establishment became seriously worried over such 'exciting' works, whether lewd ballads or radical agitation – like the Sunderland informer William Coxton who wrote to Peel in 1828 about a publican. James Kinker, who had opened a shop opposite Bishop Wearmouth Church 'in the midst of a thoroughfare, the windows of which shop are covered with infidel placards; songs calculated to bring sacred subjects into contempt; and books of a similar tendency'.[60] Such concern may have been justified over short-term political challenges, but it was ridiculous in the longer-term challenge against social and industrial stability. Those radicals who pushed for working-class 'improvement' in all of its guises, Teetotalism, Owenism, Chartism, Trade Unionism, benefit and educational clubs, socialism, secularism, they all had their own particular sincerities, but equally they all also had the destruction of the old popular culture as integral to their ends. Owenites were called infidels, whores and worse, yet look at some of their illustrations of the New Moral World; industry and factories and machinery are accepted, the pictures is one of pastoral, rational peace, the workers loll in orderly groups or pore over enlightening works or vigorously enjoy athletic games. There is no turbulence. A drunken pitman or a fighting keelman would be unthinkable in such a socialist Eden; a lewd ballad would be pornographic. The very idea of persuading working men to band together in groups at fixed times on *planned* days, to discuss *conceptually*, to sit soberly, to go away and struggle through Baxter or Volney or the Rule Book, presented common cultural problems to Methodists, radicals and 'Buffaloes' alike.

In 1834 the great radical Richard Carlile was in Newcastle. He declared battle with superstition and ignorance as much as with government and tyranny: 'Our warfare is with superstition, and human error, the printing press is an instrument to be used to that end . . .'[61] A year later Francis Place, a man who had devoted his life to radical causes, described the habits of the lower orders as 'All of a gross nature', and remembers 'where songs were sung which cannot now be more than generally described from their nastiness'. Place sees the old half-paganism as a check to men's freedom because he wanted working men to be reading Mill and making themselves capable, instead of bawling indecencies in the fug of an alehouse. Francis Place claimed to have witnessed a cultural revolution in his own lifetime:

> The ballads sung about the streets [forty years before], the books openly sold, cannot be adequately described. I have given you in writing, words of some common ballads which you would not think fit to have uttered in this Committee. At that time the songs were of the most indecent Kind; no one would mention them in any society now; they were publicly sung and sold in the streets and markets, and bought by maidservants . . . I have a collection of some of them among other materials, to show what were the manners of the people at that time. Books were openly sold in shops of booksellers in leading streets, which can only be procured clandestinely now. I have seen the Prayer Book, the Racing Calendar, and these books bound alike, side by side, in very respectable shop-windows in the

leading streets.[62]

The motive and policy of such bodies as the Newcastle Religious Tract Society, the SPCK, and those collieries which had libraries, is undoubtedly revealing. Equally revealing is the importance attached to literature in the battle for morality by such perceptive men as Carlile and Place. However, the printed word alone has a transient quality when it comes to the inculcation of morals. The colliery Methodists backed their word with the flesh: behind their hymns and prayers and tracts there lay the organisation and discipline of the society. Every Methodist society involved its adherents in functions and controlled its adherents by groups. Practical involvement and social commitment often *preceded* religious conversion: the more involved a man became with the Methodist organisation then the more difficult it became for him to disentangle himself from the moral logic of its religious claim.

Another material reason for the power of the Methodist word lay in the community itself. The Methodists dominated the inculcation of the new morality because the organised convention of their own society and its pressure on the individual well fitted the organisation of the wider society around them. There was something about the pit village that was protective to cultural patterns. Concentrated, without the scattered pattern of rural agricultural communities, it yet retained their isolation. Existing only for the colliery, the cultural identity in relationships less cosmopolitan than the town, but more claustrophobic than the country – a population that could more easily find societal consensus (and watchfulness) for their actions. A man who went tee-total and joined the Rechabites could expect scorn from his former tap room hearties; those hearties, in turn, could expect scorn, erudite scorn, from the chapel pulpit. Leifchild refers to 'clannishness and moral insulation' as reasons for 'numerous anomalies, and numerous evils, physical and moral'.[63] But what Leifchild failed to see was that this near-incestuous nature of social relationship could also work the other way, in favour of respectability and the counterculture he and his like were agitating for. D. H. Lawrence's remark on the colliery community being 'a secret people' is only true (or part true), from the outside; inside the community there was little privacy and a drive for convention.

The Methodists were effective, as well as passionate, cultural revolutionaries. And it is here, towards the end of the chapter, that we must return to the beginning. The would-be Methodist who lost his job for leaving the secular music of the colliery band, and the Methodist preacher who lost his 'cloth' for playing quoits – both men had tasted the bitterness of cultural revolution, both men had paid the price for adhering to self-images made sharp by conflict.

And yet, this self-image, conceived in the framework of conversion, death, children, and morals, remains incomplete. The Methodist personality and its reception has so far been described only in general terms. In fact, this personality was discovering itself in creative reaction to what it opposed, and what it opposed was finding social definition in reaction to the personality. General terms will not suffice for describing this dialectical process which occurred in a community already rich in self-image and identity at a time of intense social conflict. This process could not and did not leave the Methodist experience of the colliery community regionally or politically neutral. It was not enough that the Methodist personality was *received* – it had to be *naturalised.*

4 RESPECTABLES AND UNRESPECTABLES IN STRIKE

Between 1815 and the 1850s the miners of Northumberland and Durham considered themselves to be the victims of a steady deterioration in their standard of living. Although wage rates remained above prices, except in sudden slumps, the Coal Industry managed itself according to a system of speculative investment, restricted production and over-capacity within a context of increasing competitiveness from other coalfields. For the miner, this system made more frequent the incidence of slump and lay-off.

The first comprehensive and self-conscious miners' trade union of Tyne and Wear was Tommy Hepburn's 'United Colliers' in 1831. Hepburn, a hewer at Hetton Colliery in Co. Durham, was a man of remarkable ability who led the union to victory in its demands during the summer of 1831 – and who controlled the union in its defeat during the owners' counter-attacks of 1832. A Chartist interval in 1839 blended into the Chartist-inspired National Miners' Association in the early 1840s. Founded at Wakefield on 7 November 1842, the NMA recognised the growing need for a common strategy for the industrial proletariat and sought to recruit from all the coalfields of England, Scotland and Wales. Like the 'United Colliers', the NMA also saw education as one of its prime functions. During 1843 and early 1844 the union recruited strongly to an estimated membership of about 60,000. The North East was the strongest district and Newcastle quickly became the headquarters and power base of the NMA.

In April 1844, and against the better collective judgement of the whole union, the North East district withdrew their labour. There was no negotiation between union and owners, and by the September the strike had collapsed and men were back to work on the previous terms. The NMA was then systematically persecuted out of Northumberland and Durham and its leadership moved to Lancashire where it was never again to recover its old influence and strength. An 1844 North East summer of hunger, provocation, and organised blacklegging destroyed the strongest trade union of its era just as the similar summer of 1832 had destroyed Hepburn's 'United Colliers'.

I. Cadre

'I will be a swift witness against the sorcerers, and against the adulterers and against false swearers, and against those that oppress the hireling in his wages, the widow, and the fatherless, and that turn aside the stranger from his right, and fear not me, saith the Lord.' The words did not come from a pulpit directed at sinners six feet below; they came from the National Miners' Association and were directed at a blackleg called Geordy.[1]

In the last chapter Methodism was cast as a major force, not only in creating the new culture, but also in accommodating the working-class character to the new social and economic changes. But there is a sense in which the chapel's role was essentially ambivalent. There are myriad complexities attached to the blunt statement of ideological reason and impact, which when broken down come to this: some influences on working men, like Owenism or Primitive Methodism were, in their own way, double-edged to the industrial interest. Of course, a respectable chapel-going miner, in his solemn discipline, was useful to the coalowner; but Primitive Methodism had content as well as style – it can be seen as part of a new and growing working-class consciousness, nourished by and in the very womb of industrial capitalism, but opposed to it. In one sense, Primitive Methodism was accommodative, yet in another sense it was to feed the growth of formidable opposition. The Methodist cadre of miners' leaders is the *naturalising* dimension to our Methodist Personality discussed in the last chapter. Men are not made of clay. The working class reacted to the ideologies vying for attention, and took them and moulded them to suit; there was compromise and conformity but in the end, their class consciousness was of their own making. Primitive Methodism, because of its constitution for wide lay participation, suffered less compromise than most; the Zion chapels of the colliery villages evolved as their members dictated; their members evolved according to the experience of being a miner, an experience in turn made articulate by Zion. That the blackleg Geordy was threatened by Jehovah's swift witness can come as no surprise for 'He that oppresseth the poor, reproacheth his Maker'.

The story of how chapel-bred miners found expression in pulpit and strike hustings in Northumberland and Durham is famous; there is a hagiography as long as a winding cable about such men – the cadre of North East pit unionism in the nineteenth century. But the legend dwells in facts; a colliery agent in 1846 remembered two years previously:

> The local preachers, the chief speakers at these prayer meetings, were the men who, by a certain command of language, and by an energetic tone and manner, had acquired an influence over their fellow workmen, and were invariably the chief promoters and abettors of the strike. They were consequently among the first, at most of the works, to be dismissed by the masters.[2]

Colliery managers all over the two counties reported similarly to the commissioner. And activity was not only limited to the saints; at times it seems as if all those who were religious ransacked their Bibles for pertinent analogies. The long duration of the struggle? the collier's spirit was like the Widow's cruse 'that never did run out'. The Bond and wage reductions? 'the Israelites in Egypt were by Pharaoh "prest severe" '. The leaders? 'Lord let a Moses rise again the colliers to release.' The owners? 'the great Sanhedrin'. Coal measure cheatings? 'Gehazi took from the Syrian General, under false pretences, money which did not belong to him; for this he lost his health – his honour – his place – and his peace.' The rights of labour? 'the labourer shall receive the first fruits of his labour'.

But the Methodist contribution was more than a matter of scriptural analogy. The Methodist Personality carried a temperament and a demeanour which union leaders made their own and adopted for their cause. Whilst scriptural analogies were tactics for victory, temperament and demeanour were strategies for freedom.

In 1843, Robert Pearson, a pitman of Castle Eden Colliery, and Catherine Wearmouth, his lover, jointly murdered Pearson's wife. It seems the three of them had lived and slept together for some time, and on one night the screams of the wife had been heard along the terrace.[3] The murder was quickly followed by the distribution in the colliery villages of a religio-moral tract addressed to 'Ye Working men of Britain's Isle' warning them to '*avoid passion's fatal sway*'.[4] The National Miners' Association, then gathering strength in Northumberland and Durham in preparation for the strike of 1844, could in no way have found exception to this patronising little tract. In a broader context perhaps, the union's most repeated call to the miners during the forthcoming strike was to avoid passion's fatal sway. 'Keep the peace!' rings on the lips of every leader who spoke to the men during nearly thirty weeks of struggle. Whether a national leader and Chartist, or a local leader and Methodist, the war cry is the same: rebuke your former ways, trust in your leaders, in no way lend provocation to owners or magistrates or cavalry, keep the peace and let your union live. Reversion to traditional modes of direct action, sabotage and riot, would have spelt disaster for a union facing authorities well-primed for repression. And when the strike failed and the unions crumbled, the call was for colliers to learn how to read, to think and to speak and to work for their fellows' amelioration. In 1847 the remnants of the union presented a petition to Parliament for the educational clauses in the Factory Act to be extended to miners 'to assist in the improvement of their minds and habits';[5] and it is worth remembering that the concept of such education for government and owners alike was the erosion of 'those obliquities of judgement and moral disorders which have hitherto been the main source of trouble . . .'[6] Tommy Hepburn's miners' union of 1831-2 had taken an identical stance in relation to restraint of 'passion's fatal sway' and when he too failed, it is not surprising to hear him imploring his men to read and form libraries.

Hepburn, and the cohort of young hewers who formed the general staff of his union had been Primitive Methodists. In 1844 a similar local cadre of Primitives provided the leadership. The chapel had taken these men out of the mainstream of village life and nurtured civic abilities in them: some vision of Man's significance, some rhetoric of justice, some reading and a lot of speaking. Most importantly, Methodism had been a cocoon of seriousness in a pub and coursing-path world of careless enjoyment and self-mockery. The cocoon provided its own reason and reward for self-improvement – so dearly won by the miner:

> We are fifteen hours out of the house every day; I am very tired by night. I have a good appetite. I go to school at night; we are in school two hours. I hurt myself very sore to get scholarship. I am ciphering, and am at squaring dimensions. I read well. I write – I cannot say very well, but I can write.[7]

Bob Cranky, bright as a button and mad as a hatter, was not for Methodist pitmen like William Scott 'accustomed to sit in a garret for hours together',[8] struggling nightly through Wesley's *Sermons* by the shadows of candlelight. Alcoholic stupors were not behaviour fitting to a creature born only a little lower than the angels. Thus, the broad effect of the Methodist penetration was to split the mining village into two communities:

> The only place for social gatherings or recreation was a public house, formed by uniting two cottages, with a fenced cockpit and a quoit

> ground at the front, and a quiet place for pitch-and-toss just around the corner, provided opportunities for rotaries of these sports, which, with the tap room as their centre, were often accompanied by drunken brawls and fighting, with all the demoralizing influences arising therefrom.
>
> The chapel thus created was the centre of almost all domestic life. Its only competitor was the public house . . .[9]

And the effects of rivalry showed in the people themselves. As early as 1802 a local writer commented on how morbid the Methodists were, forever severe,[10] and over a hundred years later a Methodist ex-miner reflected that still gravity in his view of the 'other type':

> A reflective, contemplative man is driven inward upon himself, and in self-communion and meditation is made strong. The unreflective, superficial man, becomes a mere machine for hewing coals. The one comes to the bank to turn his dreams into realities and his visions into sober facts; the other seeks his rebound in the village tavern and on the coursing path.[11]

An Anglican vicar, writing in the 1860s of his mining parish with all the force of one of his lurid tracts, makes the villages sound like Sin Cities of the Durham Plain. Yet he finds comfort in the religious élite – 'black diamonds' that 'shine all the brighter from the force of contrast'.[12]

The cadre sang their hymns, reasoned through their texts, and expressed their class and personal aspirations in terms of the New Jerusalem. Their personality and self-image is necessarily important to us. But what of the other group, what of their hedonist counterparts? They were certainly in the majority (although the spectrum of feeling would be wide). Figures[13] for some predominantly mining areas of the region in 1851, Chester le Street, Castle Ward, Easington and Houghton, found that only 13 per cent of the population were chapel-going Methodists, 11 per cent were Church of England and 4 per cent other non-conformist groups. This is surprisingly low considering the bulky and distinguished historiography of the Methodist cadre in Durham; lower for instance than the equivalent districts of South Wales: Merthyr had a 60 per cent worship attendance, only 8 per cent of which was to the Established Church; Pontypool had 70 per cent, 55 per cent of which was Baptist. Historians have been neglectful of this 'non-respectable' group, although a majority, as active participants in the creation of class culture, overlooking that undercurrent of consciousness and aspiration that found its expression in traditional guise. The analysis of working-class popular song is again important in this context; there is not only a continuity of theme throughout most of the century, but also a continuity in the places it was rejoiced in – the music hall developed out of the public house, not the theatre.[14]

II. Class Forms

Much of the content of those boasting, manly frolics we have covered carries a latent class pride. 'The Bonnie Pit Lads', one of a series of songs published for the Union in 1844, is a well-worn toast, set in a new situation; union success and the bravery implicit combines with getting the girl:

> Then she clapt her arms around him like Venus round the vine,
> You are my jolly Pit lad and you've won this heart of mine,
> And that if you do win the day as you have won my heart,
> I'll crown you with honour and for ever take your part.
>
> So come all you pretty maidens wherever you may be . . .

The ever-jolly pit laddie has now assumed the stature of *moral* significance; the grin that was always there has opened into a smile, the smile of those only honour can crown. But even before the manly struggle of labour, in the songs the pitman's supposed ignorance is more than a doltish stupidity; it is more a shambling refusal to be a part of – typical in self-effacement, a class expression of its own cultural territory. Hence, Paganini, somehow, is not for them, and neither is classical music on the violin – so he becomes 'Baggy Nanny' and is 'reet gude' on the fiddle, the pitman adopts him as his own. Another song of 1844 reflects this; 'The Pitman Turned Swell' tells of a miner who has come into money and apes his betters; it goes without saying that the 'raspberry' is for him. The song has all the banter and vulgarity of the singing room, but the laugh has teeth which snap – if you cannot beat your betters then laugh at them; better still, laugh at yourself, for We Are The People, immutable and all pals together:

> My wife she is the worst of all, when we give genteel dinners,
> She uses neither knife nor fork, but pops in all her fingers;
> And when they hand the wine about, she tells the gents it stinks sir,

Gets full her mouth and squirts it out, and calls it treacle drink sir.

But I'm so plagued with vulgar folks since I've got cash to sport,
sir,
Why can't a pitman cut a swell since he's been left a fortune.

The pitman 'type' may not be 'clever', by his own ceaseless admission he protesteth too much the fact, but it never prevented him from having his own opinions. Neither are the opinions cast in deference: in 'The Use and Abuse, Or, the Pitmen an' the Preachers' the 'ranterfied preest . . . gets paid for his lees an' his yammer'; and 'The Keelman's reasons for Attending Church' are only to trick his religious employer into raising his wages. Those tempted to do otherwise are warned off:

Noo Dick, were ye not vera bad
When he se fine was teachin'?
Did ye not feel a' queer an' sad,
An' trummel at his preachin'?
Aw'm sure aw cud hae roar'd amyen,
Had it not been wor Willy;
For he wad jeer'd an teld wor men,
An' they wad ca'd it silly.

In fact, the chapel respectables are quite frequently the subject of spite. Confessed vulgarity cloaking a warm heart which beats good and true is contrasted to the tight little prejudices of the religious. 'Fish Betty's Account of Herself', also dating from 1844, glories in its unrespectability:

And when the folks in Chapel sit,
The nasty stinking varmint,
Aw knaw they're thinkin' mair o' me
Than ought about the sarmint.

An interesting sidelight on this daft-but-not-so-daft, wise Fool aspect of the pitmen and keelmen is given in *Jim Crow's Song Book*, a Newcastle chapbook of the period. Jim Crow, 'the daft darkie', is a negro version of the type, who on visiting the Tyne finds instant rapport with the keelmen. He mistakes coal dust for African blood, 'De keelmen shout, "Ha! blackey!" says I Hollows!/Tink him in his own country, sees so many Jim Crows!' Jim is an astonishingly liberated black

Bob Cranky: he too is 'bonny':

> Me no like the white gals,
> 'Cause their beauty faint,
> But him love the black gals
> 'Cause dey neber paint.
>
> De white ladies dey paint dere cheeks
> Vid rouge or carmine,
> But I rub mine with de blacka brush,
> And I looks bery fine.

and his good nature does not stop him from replying to insult,

> But when me get to London
> A boy cry like a good un,
> 'Oh crikeys! lookee dere,
> Dere's a valking blacka pudding!'
>
> Howeber, me soon laughee
> And I say – it werry clear,
> Dey sich very stupid people
> Dey no judge ob beauty here.

Of course there is an insidious side to all of this; unlike the pit laddie caricatures there were too few Jim Crows on Tyneside to make it their celebration. But the songs are fascinating in their resonance with the unrespectables and by no means merely mocking . . .' 'cause their beauty faint'.

But not all the songs of class aspiration were so good natured. The bar room housed the brawlers as well as the comics, and unless snatched from the burning, the hard men of the pit community would make the bar their haunt. In strike, if there was any intimidating to be done, it would come from there and not the chapel. Thornley had been on strike many months before the two counties came out in concert in the April of 1844. On the night of Monday, 12 February, the strike breakers of Thornley experienced physical attacks on their houses: windows were stoned, shotguns blasted, gardens wrecked amidst the 'rough music' of pots, fenders and hissing.[15] Robert Wrangham, an unemployed labourer, had promised to start at the colliery on the twelfth, but at midnight of the day before his door was kicked in, and while others kept watch three strikers beat him up; Thomas Wood, the viewer for the company, wrote to the magistrate, Rowland Burdon, on 8 April that 'this Outrage was planned at a meeting of a large number of men who were at a Public House not far off'. The night after Wrangham's beating other homes were attacked, although this time the blacklegs were ready – we can only presume the threat came from the same quarter. Richard Clough's home was stoned for twenty minutes; 'I was very much afraid, and my sons and I ran upstairs but found that stones were also coming through the windows there . . .' James Defty 'looked out and heard the people groaning, hissing, and throwing stones'. We can sense the feverishness of a house trapped by noise and stones in the deposition of Nicholas Wearmouth – first the front side was hammered with sticks and then the back, the windows shattered and people seemed all around, 'I left the front room and went to the back door, to stand in my own defence in case of them breaking in, which I was looking for every minute.' Along the row Stephen Bones and William Craddock had also fastened their doors and stood in readiness, but for them the attackers brought a shotgun and fired it point blank into the door; Craddock's deposition is a vivid insight into the cruelty of blacklegging: 'The door was not broken in, for as I had some fear of them for a day or two past I had fastened it very strongly inside . . . My family and myself could not go to bed after the men had left, we sate by the fire till 6 o'clock Bell rung, I then went down the pit to look after my horses . . .'

The retribution had been violent, but the men of Thornley were suffering: they had first struck in the previous November and were to be out until the following August. Not only were they and their families cheated by wholesale blacklegging, but scoundrels like the barber Thomas Richardson filched on support forthcoming from other collieries. During February Richardson toured the county pretending to be raising money for the strike. It would have broken a striker's heart to have seen Richardson lose £7 10s (ten weeks' wages for a miner) in one sitting at cards.[16] It certainly broke their tempers: the word was put about that, if found, his life would not be worth the foam he shaved with, and inevitably, Thornley made musical its threat, 'The Wonderful Shaver':

> It's oh! poor Tom the shaver, what can you get to do?
> You're forced to come to Thornley to join the blackleg crew:
> Now, Tom I'd have you to repent, while on this earth you dwell,
> If this wicked course you do pursue, you'll have to shave in hell!

Songs against blacklegs echoed their warning throughout the counties. Some, like the personal column of *The Miners Advocate*, offered direct intimidation; 'A New Song' by William Hornsby of Shotton Moor spelt out each Judas verse by verse: 'Then little *C*—— has got a face for everyone that he does talk with'; 'Then *W*—— *G*—— a Cockfield man, he is a base and treacherous villain'; 'Then *W*—— *T*—— next in the clan, for favour he'll do ought that's dirty'. And when the attack finally came, the redressers struck in the name of Rebecca, spectre of Wales:

> Thomas Johnson. Castle Eden Colliery.
>
> We are infirmed that you have Started to Brake a standing ingine at Castle Eden on the 15 of April 1844. Therefore as i have the honner to Be the Mother of so Numourous a famely i wish to take the opertunity of infirming you of the Danger that you are standing in, and you Know Not how Soon the Result May Be. As you know that youre felow workmen has Joined the Union for to Shorten the hours of labor, and to obtain an advance of wages (and you have Taken there Plases) therefore take Notice That if you Remain as you are you may Rest Ashoured that at an houre when you Think Not that your Liffe will Be Demanded in Such a Manner as you think Not if you are inclined to live a little Longer you Must Join the Union as Soun as Posable and Be As a Man in the Land of Freadem.
>
> Signed on Behalph, Mis Cromewel and your Leage Ladey. *Rebeckah*[17]
>
> From the Mountains.

'Rebeckah' moved quickly and always at night: windows would shatter, doors would burst open, and the grotesque sight of men in women's clothes, their faces blackened and revenging, would confront you. Wallsend suffered severe visits in the June of 1844, and so did a score of other collieries during the spring and summer. The terror may have been mercurial in action, but the impression is of superb planning. Thomas Wood, to Rowland Burdon in the letter quoted above, wrote of the Thornley attacks: 'The Colliers were very violent & well organized, and they kept up a continual system of terror . . . watching their Houses at night, issuing threatening placards of "Rebecca visits", going about in Women's clothes etc . . .'

The disguise of women's clothes and black smudged faces was nothing new. It had been used long before in efforts to make men dwell 'As a Man in the Land of Freadem'. The round-rimmed woman's bonnet was useful in protecting (and hiding) the poacher's eyes from the night glare of his torch as he and his accomplices stalked upstream with trident and net for bull trout; a face in shadow, and the figureless form of a woman's skirts made identification impossible should there be a skirmish with the keepers. Could the fact that Rebecca's family were all daughters be explained by this? Poaching was a standing habit of the pitman, but few Methodists would do it – in Weardale permission for chapels was given by gentry on promises that it would decline in the face of the new influence – poaching parties were planned and shotguns admired in the pub: by 1844 only the 'unrespectables' would take the game, as only they would bait blacklegs. Stephen Bones had leapt in shock when 'a gun was fired twice at the door, I saw the flashes under the door'; the flashes were surely those of a gun used for less exotic game.

Hepburn's strikes of 1831 and 1832 had similarly given rise to songs in threat of blacklegs. Probably the most famous was 'The First Drest Man of Seghill', here a printed broadside dated 31 March 1831:

> But I will tell his travels here
> As he went from the binding;
> They stript him there of part his clothes,
> And left his skin refining.
>
> But remember you that come
> Unto Seghill to bind,
> You may think upon the man
> That we have treat so kind.

But come they did and the promise was kept; after the defeat and scattering of the union in 1831, Seghill was the scene of pitched battles with picks and staves between unemployed union men and immigrant labourers. The February of 1833 witnessed the most savage of these battles at Wideopen Colliery.[18] The affair was a calculated attempt by native pitmen of the village to lure and provoke immigrant miners out of the pub and into the street to fight. The ferociousness of the assault which followed, with pokers and fire irons, is staggering. An atmosphere of the silent hatred which pervaded the village is set by a Staffordshire man; ' . . . we went into the Tap Room. Some of the Old Pitmen were there, we called for some Beer, We had no conversation with them . . .' Brooding over their glasses and nervous for the fight, the native men sat and listened to the immigrants singing; Edward Cook, a Yorkshireman, reported ' . . . one of the old Pitmen of the name of Henry Temple came several times and used very abusive language, and said he had a Man in his Company who could sing better than any Man in the Ship or that came out of Wales and Staffordshire . . .' Arguments were slow to come, more beer, and one had to be started: a challenge match for 6d at 'pitch and toss', a traditional North East pitman's game, was arranged, money to be spent on beer; the natives won and kept the coin; complaint was the signal for revenge: '. . . struck at Saddon, the man who played, Evan Jones a Welshman then got up and he was likewise struck at and knocked down – A general Row then commenced, & Witness saw the defendant Mordue, he was stripped and had nothing on but his Trousers.' As soon as the uproar was heard, native men and women of Wideopen flocked to the pub doors ready to assist. George Walker, from Staffordshire, was dragged from the pub and thrown into the lane:

> . . . the old Pitmen kicked me over the Head and Temples until I had scarce life left in me. My mother was sent for who came to me when she heard me crying out and James Shakespeare [another Staffs miner] . . . held me upon his knee and my mother was standing by me she begged of them not to injure me any more as they had given me plenty . . . [four men reapproached with pokers and scrapers] . . . and they all struck me very violently over each arm, on the Fore part of the Head and on the Back . . . must have been with a Hot Poker as my Back was burned, when I was knocked down I became insensible . . . My mother had hold of me and my mother at this time received a violent Blow.

Job Davies, a Welshman, rushed from his home only to be confronted by a woman brandishing a poker – the next thing he knew he was down and bleeding only to wake the next morning on the slag heap of West Moor pit, a quarter of a mile away. By this time the immigrant women were out of their homes and screaming; some went for help – the information of Edmund Godber, from Derbyshire, 'That on Friday night last about 11 o'clock he was in his own house & was just going to Bed, when a Woman came into the House and said "Edmund for God's sake go out for they are killing all the Staffordshire men".' He did go to find some like Davies, insensible and being kicked; others like Walker, held and being brayed with scrapers. There was nothing he could do.

The chapel folk of Wideopen, Hepburn himself (he was then reduced to selling tea through the villages) and the cadre of 'respectables' who had staffed his union, would have felt only disgust at these scenes.

Tactically it did not matter any more; the union was dead, its leaders victimised, many of its members unemployed. But respectability for them was more than a social vision or a personal ambition; it was a reason for living itself. They were out of the morass; respectability had become a means and an end, it had given them the confidence to be confident; fighting in the street, blowing heavy with beer, was typical of the 'vortex of sensuality' they were to spend their lives avoiding. Robert Forbes, a Scottish miner, was one of the most regular contributors to the *Miners' Advocate* through 1844. In many ways he represented the archetypal self-educated, rationalist-respectable élite, next to the religious respectables, predominant in the NMA leadership. Writing here on October 19 when the union was beginning to crumble after the Northumberland and Durham collapse, and there were real dangers of physical conflicts, he casts a prophet's dream of the New Reason substituting the Old Sensuality. The working class must 'KNOW THYSELF' by 'the queenly power of reason'; and knowledge pure and undefiled is equated with morality, his morality, ' . . . causing the pure rivers of knowledge to burst forth and fertilize the moral desert by invoking the assistance of the goddess of reason'. A coalface Zimmerman, a Scots Volney, Forbes takes delight in words; he writes heavily, he poses his bust of knowledge in the classical profile and his elaborate asides are overladen with the conceit of a man only one step out of the morass – but for all that, an unmistakably honest pleasure in the act of self-expression is revealed. His most common image of unrespectability is mud: it is an obvious truth that the working classes slumber on in degradation, 'wallowing in the stagnant pool of ignorance all besmeared with its mud, which is PREJUDICE'; the way out is by the choirs and sisterhoods of Science and the Arts who stand as pillars above 'the muddy, deceitful waters of sensuality'.

It is clear that the visions of Man held by a George Mordue who stripped to fight blacklegs in the Ship at Wideopen, and a Robert Forbes who contemplated blacklegs as in 'want of principle and economy', were startlingly different. If they were partly self-images, then, although obviously to lesser extents, they must also have been self-ambitions. It seems worth asking to what extent such ambitions encouraged or opposed each other in their rival claims upon the pitman's imagination and realities. Certainly, the gay young rake stereotype of a Cranky came nowhere near ambitions of piety or knowledge, and for some bordered on outright sin. It was, however, an important collective spirit in time of strike, for was not the bonny collier lad as invincible as he was arrogant? Who dares to put him down when he has had a few beers and is with his *marras*? No one, except a buxom lass who might break his heart! Anyway, the truth is that both styles transcended immediate differences to form a wedge of class solidarity during the strike of 1844, the like of which was unprecedented. The tensions were still apparent, but now, and without niggle, they were directed against a common enemy: The *Miners' Journal* of 18 November 1843, five months before strike action, could exhort 'get knowledge and read', and 'worship at Reason's shrine', and at the same time carry an editorial snorting class hatred in a most non-rational way: 'He [the coal owner] grins again! his wife chuckles, poor soul, the "partner of his bosom", and little Susan has a new pair of dancing shoes.' Even the marble logic of Forbes could melt emotion; without the miner's labour ' . . . your pampered aristocrat, your fine ladies and your upper and middle classes would be the most abject, most helpless wretches.' Working-class differences of 'respectability', in a brief flush of consciousness, resolved themselves into what was more vital, to stand united.[19]

III. A War in Print

In the silent fury in which the strike was waged (the owners refused throughout to talk to the union), it became a war in print: the region was bombarded with tracts from both sides, everything from the most intricate essays on weights and wages, to the most caustic polemics.[20] 'Knowledge is Power' headed the *Advocate's* every copy, and miners were repeatedly urged to contribute. The paper was showered with mathematical calculations from every branch, bringing down to Q.E.D. proportions exactly how much to the penny had been deducted from the collier's wages over the previous years – in sixteen pays Thornley reckoned about £606 13s 4d to hewers, a £93 6s 8d loss to putters, and £24 loss to drivers. The minds of Joseph Hall and Joseph Walker, lodge president and secretary together, reveal that shrewdness typical of the intelligent uneducated. Apart from the mathematics (and paid by the piece in weight, the miner was a mathematician every day), the fullest contribution was in songs and poems; the greatest number of them testifies to the existence of an already richly ingrained collective consciousness. Some were written and distributed merely for amusement, but they were a minority form. Of the others, predictably, some were hymns, some were ale house ditties, but both bristled with the matter in hand.[21] 'Verses on the Cruelty of the Masters to the Pitmen' is a hymn yet it carries all the images: the Bible is invoked:

Thou heard the Israelites of old,
And led them to a blessed fold,
Deliver us from slavery
And set the sons of Britain free.

and the true patriotism of radical politics will help:

Does not the trumpet sound reform,
And are we not free Britons born?
We want to have a jubilee,
The slavish Pitmen now set free.

The strike is only against one aspect of many years' encroachment on the people's rights:

As lions greedy of their prey,
They take our rights from us away,
To starvation we are driven,
Pale and wan we are ill thriven.

Who is to blame? The song gropes forward to socialism and points at capitalists, but in the rhetoric of old:

As cannibals they eat our flesh,
Their bellies swell to great excess,
To quench their thirst have drunk our blood,
And left us wallowing in the mud.

Another hymn, this one to the tune of 'Auld Lang Syne', was written by Thomas Nicholson of East Holywell colliery. In stately fashion, the first national miners' union is rejoiced: Welshmen, leeks and Liberty!:

Come, let us make a Union Knot,
  Round every heart to twine,
When carried to the Miner's cot
  It may his cause combine.
The first is 'England's bonny rose',
  Then 'Scotland's thistle's' seen;
The twain will heal a Miner's woes
  And make his heart serene.

Truth, like a rock adamant,
Will ever stand secure;
The Union, like the shamrock-plant,
For ages will endure!
The valiant hosts for liberty
Are neither cold nor bleak –
Firm in the bands of unity
With the Welchman and his leek.

William Prowting Roberts was a West country solicitor and Chartist who had fought a number of successful legal cases for the union. His victory for the Thornley men had secured the release of their leaders from prison and made his name hallowed among miners in the two counties. Daniel O'Connor may be 'the Lion of Freedom' and Oastler 'King of the factory children', but Roberts was 'The Miners' Attorney General' and in an anonymous song, 'The Pitmen's Union', his friendship with the miners is shared with another:

Long, long, may Mr Roberts live;
Long may our Union last;
May God our souls receive,
When all our toils are past.
O, may we all to Heaven ascend,
And reign, with Christ, the Pitmen's friend!

On the original manuscript in the first line of this verse 'Mr Roberts' has been written over 'HEPBURN'. Other songs, though as grandiose as the hymns and mixing Enlightenment philosophy with English rights and Old Testament wrath, have traces of the dramatic personalism of the stage. Arm to forehead and looking away, this anonymous piece carries melodrama into the humble cottage:

'Speak not, my husband, thus', she said,
Then sighing faint, she droop'd her head,
And died – OF HUNGER DIED!
My helpless babes, your mother's gone,
The spirit from starvation's flown,
From Grief and sorrow's tide.

But can we thus in hunger waste,
Our wives and children pine to taste

The joys of daily bread.
Rise, Britons, rise! let despots know
That Heaven will deal the avenging blow!
Our hearts too long have bled!

In sharp contrast to this dirge of an anthem the irrepressible Bob Crankey is invoked, this time called Peter Pluck. No one can knock this marra down; the 'Dialogue between Harry Heartless and Peter Pluck' by a miner from Framwellgate Moor, has him remembering the victory of 1831 as reason to be of good cheer:

. . . Thous kens weel as me at the last greet lang strike,
The Maister's behaviour was just the same like,
Ane thief the —— aw'l not tell his name,
He said to the men they might all be gann hame,
For what they were axin he never wad pay,
They got all they ax'd for the very next day.[22]

'Restriction', by *Junius*, is also in dialect and bounds along in tap room sty el. It calls for good heart in the traditional tactic of withholding production at the place where the miner exercised complete control, the coal face:

They say that we are not aggriev'd,
An' hev ne wants to be relieved,
But that we are by knaves deceived.
What monstrous fiction!
But yet we canna be retrieved
But by RESTRICTION!

They think that they can saw division
Amang wor ranks by competition;
But there's a word in wor commission
Of purer diction,
That we should force upon their vision –
By name RESTRICTION!

Songs such as 'The Wingate Grange Blue Hounds in Pursuit of a Fox' set to a popular tune of the time and mocking of the newly summoned rural police, were merely comic cuts; but another anonymous piece, 'The Owners Vend and the Miners' Union' (1844), in three verses.

sets out in rhyme the exact issues of the strike – wage reductions, restrictions, the owners' monopoly called the Vend:

> The last four years we know full well, our wages have come down,
> As far as 25%, five shillings in the pound;
> The cause of this we do not know, but we feel the effect,
> We're meanly fed and poorly clad, and treated with disrespect.
>
> Our masters say we might have earned, more money the last year
> But live and let our Neighbour live, this is the course we steer;
> Had we not restricted ourselves that each might have a share,
> One-fourth of us would paupers been to live on Workhouse fare.
>
> I wonder how the masters can find so much fault with men,
> For joining in a Union themselves for to defend;
> These twenty seven years or more they've had their monthly Vend,
> For to keep up the price of Coals, which they to market send.

The minutiae of struggle is admirable, but the owners' silence on negotiation is deafening, and renders it useless. In the miner's day-to-day exposure to moral attack, physical provocation, eviction, hunger and idleness – the *waiting about* of a long strike, interminable days lounging about the house, shuffling through the village, squatting against the wall – such facts were legalistic, even pedantic; they did not relate to the facts of industrial dispute which is not about fairness, but power. What was much more likely to relate was the sort of song, ditty or hymn, that celebrated the miner as a man, that boosted his ego and thus sustained his will. Endurance was what mattered, and here the boisterous cheeky chappie Cranky, or the child of God self-imagery must have been much more significant. 'The Miner's Prayer' equates salvation with three freedoms:

> Ours was a wretched state exposed,
>   To men and angel's view,
> A slave to man, a slave to sin,
>   A slave to satan too.

The gritty determination to hold off Satan and to shun sin meant equal trouble for any Lambton or Londonderry intent on making him 'a slave to man'.

The two poles of consciousness, channelled through song, naturally enough reflected in the leadership of the union. Manchester was the venue in January 1844 for a national conference of the Miners' Association. Amidst the welter of debate on relations with Chartism, principles of Restriction, whether to stamp the *Advocate* and the strategies of strike, a recurrent theme was on the recruitment of paid, full-time lecturers for the union. The Staffordshire delegation was insistent, 'If the lecturer is of good moral character, the Staffordshire men do not inquire much about the rest; but we must have men of good moral character to do this work.'[23] Two lecturers were dismissed for moral laxity with all the gravity of a Wesleyan Conference. But parallel to this, much humour was made of the Staffordshire allowance of two quarts of ale to every miner. To conference laughter, one delegate referred to it as 'pit wash' or 'water-in-fits'; but we can be sure another delegate, the Durham Primitive Methodist Christopher Haswell, was not laughing; as early as 1832 his Methodist Conference had recommended abstention. The *Manchester Guardian* praised the delegates as '. . . a credit to the class; and a proof that those who sent them were not destitute of judgement as to who were likely to serve their purpose'. At the same time the *Guardian* recognised the differences in the style and assumption of this high quality: 'Amongst the delegates were included three or four preachers of the Primitive Methodist and Baptist denominations; and, as a contrast to these there were not wanting one or two men of mirthful propensities, ready upon occasion to throw in a jest which set the table in a roar!' This is an under-estimate; of the Northumberland and Durham contingent alone, there were four Primitive Methodist lay preachers, George Charlton and Thomas Pratt – probably the most active speakers in the forthcoming strike – Christopher Haswell and Mark Dent, whose brother was a professional minister.

In the end the English labour movement adopted anthems as its songs; given the sturdy Nonconformity of the men who first shaped it, it could hardly have chosen popular ditties. And it was Blake rather than Connell who was chosen, a Jerusalem rather than a Red Flag. Not that it really mattered as they were both hymns – indeed, Connell had originally set his words to the spritely music of 'The White Cockade' but the atheistic worthies of the Social Democratic Federation, marxist to a man, preferred the German hymn tune 'Tannenbaum'.

It is 13 August 1844: the strike is beginning to fold; Durham will go first, find many jobs lost to blacklegs, panic and cross the Tyne into Northumberland to seek work there. The house of cards that the union had been for a week or so will finally collapse. However, on that evening of 13 August, in Nelson Street, Newcastle, a 'Musical Melange' was being held to raise money for a sapping union. There was singing with Mr Sessford presiding at the pianoforte, the Shincliffe Instrumental Band and the Bell Family Quadrille Band with a nice selection, and at the top of the bill, Mr Joseph Fawcett recited 'the Battle of Minden' and 'The Miner's Doom' in his pit clothes.[24] The National Miners' Association, monster creation of half-savage pitmen, trauma for middle-class neurosis, fiend to be killed to the local establishment – with five months of struggle and two years of preparation crashing around its ears – this union was leaving North East history with all the pianoforte politeness and prim graces of a bourgeois parlour.

5 PREACHING IN THE BAROQUE

The movements of the English working class during the first half of the nineteenth century shared a need for relief and a hope for reconstruction. Industrialisation was disruptive and embittering, and a millenarian aspiration of justice matched the need for relief in the movements which sought to cope with it. Also, industrial capitalism was still a minority system revolutionising 'traditional' society in a way which made immediate the prospect of radical reconstruction. Working class need for relief, and hope for reconstruction, were given some license in the idea of labour value as the source of all wealth. The labour value concept was part of political economy, but in the 1820s the journalist-economists Thomas Hodgskin and William Thompson had re-interpreted the orthodoxies within a radical dimension. Robert Owen and the 'Owenite' movement were early propagators of the theory.

The North East had two major bouts of popular Radicalism: in 1819 led by the Political Protestants, and in 1839 led by the Chartists. Although there were Owenite and other sympathies in the area, most working-class social vitality went into trade Unionism, Friendly Societies and Methodism. The Teetotal Movement enveloped political, 'friendly' and nonconformist aims and styles. Beginning on Tyneside and missioning outwards, North Eastern Teetotalism enjoyed its most expansive phase in the first ten years, 1835-45.

For the miners, their conditions were dramatised by the 'First Report of the Commission on Children and Young Persons' in 1842. The Commission had intended to shock sensitive parts of 'public opinion' and the ensuing bourgeois outcry revealed more about their ignorance of the working class than their exploitation of it.

After the 1840s society staggered into a relative prosperity. With ensuing entrenchment, the middle class was able to develop its share capital, and its mores – and the state's role in educational provision for working-class children became an area of growing concern. The working-class movement remained, but it was forced not only to accept but also to constitute part of the system. Under these conditions Liberalism became the political voice of working men.

The Nelson Street soirée could never have been held by an institution – moreover, a union that to all concerned was clearly finished – that did not in some sense systematize attitudes that were already there. The union was raising funds in the same manner as a hundred Tyneside 'improvement' clubs, as any Mechanics' Institute, as every Methodist Chapel. However, while Joseph Fawcett played 'The Miner's Doom' in his pit clothes to raise money for the salvation of his class, other union men huddled together in conspiracy to thrash blacklegs to within an inch of their lives; that was their reaction. And yet, the two *styles* of class action had been brought to life on ground much more common than they would have cared to admit. If we have up to now over-stressed distinctions between the two cultures; if we have crudely portrayed the institutions of amelioration as only driving a clean wedge into the old and fixing boundaries of attitude (a sort of cultural Rubicon), which one crossed and changed forever – if we have done this, then this chapter will attempt balance. For in these years of the making, the sphere was volatile, its actors human, and in origin as well as development, in confrontation and collision, the relationship of the two orbits of consciousness was not separate but dialectical.

It is with this dialectical relationship – a three-cornered relationship between the old culture, the new culture and the various bringers of new culture – that this chapter will concern itself.

I. Labour Value

Ideologically, the National Miners' Association made an impact on the miners of the two counties that was to last for over fifty years. The union saw itself as an educative as well as a militant body, and its success in this rested in a refusal to make the mistake of other organisations (then and today) and dole out the 'truths' as a gospel from heaven. With insight, the union latched into the attitudes of the mining community as it found it, and then sought to go beyond – not so much to educate as to *re-educate*. Of course, distinguishing between this as a conscious and a subconscious process is tenuous: a lurching atmosphere of discontent, circumstances of an existing collective spirit among miners and a democratic consensus, made for invisibilities between leaders and led. But, having said this, the local leaders, even those who merely contributed to the newspaper, did constitute an élite – who by their very nature were self-obliged to teach and to preach. Therein lies the insight, the keen sense of communication, razor sharp in its appreciation of the miner and all his ways: these ways and how they were used is the subject now to be considered.

In 1832 Major General Bouverie was officer in command of northern forces; a letter of his to the Home Department explained the movement of four cavalry troops to Newcastle in words seeking to justify the greater dangers of Hepburn's union to strife in Lancashire: 'If the Pit men continue refractory they will be awkward persons to deal with, one pit man being equal to 3 weavers at the least . . .'[1] This would have merely confirmed government fears of the miner's capacity for bravery; it only reciprocated the miner's view of himself – some thirty years later, an account of colliery life tells a story of 1844:

> The men on strike were in great glee at the notion of a feeble little tailor who had accepted work in the pit; and while we were being told of this pretender to the character of a hewer, he passed by accompanied and guarded by a rural policeman. This ceremony they obviously did not like. 'Had we wished', they said, 'to injure the man, would it be a single policeman who would prevent us?'[2]

Much of the popular song material covered in Chapter 2, dialect, caricature, patriotism, is written in the tone of *virility*. Culturally this was no myth but integral to the pattern of mining village and family life. There were many reasons for it, the main one being that capitalistic divisions of labour in the industry reached the North East early;[3] but ideas of manliness and adulthood being equated with the job, which was, after all, a physically demanding one, were rife in the nineteenth century.[4] To most bourgeois observers of the pitman during the period the exercise of manual labour, any manual labour, was an experience and a mystery which they had not shared. Moreover, the idea of physical exhaustion beneath the ground was a rite completely outside the bounds of their comprehension – even Cobbett, with an acute eye for the motions of labour, even *he* got it wrong – he thought the miners and their families actually lived (albeit seasonally) underground. The general effect was that writers and popularisers of the colliery districts transferred their profound feelings of alienation about what to most of them was a hole in the ground, on to the impulses and feelings of the miners themselves. Considering that to drop by a rope into that hole was a normal, daily experience for the miner, the result was an exaggeration of the fears it held, and therefore of the courage required to do it. A sense of the sweated terrors the pit signified for outsiders is given in a suggestion of 1786 for imprisoning convicts there. The writer to the Home Department considered the mine, its gloomy cavern, the best punishment 'likely to Bring the mind of man to sincere reflection'. He is prompted by Holy Writ: sinners are the sons of eternal darkness outside the bounties of Nature: '. . . where they will Sigh in perpetual darkness, and the whole Length of their Slavery, will be One Mournfull Alternative, of in-sinsibility and Labour, where not even the smallest hope of Escape can ever Reach them.'[5] The pitmen may comprise one of the highest paid groups of labour (he estimates about 18s per week), but they, poor souls, should be rescued from their torment – and anyway, convicts would be much cheaper. As mining expanded and government became more efficient with inspectors and committees of enquiry, so gradually did the popular horrors of mining diminish. However, we should not forget the genuine shock of middle-class opinion on the report of 1842, and, as late as 1892, an observer could remark that 'Few persons, even of those resident in the coal district, are possessed of sufficient nerve to descent a pit'.[6]

None of this is to say that there were not elements of bravery in the miner's character. He would have found reluctance to 'ride the loop' down the shaft a cowardly and a laughing matter. He might have been more tolerant of a man unwilling to squirm in the wet dirt of a thin seam and chance his strength and skill with the whim of a living earth; this presented daily battles and daily courage. And when the mine exploded and licked flame, or collapsed to bury, then the tiny battles became a big one and presented a scene of courage at which observers could only gape. When the St Hilda Colliery at South Shields exploded on 28 June 1839, the town merchant and philanthropist, James Mather, admitted of a heroism he had never seen before:

> The men who were exerting themselves for the recovery of their unfortunate friends, acted with a solemn, high-wrought, steady courage, without bustle, scarcely with a remark, and what remarks were made were such as were necessary, brief and decided, and generally in a subdued tone . . . Their companions were brought out insensible from the overcharged atmosphere, struck down at their feet almost without life, yet it produced no fear, no flinching, no hesitation, but they stepped gallantly forward to the same spot, with an almost certainty of suffering a like attack.[7]

That such unquestionable bravery was more than moral obligation alone, that it was characteristic of men confident in their virility, is given formal recognition seven years later by Dr J. Hutchinson, a district veteran of mining disasters. As the classic example he quotes the Sheriff Hill Colliery explosion of 1819, when four brothers died in succession following each other into the 'after-damp', the gas that is sicked up by the workings after the 'fire-damp' has exploded:

> The miner rarely considers that the after-damp is a CERTAIN POISON; he considers that it is something which he can resist by some inherent strength, and they go into certain parts to aid their fellow-workmen, and thus they perish . . . They *will* rush into the carbonic acid, or 'after-damp' air thinking, 'I am stronger than you!' but they are sure to perish, for this is nature's law.[8]

The community existed for the colliery and the colliery was the domain of men. The Act of 1842 disqualified women from working there but it is unlikely that women had worked underground in the North East for any of the nineteenth century, and well before. Structures of family life starkly reflected economic organisation; Cooke's topography of 1842 talks of quick wages, rapid manhood, '. . . and the boys, by their hard labour, having a right to indulgence, soon became the masters'.[9] Dr Elliot, a colliery doctor, mentions in 1842 the anxiety of young lads to start work, '[they] . . . very naturally regard it as an era in their life to be associated with their father at work';[10] and George Parkinson first rode the loop on his father's knee at the (comparatively late) age of nine in 1837. Parkinson remembers with what manly pride he first donned the blue flannels, took his 'bait poke' and candle box, and scurried into the morning darkness at his father's side to 'be initiated into what seemed to me the mysteries and the manly phraseology of a pit boy's life', pausing only to pity those children who yesterday were his school friends. Parkinson's father took a different view, mumbling 'Aw wish ye'd byeth been lasses'.[11] About fifty years after, things were still dominated by men and the status of 'pitman': Jack Lawson's day of initiation into the brotherhood was at Boldon Colliery in north east Durham; he explains a paradox:

> Still, I was a man, and I knew it. There was no more drudging at home. I was entitled to as much meat as I wanted, and others were cleared out to make a seat for me . . . No more elder brothers' reach-me-downs, or cast-off boots. I sat up to the table with my elder brothers and father, black from pit, paraded my knowledge of pit technique, and generally tried to live up to my newly acquired

> status . . . Thus ten hours a day in the dark prison below really meant freedom for me.[12]

The fifteen-year-old sister who 'dadded' her twelve-year-old brother's 'hoggers', and ate after him at the table, and washed his pit shirt, knew the paradox not only of his life but also of hers well enough. She had no sovereignty over her life: it was only to be the other side of the grimy coin that was her brother's.

Coincident with this community equation of manhood with miner, was a traditional national awareness of the importance of coal. By the eighteenth century the Northumberland and Durham coalfield was easily the greatest supplier of the nation's coal; most of it carried by sea from the Tyne and Wear to London for the domestic market. In 1710 a coalowners' monopoly agreement on price and output was reached in Newcastle, and for the best part of the following 135 years annual agreements were formulated; sometimes discussions broke down and the trade lapsed into competition, but generally, the Vend, as the monopoly was called, carried the day. At crisis moments London begrudged the Vend and pamphlet-petition wars would rage between interested parties in the capital and those hard-hearted barons of the north. By the beginning of the nineteenth century, with an economy of 'carboniferous capitalism' gaining momentum and the market expanding, plus the rapid growth of London's domestic market, Parliament set up inquiries into the Vend. Reports of 1800 and 1828 were not favourable but nothing was done. Well earned was the Vend's nickname of 'The Newcastle Parliament'. In the end, the monopoly collapsed not because of notions of justice or fairness but because of brute power: the miners' strike of 1844 knocked awry delicately regulated agreements between collieries, and the railway called into feasibility other coalfields. But the overall effect of over a century of monopoly was to propagandise into national awareness the vital role of North East coal. An *Essay* of 1803, published in London, criticises regulation on the hypothesis that 'upon the cheap and regular acquisition of fossile fuel, our national improvement and prosperity eminently depends'.[13] There had been, and were to be, many pamphlets like this, and not surprisingly some of the fame rubbed off on to the pitmen themselves.

In 1818 a Home Department circular warned authorities of a professional begging trick to pose as an ex-Royal Navy seaman, such was the brief, glorious moment of national indebtedness to him after the War.[14] The miner's national fame was less picturesque but more sustained: 1842 dramatised his plight to sensitive parts of middle-class opinion, and 1844 saw much of the national press on his side against the wicked monopolies – Londonderry's half bullying, half patronising threat to his men contained too much of the braggart for the liberal press. To the *Weekly Dispatch* it smacked of 'cold-blooded cruelty!'; *Punch* saw him as 'smitten with the fatal charms of pen, ink and foolscap'; and the *Dublin Monitor's* jibe would have been beyond most pitmen though the support was welcome – 'Bombastes Furioso'. The miner, unless he was too naughty, was on his way from being a hump of national sympathy to being almost a cliché figure of national neglect; a writer in 1855 was near to plagiarism when he spoke of the miner, 'He troubles not our repose, – the tales of his distress hardly reach our ears – he is poor – he is far away – he dies – but he is our fellow-creature and our fellow-countryman'.[15] The sentiment finds perfect expression in a late nineteenth century poem by Alexander Barrass, an ex-Durham collier:

> He seldom thinks, that sits at ease,
> I' warm an' cheery room,
> While at his feet the big coals blaze,
> O'Geordy's dreary doom;
> He's grummell'd ower thor money cost,
> He's analyzed an' view'd them;
> But seldom thowt the man wiz lost,
> Or might hev been, thit hew'd them.[16]

In his manhood and in his work there were thus traditional grounds for the exceptional status of the miner; but the Methodists were also, besides other things, propagating ideas of his significance before God. Primitive Methodism, at grass-roots level, was a lay church; in practice as well as in ideology the tenets of free grace and spiritual egalitarianism were exercised. In a letter from William Hamilton of Willington Colliery to the *Advocate*, we can hear the eloquence of pulpit rhetoric personalising a local struggle by the universal truths of the Good Samaritan:

> Shall I show you men stripped and wounded, and left half-dead; they may be seen in our cities, as well as in the highways between Jericho and Jerusalem – and shall I show you the tears running down the cheeks of the orphans and widows – shall I call you to hear the cry of the hire kept back by fraud or violence . . .[17]

A speech to the union in 1832 went further than identification (though this was the commonest gambit). Ralf Atchinson insisted that not only were they equal before the Almighty but that He was actually on their side. The Old Testament was far from mumbo jumbo to the erudite of Methodism like Atchinson, and what language could they invoke!

> They had no more right to doubt than Hezekiah had when he sat within the walls of Jerusalem, and the army of Sennacherib was without; as the Lord delivered Hezekiah, and caused the army of Sennacherib to perish in a night, so would he deliver them (APPLAUSE) . . . Who were their opponents? They were only an arm of flesh, whilst with them (the men) was the arm of the living God.[18]

It was confidence of this dimension which made men lions, though they had the whole of the local establishment ranged against them – naturally the owners, with their apologists in the press, clergy and at the magistrate's bench; with some orthodoxies of political economy stating *a priori* that trade unionism was an impossibility – the level of wages had nothing to do with the trivial activities of men but rested in the iron cradle of the laws of supply and demand; with victimisation in defeat a certainty – such confidence provided the arbiter and final appeal for self-assertion. Deference was shrugged off and miners talked of Lord Londonderry himself spending a day in his shirtsleeves shovelling coal into wagons to see what it was like.

The leaders of the NMA and the community élite who officered the union knew this dimension and sought to inspire others with it. To do so they took their cue from the traditional mentalities of colliery life: if the miner was so exceptional as a man and a child of God, and if his work was so vital, then why should he be oppressed? Manliness; Work; Religion: the educational activities of the union, relying on firing a *self-dramatisation*, brought together all three strands in a popularised version of labour-value theory – the prime apologetic of the NMA. Bob Cranky cheek and chapel faith was not enough; they ran a strong current but positive industrial action demanded another impetus and more knowledge, and here we are almost privileged with an ear to the proselytising debates that must have raged in cottage and pub.

The NMA was clear-sighted in its aims from the beginning: a poster of 4 October 1843, *Miners' Journal and the scourge of tyrants*, declared that the *Journal*

> . . . is meant . . . to point out to the Miners their real worth, and to compare their worth with that of their Masters, and to shew them

> that instead of their being dependent on their employers, their employers are dependent on them.

The aim was easily declared; but the problem was not one of declaration – it was one of *communication.*

Firstly the union integrated their themes with the base of manhood; as God's sons and inheritors of His glory their action was right:

> . . . it is a complete frustration of the designs of Divine benevolence that such men should have to fritter away nearly the whole of their lives in ill-paid, toilsome labours to the neglect of the cultivation of those powers which distinguish him from the brute creation . . . an insult to his Creator.[19]

The theology is a mealy-mouthed rationalism of deities and divine providences typical of the *Advocate*, a world and a heaven away from the hot gospel of the Methodists. However, some of the language and certainly the theme would have connected as familiar.

As well as God's sons, the union sought justification for its claims by the old radical criteria of free-born sons of England. A song, 'The Poor Tradesman's Lamentation', demands public support because the miner is a Briton, not a Heathen, Savage, Jew or Turk; and the same stance is used in appeals to blackleg labour – especially the Welsh and Irish. 'We appeal to the warm and generous-hearted sons of the Green Isle to remain at home . . .'[20]

Miners were also proud sons of the working classes. The *Advocate* delighted in 'impartial' snippets of useful information, and, with dubious historical licence, informed readers that Shakespeare, Franklin, Ferguson, Burns, Pope, Arkwright, Aesop, Homer and even Virgil, were all out of the working classes. Sheer joy that Luther's father was a miner![21]

Child of his Creator, of England, and of a class, the miner also had a right to pride just as he was, a man – his small, stocky physique was well-known:

> Show me a big fellow in any situation of life and ten to one but I show you a big booby; but introduce me to a little fellow and I'll recommend to your notice one that knows 'what's what' and one who has plenty of brains in his head, if he has not got too much to boast of in the matter of legs in his breeches.[22]

The business of creating a kind of social warrant for union existence by infusing pride in manhood was closely linked in totality by the encouragement of dignity as workers. The miner was not to be downtrodden, he was a vital and irreplaceable factor in the nation's wealth, prestige and strength. Theories of labour value are not used merely to reiterate an economic 'truth', but to cultivate a cultural climate for social assertion. This was nothing new in the radical strategem: agitators as different as Cobbett and Owen argued social radicalism from the platform of labour value; Corbett harking back to honest trencherman days of labour's dignity, Owen outraged at labour's depreciation in a contemporary competitive jungle. Political reformers in the 1820s and 1830s, especially in London at the Rotunda or the offices of the Poor Man's Guardian, all hammered out arguments that put together winning the vote with securing to labour the full wealth of its produce. During the 1839 revival of popular radicalism among the miners, one of the central tenets of Durham Chartism had been the connection of suffrage with labour value. George Binns, the Sunderland Chartist, had preached to pitmen and others:

> And what he [lord, parson, or 'middleman'] pays is not one particle of remuneration; for the grandeur which he displays dishonours society because it exists upon the misery of the people. Their grandeur emanates from your industry; and if the loom were shut up tomorrow . . . and each labourer were to demand the Charter before he cut it [the golden harvest] – and if every department of industry were stopped at its source – I ask, how these middlemen would shrink into the littleness of their nature, when they saw all their wealth & grandeur in society was a humbug.[23]

Indeed, initially, the general strike, or 'sacred month', was to be the weapon for the Charter, and the militant collieries in both counties had actually struck for a short time – some even barricading the village to defy the Hussars who must surely come.

Five years afterwards, on 8 April, the strike opened on a shout of labour's rights. Twenty-five thousand men and women stood on the natural amphitheatre of Shadon's Hill, stamping ground for unionism, and in a stiff breeze beneath the flapping banners heard their leaders state the case. George Charlton from South Shields resolved that oppression had filled the moor and made claim to 'the lawful and inherent right' of the workman to be justly paid for his labour; Robert Archer from South Hetton seconded their legality, by

Holy and constitutional law; and John Tulip from the same colliery declared that 'they were the bees who produced the honey'. As he assured the meeting there would be few blacklegs the men of Murton arrived on the moor to great cheering; this was cause for confidence indeed as these men had been expected to shun the union. Further speeches, and Charlton returned to the hustings. Enjoying himself now, with distaste merging into contempt, he warned of 'oily-tongued slave-drivers'; he would like to see the owners strip, sweat and fill wagons to understand what labour was, and, joining in the laughter, Mark Dent told of a master who tried hewing, a pale wan thing who 'blushed' his hands! Later in April, Robert Archer, probably the most eloquent of local leaders, was speaking again, this time at Black Fell, between Birtley and Washington:

> But they were assured on the authority of God that the servant had a right to be paid for his labour . . . They had been the means of making many rich men; they had made the land to flow, as it were, with plenty, but it had all rolled into certain hands; they, the producers, shared in none of the benefits.

And this was the tone of speeches throughout the strike.[24] Although much of the language of labour value is in the rolling tongue of the Bible, the union's understanding of it was warped by a social philosophy that was crudely eighteenth-century *philosophe*. Labour value theory by Hodgskin and Thompson, extended by Marx, regarded exploitation as in some sense intrinsic to the system and a precondition of capitalism: exploitation is then a fact by which 'the surplus labour of one man becomes the condition of existence of others' (*Das Kapital*, vol. 1, pp. 482-93). This conceptual analysis and others like it was very different from that reflected in the ideology of the NMA. From its speeches and publications, in no way was exploitation cast as intrinsic, and neither was the capital 'risked' by the capitalist merely embodied or stored labour value: the union granted the capitalist his right to remuneration. Instead, their grievances were formed in the traditional style of 'a fair price' founded on custom. They were not wage slaves fated to innate exploitation, they were the victims of criminal cheating extraneous of any *system*, an aberration, not an integral mechanism.

The proof of labour value was in the pudding of ostentatious wealth; hence the weekly calculations of excessive fines and wage skimming over the previous five years from each colliery submitted to the

Advocate. Classical labour value theory, considering division of labour, would have been suspicious of such lucid sums owed to the miners – but the union used its eyes and popularised labour's creditor status:

> If the trade will not afford a fair remuneration for the Miner's dreary toil, how comes it about that it *will* afford carriages, gigs, horses, and splendid halls for Owners, Viewers, Overmen, etc. and allow them to give fortunes to their sons and daughters?[25]

This editorial comment hints to us that the *Advocate* was a little more aware of the systematic nature of exploitation than most of its readers – as Thomas Pratt's statement to the *Durham Chronicle* clearly reckons the exploitation at £934 6s 11½d for hewers in the main seam with a drop in score price of 1s 4¾d between 1842 and 1843. It must have been obvious to the editorial above that the fine palaces and vast fortunes were not accrued in one year, nor on sums of £934; but the miners seemed to feel their exploitation differently – only as an encroachment, not a *raison d'être*, as the men of North Hetton: '. . . the necessity of renewing our understanding with each other again, in order to bring round to ourselves, our wives and families the comforts and happiness equal to that which we enjoyed in the good old days of 1831'.[26]

The rationale of dispute centred round the notion that one party had erred, become too strong and must be made to go back. The *Advocate* and union executive knew that it was more than a matter of filching, as many of the collieries appeared to see it, and sought to use, but go beyond, this tormented base – but when they do talk of changing the existing order, it is usually in the let's-have-goodwill-and-be-reasonable terms of Owenite philosophy. The two evils of society are competition and over-production: they are held, as concepts, in abstraction. They are faults, irregularities, hydra-headed monsters, almost as if possessed of a personality and existence of their own, and if only Man would regard them as outside his best interests, harmony would prevail. Likewise Londonderry, one of the 'big three' coal-owners, is more often called a 'Despot' than a capitalist. The battle is not against economic formations, but against 'Tyranny'. Predictably, the argument-from-patriotism theme is woven in, the myth of the freeborn Englishman carried economic as well as civil connotations; as Free Britons we demand our long lost rights. William Tell, Swiss patriot and hero, whose story is told by instalments in the *Advocate*, may be Swiss, yet he fires an English longbow and is every inch an International

Enlightenment Hero seeking LIBERTY, TRUTH and FREEDOM. The theory was hybrid and often contradictory, but as a *sentiment* there can be no doubt that the union succeeded in popularising it as a species of moral economy: the strike rings with outrage rather than erudition.

For others in the religious camp, imagery swamped sentiment in a 'theory' of labour very close to Evangelical doctrines of Sin, an irreparable condition. A song by William Johnson of Framwellgate Moor calls in Adam's Fall as a proof. ' 'Tis true that the curse to labour hath bound us'. The local establishment tried to use this Biblical proof of the blessedness of hard labour (and poverty!) 'all the days of thy life' as a lever against the union's contending theories of labour value. Newspapers enjoyed it as a catspaw for almost anything; and the owners, as part of a venomous personal campaign against the leadership, rebuked 'their continual croaking about evils which are, after all, only the penalty of Adam'.[27] Reverend John Burdon of Castle Eden wrote a pamphlet which hung labour value over the flames of Hell:

> You are resisting, not the oppression of your employers but the Will of your Maker – the ordinance of that God who has said that in the sweat of his face shall man eat bread, and who has attached this penalty to the refusal to labour, namely, that if a man do not work neither shall he eat.[28]

The owners' side, however, did not bargain for the percolation of union efforts through the movement. There were many Biblical quotes that could flatly contradict the argument, but 'Robert Forbes, miner', held fast to union principles and replied in a theological tit for tat:

> I am aware that ever since the introduction of moral evil into our world, 'that out of the sweat of his face man must eat bread'; although this is the case, it does not follow that this is the only design for which he was made. Let those bear in mind who make the assertion, that the miner possesses a body capable of developing the faculties of his mind – possesses a Soul endowed with rational powers, deathless and endurable as eternity itself, and will survive the struggles of expiring nature and when the world has ceased to be – that he is part of that link which connects the material with the immaterial world – that he is a being 'who is not dictated by brute instinct' but by the high and ennobling hopes, or the dread

> and horrifying fears which alone can operate upon an intellectual being before they arrive at a conclusion that the miners were only made to sweat for a scanty subsistence and then to sleep – and sweat again.[29]

We can be certain not all replies were of this quality, indeed we have seen some of the simpler (yet as forceful) ones; but the union delighted in its success – that existent streams of consciousness had been harnessed, and in some cases remodelled, to suit the fight and make reply. An NMA broadside, *Dialogue between 3 Coal Viewers after being in search of Men*, positively dances with joy at this capacity to join battle:

> *Mr D:* Well sir, you see it is now as in the year 1831, they are so well disciplined, contrive what plan we will, they are sure to lay a deeper one; they have long been called ignorant, but they are quite the contrary; they can lay their case so plain before the public as to make a very weighty impression. Then they have a few tallented fellows amongst them that if we had to enter into public discussion with them, they would be sure to make fools of us; indeed they are so much better educated, that it's astonishing how they have got it.
>
> *Mr F.* I quite agree with you Mr D, concerning their tallents – there is a number of Delegates who are local preachers, and some of them can ransack the bible between backs; another thing is that they carry on their financial affairs, that the most ignorant of them may understand; besides this they have got their legal adviser (and he is really a clever fellow) who is so humble as to tell them anything they ask, that I humbly believe we will be forced to yield and quit the field, leaving them to enjoy their union.

But the fact remains, and in a way it is the only real fact of the strike, that the union was defeated, the strike in vain. The broadside quoted above goes on to discuss means out of the conflict, how the owners could back down with honour. The union needed peace. The miners of Northumberland and Durham, against the better judgement of the national association, had gone it alone; unable to wait for a national effort, they paid the price in practical terms of not appreciating their value and power as workers in an identification of *class*. Instead, and the point is ironic, they had felt sufficiently confident as true-bred pitmen – Sons of the Tyne, inheritors of Cranky – to fight an action that could only have been won by a broader, more comprehensive estimation of labour value and class power. The days of Cranky, the days of a craftsman miner socially celebrated were dying parallel with the North East monopoly, the Vend. If Northern coal was not forthcoming then it was coming from elsewhere; Welsh, Scots, Yorkshire, Staffordshire and Lancashire coal was filling the gap – 'Geordie' now had to take his place with Big Hewers with other dialects, and even with the railwaymen who carried it.

Mr Joseph Fawcett, in his pit clothes, reciting 'The Miner's Doom' to raise money for a flagging strike is uncannily symbolic of what was happening. Moreover, the poem speaks of a labour value by occupation rather than class – a sentiment, if he only knew it, whose days were up:

> But who regards the mining slave, that for his country's wealth
> Resigns his sleep, his pleasure, home, his freedom and his health?
> From the glad skies and fragrant fields he cheerfully descends,
> And eats his bread in stenchy caves where his existence ends.

II. Radical Religion

If the *rapport* between the union and traditional community mentalities was organic and not separate, then it was the same for other cultural forces. The NMA had offered conciliatory and accommodative responses – perhaps with a gentle cuff here and there for the quick-tempered or the religious fanatic – and so the lines of union penetration into the mass are at least identifiable. Methodism, on the other hand, offered only confrontation with the existing milieu. In the shock of conflict that followed, Methodism absorbed cultural patterns as a tactic to communicate and the Methodism that came out of the clash was very different to the godly élite Wesley had envisaged. In part, for Methodism, the medium became the message.

John Wesley in his preaching tours amongst, for instance, the 'half-savage' pitmen of Kingswood and Tyneside, was often acutely embarrassed by his apparent ability to induce hysteria. His journals love the word 'calm'; there is some repugnance in descriptions of revival scenes. Reverend Dr Adam Clarke equally distrusted such exhibitions, but in a letter displays a clever sociological insight into the cultural interplay that was at their root:

> The common people, who have never had the advantage of mental

> cultivation, hear through the medium of their passions. Everything that affects them, arrests and fixes the attention, and then sacred Truths have, as we phrase it, fair play in their minds . . . We have had hundreds converted here, and yet we have had very little extravagance of any kind. This, we consider, as a peculiar mercy of God; for, if it had been otherwise, we should in all probability have had bad work with Sailors etc . . .[30]

The 'medium of their passions' could be inflamed by drunkenness. Adam Clarke's thesis had been supported in 1810 by Thomas Trotter, an enlightened Newcastle doctor, in his *Essay, medical, philosophical, and chemical, on Drunkenness and its effects on the human body,* where he slyly attributed religious hysteria to drunkenness: 'Religious enthuasiasm is apt to occupy the imagination of fanatics at this time and they burst forth with blasphemous and familiar addresses to the Deity . . .' (p. 33). There had been all kinds of interpretation since Pentecost, but it is undeniably true that Clarke was an intelligent impresario for Methodism; he recognised that as a cultural rather than a religious movement it could not strike into the heart of a community without spilling blood on its own hands. And, in moments of social upheaval when Methodism recruited strongly, if unevenly, fixed structures of behaviour seemed to suspend themselves to form an excitable amoeba of shifting patterns of belief and loyalty. Methodism, because it was represented by a barking preacher in such situations, found itself in the open – free to change and be changed. The historian of Primitive Methodism, looking back on the 'genetic moment' of 1816-20 expresses this vulnerability:

> Churches of long standing naturally made it their chief solicitude to keep their people from being 'drawn away and enticed' by the lawless spirit abroad. They drew a cordon around the fold and tried to isolate their flock. But as yet our missionaries had no such necessary work to engage them. They themselves were outside the cordon, and any work they did must be carried on within the infected area.[31]

But the areas of crisis into which the itinerant missionary would tramp were a buffeting, huckster world of social quacks and prophets. Often he found himself just on the heels of a Southcottian who had moved on, or a teetotaller or rival evangelists who were preaching in the adjoining street: as the Primitive itinerant, Nathaniel West, recorded in his journal for Houghton on 25 April 1824, 'somewhat disturbed by a society of people who came just under us at our time of service and commenced and carried on theirs. However, the Lord was with us'.[32] But the most cogent cultural dialectic seemed to be found with the radicals. Vying as they did for attention, both working men with thick accents, both with street corner voices and plain argument, both calling for a sober adherence – din din dinning words of salvation and a New Religious-Moral World to be stepped into – there seem to have been times when the face in the crowd found it difficult to distinguish between them in what they demanded of *him*. When Thomas Batty, Primitive itinerant, slithered down the path into the North Pennine lead mining villages of Nenthead and Garrigill and began to preach the Word, he remembers he was at first mistaken for one of those 'outlandish men' or a 'Political Radical Reformer' under a new name. The miners listened attentively and then proffered payment for the performance! It *was* a performance; we must be careful when considering such volatile years not to inflict on the actors too sharp an intellectual discrimination. It was often a question of people congregating 'to see', and here names are important: Hugh Bourne, co-founder of Primitive Methodism, remarked that the nickname 'Ranter', because of its unfamiliarity and curiosity, had greatly helped mission; 'radical' in the Tyne shipyards in the 1820s was the epithet for blackleg. A story from the Midlands in 1816, recounted in 1872 is, in spite of its cosy way of telling, instructive:

> Joseph W– was a very wicked man, and usually spent the Lord's Day in wandering from one public-house to another. One day he heard a person say that the 'Ranters' were come to – Hill. 'Oh' said Joseph 'it is only the Radicals under a feigned name, I will go and hear them'. And so he did on the next Lord's Day: he listened very attentively, and thought he heard very little Radicalism. The preacher gave out that he should be glad to meet in class as many as would join him, at a neighbouring house. So, thought Joseph, he will explain his views more clearly . . . I dare say he has some private communication to make about a general rising. So in he went; the preacher sung, prayed, and gave his experience; Joseph's eyes began to open . . .[33]

The facts of the tale had probably suffered with the years, and old Joseph must have been under the influence of more than Ranterism or Radicalism to be so stupid, but the manner in which interest was engendered is illuminating. At times, the exchange with radicalism (in men or ideas) was so reactive that it must have seemed to the Primitives that they were to be beaten with their own weapons. Thomas Cooper,

Leicester Chartist and sometime Methodist, recalls:

> During the summer of 1842, I often led the poor stockingers out into villages, – sometimes on week-day evenings, – and thus we collected the villagers of Ansty and Wigston, and Glenn, and Countesthorpe, and Earl Shilton, and Hinckley, and Syston, and Mt. Sorrel . . . and inducted them into some knowledge of Chartist principles. One Sunday we devoted entirely to Mount Sorrel, and I and Beadham stood on a pulpit of syenite, and addressed the hundreds that sat around and above us on the stones of a large quarry. It was *Gwennap* – Wesley's grand Cornish preaching-place on a small scale. Our singing was enthusiastic; and the exhilaration of that Chartist 'camp meeting' was often spoken of afterwards.[34]

Joseph Parker, as a boy in the Northumberland market town of Hexham, remembers Cooper coming to speak of 'Paradise Lost' in the Mechanics' Institute during the 1840s. There was a fear and fascination for Chartism in the town; no one really knew what it meant: Stephens had talked of Edinburgh into flames and Glasgow into ashes and that was horrible, yet Parker's father, a respectable stonemason and contractor, had Rev. Stephen's portrait on the wall as a sure Dissenter and enemy of High Wesleyanism. Hexham at the time had an atheist sunday school and 'Feargus O'Connor was nothing where a burgling Dissenter came'. Cooper, Chartist, gaolbird and atheist-to-many, was to speak on a religious subject in the hall of the respectables; and it was with 'Palpitating heart' that the young Parker stole down to the station to witness this amazing creature:

> The train stopped! That was the moment of agony! Out came a large, pock-marked man; a man with a swinging walk, and a kind of smile which divided itself between hope and doubt as to the public reception in store for him . . . Yes, there he was! And I, at a safe distance, quivered with doubtful pride as I walked behind Thomas Cooper . . .[35]

For all the confusion one can see that the temper of Ranting and Radicalism was the same. Of course there would be differences between a pit village and a Manchester, and between periods, but from ground level looking up to the movement (instead of looking down at the people from the movement), the style of one was the cue for the other. In 1817 a nervous army officer at Wakefield wrote to the government drawing their attention to an evangelical tract that was martial in language and imagery – he considered it dangerous in temperament, 'the language altogether being so different and novel to the mild scripture phraseology'.[36]

Primitive Methodists, in the first half of the nineteenth century, collided with local establishments almost as much as the radicals did – although it was much worse in other parts of the country than in the North East. The journals of missionaries, especially during the 1820s and before, are full of running battles with England's squirearchy. In their determination to reach ordinary men the preachers exercised an outright testing of the free-born Englishman myth. They refused to let it remain a convenient legend for vicars and squires but asserted it spiritually and practised it socially. Many were offered safe conduct from villages on promising never to preach there again because, really, their agitation was so very 'irregular'! The answers given would not have been unlike those tossed in the face of a Leicestershire magistrate in 1821: 'Was not our Lord's rebuking the Scribes and Pharisees . . . very irregular? . . . Was not the course of the apostles, and of Stephen, and of many of the Evangelists, very irregular? Were not the proceedings of Calvin, Luther, and their fellow-workers in the Reformation *very irregular*?'[37] Answering that and keeping to the Thirty-Nine Articles would have risked many a vicar his cloth. Other members of the gentry were more imaginative in opposition. When it was heard at Aldbourne, Shrewsbury in 1829 that an itinerant was to preach, the squire and his friends hired a song and dance acting group, 'merry andrews', to counter his exhortations. Battle commenced at 7 a.m., preacher at the market cross, squire and company at the Bell Inn. After a slow start with laughing children the preacher had gathered a crowd – but the antics of the 'andrews' lost him it; the show finished and there was a move back to the preacher. Exasperated, his rivals climbed up behind him and banged a drum in his ear whilst the parish officer marched round him with a large bell encouraging the children to scream – 'Amidst this disturbance the youthful preacher continued to proclaim the solemn truths of revelation and with increased feeling and power'; his lungs proving stronger than their patience and the battle was won – though without converts.[38]

However, as we have seen, preachers like this young *enragé* were out to combat more than merry squires. Methodism also found itself in exchange with the popular culture of the people; as it sought to oppose it, so was it half-absorbed into it. A good example of the religious alternative posed in the form, the admittedly attractive form of the enemy, is a Methodist poster from Lancashire, dated 1810. Fighting against the sinful theatre it quotes Bishop Burnett: 'The Stage is the great corrupter of the town; and our Plays are certainly the greatest debauches of the nation.' The chapel, it is announced, will provide its own play in three acts: first, The Archangel and the Trump of God; second, the Saints in White; third, the Assembly of the Unregenerate. 'The MUSIC will consist chiefly of Cries; accompanied with Weeping, Wailing, Mourning, Lamentation, and Woe.' Thus assured it is not a comedy production, the theatregoer learns how to gain admittance:

> To prevent inconvenience, there are separate doors for admitting the company; and they are so different, that none can mistake who are not wilfully blind. The door which opens into the *Gallery* is very narrow, and the steps up to it are somewhat difficult; for which reason there are seldom many people about it. But the door that gives entrance into the *Pit* is very wide, and very commodious; which causes such numbers to flock to it, that it is generally crowded . . .
>
> TICKETS for the Pit, at the easy purchase of following the vain pomps and vanities of the fashionable world, and the desires and amusements of the flesh: to be had at every flesh-pleasing assembly . . .
>
> TICKETS for the Gallery, at no less rate than being converted, forsaking all, denying self, taking up the cross, and following Christ in regeneration.
>
> It will be in vain for one in a tinselled coat and borrowed language, to personate one of high birth, in order to get admittance into the upper places; for there is one of wonderful and deep penetration, who will search and examine every individual . . .[39]

Manchester magistrates thought the poster a blasphemy; they were not to know what the Primitives were to do with the hymns.

In 1840 an observer compared the Wesleyan and the Primitive Methodist communities in the farming and leadmining regions of Weardale. He thought the Wesleyans a credit; their fine chapel, their nipping respectability, their dedication to singing and music. The Primitives were distasteful; too much 'phrenzy', too boisterous, too working class in an amotional way of faith:

> In prayer they work themselves into a complete phrenzy; sing at the stretch of their voices their hymns to some of the most popular tunes of the day . . . and it does not matter whether he or she in the pulpit

> be preaching or praying, loud 'Amens' 'Praise God' 'I do believe' resound and ring throughout the building.[40]

In Weardale Wesleyanism, 80 years after Wesley's first visit, there are signs of that institutional paralysis that was to creep through the national body as the century wore on – declining missionary success, and talk of the appointed minister delivering his 'crack' sermon. The Primitives, however, were still loose enough to be in mutation; why, they even adopted hymns to popular, secular tunes such as 'Scots wha hae wi' Wallace bled'! If Weardale had a taste for the Scottish, other areas had a taste for Chartist: O'Connor's 'The Lion of Freedom is come from his den' had been originally taken from a traditional melody – the Primitives not only copied the idea, but followed the words to produce their 'For the Lion of Judah shall break every chain'.[41] That the Newcastle Sunday School Union should have devised one of its favourite hymns from the tune of 'Weel May the Keel Row' comes as a surprise to nobody.

Joseph Leighton, a Tynesider, had been converted when eighteen by the first wave of Primitive mission in the area. Clowes and Nelson began the tremors of salvation and until his death at Ballast Hills, in 1857, he remained steadfast to the movement. In him one can feel the essence of Primitive Methodism: '. . . he loved plain preaching, lively singing, and short praying, and was opposed to all innovations'.[42] Leighton would have been no conservative in the sense of static institutionalism; it was from minds like his that the movement encountered its greatest difficulties in later years when trying to introduce greater professionalism in the ministry, greater respectability in the services, even a theological college – these were the 'bourgeois' innovations Leighton and his generation opposed. They loved instead the fierce preaching and popular music of their religion, the *form* it had absorbed, fed on and reacted to, when seeking out the miners and seamen of Tyneside, the form that had given it an audience. Rev. George Herod, in his *Biographical Sketches*, remembers Nottinghamshire mission between 1816-19; understandably, he exaggerates the clinical character of penetration:

> At this juncture and crisis (industrial and political) the P.M. missionaries brought a counteractive influence to bear upon the masses, and in multitude of instances destroyed the baneful virus of infidelity and insubordination . . . Their manner of entering a town or village also produced great excitement; in general the missionary was

> accompanied with a number of warm-hearted singers, and so soon as they entered the place of their attack they commenced singing down the street, and continued so doing until they arrived at a place of rendezvous; as nearly every town and village have places where men and youths meet to discuss different subjects, thither the missionaries would make their way . . . Had the preacher with his supporters sung a hymn or psalm in Martin Luther's favourite tune, or one commonly used in a place of worship, it would have been said – 'Oh, it's some Methodist preacher; it is nothing new'. But the course adopted led to a different result. Hundreds, and in some instances, thousands (and especially on a missionary's first visit to a place) were collected together through the novelty of lively singing.[43]

Here the poaching of popular music is described as a deliberate tactic to sharpen curiosity; often, in retrospect, the gimmick is sanctified as part of the holy work – of Richard Jukes, a prolific Manchester Hymn writer, Mr J. Ireland could remember:

> Before the Primitive Methodist came to this city, and for some time after, it was very common to hear lewd or ribald songs sung in the streets . . . But our movements drove them away by putting something better in their place. We used to pick up the most effective tunes we heard, and put them to our hymns . . .

More often it would be merely a lilting melody on the ears and a quick claim of patent, as Rev. Henry Higgenson of Walsall who bought 'rights' for a penny from a lad in the street who sang the tune till he knew it – 'I've got the tune, and the devil may take the words'.[44] For a penny, it seems, the devil was well cheated.

The spectacle of religious cabaret at street corners, quaysides and markets was undoubtedly successful whether deliberate or natural. Joseph Spoor, a Whickham keelman who became a legendary figure in the North East ministry both for his fists and his tongue in defence of the gospel, was first attracted to the Primitives by the evangelical singing of Mr and Mrs Suddards at Blaydon. Between 1827-30, 'Their spiritual songs set to popular airs (and they were both excellent singers), their earnestness, and the divine influence attendant upon all their exercises attracted these three young people . . .'. William Thompson, a miner, of Murton and Seaham collieries, also owed over sixty years of Methodist loyalty to being first 'attracted by their hearty singing, and receiving the word of truth into his heart . . .'[45] in the 1820s. There were many others; for some, the chapel, in its neighbourhood drama and sociability, would have differed little from the fug of the tap room: publicans were well-attuned to common pleasures; a Manchester man, in 1834, mentioned the increasing custom of licensed victuallers employing musicians and singers 'to beguile the weak'[46] and the new practice of pub psalm playing on Sundays reassures us of the dialectic at work. Later, 'The Holy City' or a solo 'Ave Maria' became among the best loved songs of a workingmen's club; a beery gush of emotion from people never seen inside a church. Never mind about the words, get on with the tune, became continuities common to club and chapel alike.

A measure of their days, a monument to their conversions, a guide to their new life, the hymnal ran deep into the Methodists' consciousness. Primitive Methodism in Carlisle was founded in 1822 by an old woman who had shuffled the 44 miles from Kendal to show a relative her new hymnal. Printed by the thousand, the classic reward to zealous Sunday Schoolers, 'Presented to John Eastwood by his Teacher for Good Attendance at the Primitive M.S.S., Barnoldswick, Oct. 4th, 1891',[47] the hymnal represented the democracy of faith. It was Joseph Fawcett and George Charlton, both prominent in the great miners' strike of 1844, who headed an *ad hoc* committee at the Newcastle 1853 PM Conference to secure the withdrawal of the new hymnal: 'The indifference manifested to Connexional Opinion in that the new Book was authorized, *stereotyped*, and issued without an opportunity being given for the Connexion to judge of its suitability.'[48]

We know now that Joseph Fawcett had tastes and loyalties that stretched beyond 'The Miner's Doom' and the National Miners' Association, but he was to wage a losing campaign as Primitivism and society moved into entrenchment and stability. Once the chapel was built (after 1850 and especially 1870-90 was the great era of chapel funds), and social discontent lost its popular expression, then the time of cultural exchange was over, doors could be shut, the iconstasis could be erected. As early as 1835 professional Wesleyanism in the area rapped the vulgarity of working-class influences on religious worship. It is ironic that the outspoken critic, Rev. James Everett, had made his reputation and won his preaching spurs around the collieries in the early nineteenth century as an evangelist of extreme emotion. His hysterical exhortations had earned him the title 'Hellfire lad', and yet here he can talk in mellow tones of the

> ... vitiated taste ... often found in humble life, and among persons possessed of stirring qualities, with an inclination to revivalism. The introduction of tunes more fit for the circus and the chase, than the house of God, is a subject of occasional regret; and the misfortune is, when once they find their way among persons similar to the originators – possessed of bad ears, weak heads, and warm hearts, they become exceedingly offensive, and are not easily abandoned.
>
> If the persons who take a lead in the singing, in Wesleyan chapels, were to familiarize themselves with the tunes in Mr Wesley's 'Sacred Harmony' and in the Hymn Book, published in 1761, with the 'Tune Annext', the Body would be preserved from much reproach ... compare, it is reiterated, some of these, with the horse jockey abominations, which move in the current of persons of bad taste ...[49]

Everett was an old man venting his spleen and forgetting the influence of his creator in the days of his youth. If he was right in thinking 'hurrah songs' in bad taste then so was much else of Methodism. Wesley himself had created the famous Watchnight Service out of the habit of Kingswood colliers' sitting late on a Saturday night at the alehouse. By having hymns and prayers in the schoolroom far into the night, Wesley had learnt a lesson and laid a bait – the community gave the style, Wesley would change the direction.[50] A siege concept of salvation so obsessive comes unruly on us: the Watchnighters would sit over the revellers in judgement and rivalry till they were finished. When, in 1818, Sheriff Hill in Co. Durham found itself with a dancing school, the pitmen Methodists of the colliery immediately countered with a Sunday School – the evil was eventually arrested.[51] Probably, the most famous 'inheritance' from popular culture was the rowdy singing of psalms and hymns round the bed of the dying. In 1825 Mackenzie admits that the lake-wake was still observed though now taken and implemented by the religious.[52] *Lic* was Anglo-Saxon for a corpse, and *wacce* for a vigil; traditionally, we are told in 1898, the vigil had declined into a hard-drinking excuse for 'indecent revelry' around the flower decorated coffin.[53] The Methodists banished the drink but – and the 1898 writer does not appreciate the fact in an age of chapel propriety – were at the time widely criticised for replacing it with their own brand of 'indecent revelry'. Featherston finds objectionable, in 1840, the 'din and disturbance' of chapel groups in a situation demanding sweet, gentle prayers. Predictably, Irish wakes come in for the same disgust.[54]

By the 1840s Primitive Methodist confidence grew as stridently as their numbers. The Sunderland Circuit was founded in 1823 and ran south along the eastern half of the county – through Houghton le Spring, Hetton and the developing colliery district, past Durham City and on to Hartlepool and stopping as far south as Stockton on Tees. Eleven years later there were 1,400 members in the circuit; Stockton formed its own in 1837, and Durham in 1839. But there was a world to conquer: a mission was despatched from Sunderland to Edinburgh, and by 1843, with supreme provincial confidence, the circuit looked to Catholic France. As a jumping-off place into Europe, preachers were sent to the Channel Islands. One of these preachers was George Cosens, a West Indian, sent because of his colour which would attract in open air services. This is a vivid insight into policy: the brunt of mission fell on field preaching; in a society which was predominantly illiterate, and for a cause that demanded personal response and had no buildings in which to weave its craft, communication with the people was primarily audible and visual. But, to win crowds, it also needed that magnetic element of *spectacle*. Spectacle, show, a 'big-drum' invitation to come and see, the trappings of wonder – they had long been integral to the business of popular entertainment. Moreover, they were a shameless side to much retail trade – from medicines to marketing. Similarly the state had well appreciated spectacle as a means of social control – from the stately theatricality of the Assize parade to the human drama of the hanging: Dick Dastardly repenting beneath the rope and will the king intervene with mercy? This and much more made the grand spectacle the key instrument of popular communication; sharpened with the edge of Hell, and made quick by the nervous decay of a social order, Methodist preachers made it their own during the first half of the nineteenth century. If lively singing attracted crowds then it was the preaching that was to hold them.

Mary Dent was converted as a young girl near Darlington after first 'hearing strange and exaggerated rumours of the method and manner of these men, she went like multitudes, to see and hear for herself'. That her action was typical can be seen from the Primitive Methodist Magazine report on the Weardale revival of 1823-4: 'There has been such a falling down under the word, and in the prayer meetings, that young men would say to their comrades – "Come let us away to Ranter Meeting and see them tumble down".'[55] John Kirk, a Weardale leadminer was converted in 1824 on reputations of preachers like John Oxtoby who had recently presided over wild scenes at neighbouring villages. His first impulse was to go and see: 'When it was rumoured that he was about to visit the dale, and that his praying and faith were often nearly irresistible, a general desire to see and hear him was excited among the people.' Joseph Spoor, the keelman, was first stricken with 'longing' after casually hearing the preaching spectacle of Rev. Hodgson Casson: 'This noted Wesleyan Minister, whose personal and pulpit eccentricities were only exceeded by his devotion . . . created a great sensation in the Gateshead Circuit . . . crowds were attracted by the notoriety of the preacher, who "tried each art, reproved each dull delay" and multitudes of "fools who came to scoff remained to pray".'[56] After two weeks in the Slough of Despond, Spoor came to full rapture – though later it was Primitive singing that was to lure him from Wesleyan preaching.

William Crister, pitman and local preacher, killed in the Wallsend Colliery explosion of 1835, was tinged with the same notoriety, half fear, half excitement, that was Casson's. He was shrewd enough to know that revival emanated more from an expectant reputation than mere words. Preaching in a lull, with the circuit in need of a boost, he alluded to a recent outbreak, 'the other day', where 3,000 had fallen to the Lord in one session. After the service he was implored to tell where this had happened; forced to answer, Crister replied, 'Pentecost'. He clearly understood the currents of revival, how an 'outbreak' in one place could reverberate in emotional shock waves throughout a whole district. What was one white lie to the good it might reap?

But Crister also appreciated the dynamics of bold preaching. Bent like a spring in the pulpit, finger in the air, sweating hard and beyond reason himself, Crister had brought many a weeping penitent to the floor. He liked preaching that came as a thunderclap, where the preacher makes spectacle of the physical fact of the spirit's restless presence within – without it his biographer refers to 'the *cold* and the *dead* . . . there are no *signs* – no *effects* – you *feel* nothing; and though you *hear* the voice, it is from the *tomb*. And are the *lifeless* to set themselves up as judges of the *life* of others?'[57] They were not; Everett the past master hails Crister's visual arts as the stuff of evangelism:

> Just at the moment he had strung the people up to a certain point of highly excited feeling . . . he suddenly stepped forward with one foot, inclining his body in the same direction, like a person about to throw himself headlong over a frightful precipice, and exclaimed, 'O bless you! I love you so much, that I could dash away downward, and take a dip into hell for you, if it would only be the means of saving you' [then] he quickly started back – as if he had just touched the liquid mass, and felt it too much for him to bear for the *moment*,

> and therefore too much for them to endure for ever, exclaiming in an altered tone – 'but, mind ye, I should not like to stop there'. The sensation produced was beyond description . . .[58]

And yet, for all his praise, Everett maintains a note of apology for this pitman firebrand. Crister had swallowed his religion whole; added to this he expressed it with all the unruliness of his class: his was a blunt affirmation of forthright pleas and interjections, loyalty and spontaneity – he thought nothing of breaking up a meeting that was 'unscriptural', he exercised no sense of etiquette or deference to those of a higher class, money was no disinfectant for sin. To a man of the Wesleyan ministry (and Everett was by no means the worst), who had dedicated his book to Mr John Reay, 'A Promoter of Religion, Sabbath Schools, and Civil Order', much of Crister was an embarrassment, and was to be an increasing embarrassment to Wesleyanism as the century wore on. When Everett apologises for Crister's 'outbreakings of quaintness', and remarks that 'the contrast between the ludicrous and the sublime was often so striking and sudden', and judges that 'he was not the man for persons of grave habits; and that he would have been open to still severer censure, had he been tested by his *expression* and *manner*, rather than by his *sincerity*', then he is not so much expressing doctrinal differences as cultural ones. Crister had responded to Methodism with all the flamboyance that had prompted him to join the Volunteers for its parades and tambourines. On conversion the flash of the Volunteers was given up – that was the Puritan in him. Its temperament found outlet in a religious theatre – that was the Harlequin in him.

When, in the second half of the nineteenth century, Methodism settled into a more comfortable, more respectable middle age, the importance of preaching remained high in the totem, but in static form. It is in 1868 that Hetton's famous Good Friday Concerts begin. Ostensibly the concert is to raise money, but the event is really a glamorous social spectacle with guest singers and hired musicians. It is also in 1868 that street singing among the Sunderland Wesleyans – only a few miles from the Hetton Primitives – is under attack. Rev. John Broadbent finds it necessary to defend Methodism's own birthright from its own members:

> It is to be deplored and deprecated, when individuals stand aloof from a revival, because the chief instrument in the work is not exactly what they would desire, and does not meet their peculiar views as to the mode of conducting the services.

> . . . whilst passing along the streets, thus testifying for the truth, as I have been leading my 'hallelujah band' persons have stopped me to tell me of their conversion by my preaching . . . There are thousands who are now sitting under the sound of the gospel in this town, who would not have entered the house of God had not street-singing, joined with short, pithy exhortations, and the Total-abstinence Pledge, been used to gather them.[59]

The former impatience and vitality was clearly fading, a good service was a cabaret – 'The pale horse in Revelations is considered his grandest display.' Those of the working class who had risen to the ministry and were old men in 1890 for whom preaching in the baroque was natural, increasingly found themselves anachronisms in a new order. A good example of this is Rev. Peter Mackenzie.

Mackenzie was born in 1824 of peasant stock in the North Highlands of Scotland. He immigrated, like so many, to fill the gaps of a Durham mining disaster, moving to Oxclose Colliery, Washington, in 1844 during the strike of that year, and shifting from putting there to hewing at Haswell colliery in 1845 after the explosion there that had decimated its labour force. Married in 1847, Mackenzie was converted by the Wesleyans in 1849. Ten years after, he was appointed minister, which he remained till his death in 1895. The most important fact is that he was converted in 1849, the tail-end of the turbulent years – and in a backwater; the Wesleyanism of Haswell was more 'vulgar' than anything Rev. Dr Jabez Bunting would have tolerated. When his 'great reward' came in 1895 we are at the high point of Methodism's influence and respectability; Mackenzie, in style and origin, was a rarity. The biographer's approach is lovingly patronising: 'the impetuous miner . . . this unlettered and somewhat boisterous working man', 'What a happy eccentricity was his!'[60] He was certainly an eccentric, probably huffed many people, got 'carried away' too often it is true, yet he was a good and honest worker in God's vineyard. But the truth is that Mackenzie's brand of Methodism, the plain speaking of the uneducated, without refinement, was not eccentric to his age or his class. Society had changed, not Mackenzie; it had settled into mature relationships, and the stability and certainties of late Victorian society reflected themselves in a nonconformity of *reasonableness.* How this rough Haswell pitman in a collar had upset suburban congregations!

> This *abandon*, the losing of himself in his subject, was not only the secret of much of his power, but serves also to explain those vergings

> on the indecorous, almost the vulgar, to which at times he was perilously liable. Intoxicated with the enthusiasm of his impersonation, he occasionally allowed himself to be carried into an extravagance of utterance and gesture, that detracted from the grace and dignity of his performance . . . There were people who went to hear him once, and because of these minor delinquencies would never listen to him again.[61]

It is in this light that the examinations for entrance into Didsbury Theological College for which Mackenzie had made his London trip in the summer of 1858, are near farcical. He sat two papers: one 'literary' paper on languages, maths, history and geography for which he received a blank; the other on theology for which he was one of the highest. To the bright young men around him, Mackenzie was an eccentric praying man, forever amusing and embarrassing them with his alacrity to kneel and pray at all opportunities regardless of time or place – 'Down on your knees brother!' Somewhat bemused himself, asked how he was faring during the examination, his reply was, he would prefer to turn it into a prayer meeting.

Once in the ministry Mackenzie remained steeped in the preaching traditions from whence he came, and yet compromised with the slowing pace of Methodist expansion and the ethos of a primness that had formerly been a bustling crusade. The result was that he became a pulpit entertainer *par excellence* – and as the century progressed, more entertainer than converter. Working nightly in an atmosphere of lights and applause, Mackenzie recognised the uses of burlesque; newspapers and periodicals were studied for witty humour; 'All the wit that sparkled in Mackenzie's lectures was not brewed on the premises.'[62] But the old idea of spectacle that had won him, and once thrilled Durham mining congregations, never really left him; and when it did appear, it rang incongruously on an age that neither understood nor needed it. Preaching in 1868 at Spitalfields on Samson's encounter with a lion, the patriarchs of local Wesleyanism were stunned into speechlessness at a performance that must have seemed to them (as they scrambled for cover) a form of madness – the gallery loved it!

> '. . . Did you ever hear a lion roar my friends?' Then he began with a loud growl, rolled his eyes and tossed his head, his being worn a little longer than in recent years. Growing more excited, he swung his arms, and by some means drew one arm out of his coat sleeve. Then he pushed aside the table and began prancing round in a

> circle on the platform. Speedily his hands came perilously near the faces of the gentlemen who sat around, and who wisely gave him a wider berth. On he went, treading on the chairman's toes, tapping slightly on the ear of another, and stepping on the feet of a third. Every moment the circle grew wider, chairs and their occupants became all alive, and the audience, entering into the humour of it, cheered vociferously. At length one brother climbed over the rail onto the floor, and another down by the steps. This created roars of laughter, and Peter, taking in the situation, enlarged his revolutions until, amid the enthusiasm of the audience, the platform was cleared, and the roaring lion left, like Selkirk on his island, monarch of all he surveyed.[63]

Mackenzie was embarrassing his bourgeois betters on the grand scale; others (labelled as 'characters' by those who mentioned them in books later), were doing it more innocently. Men like Richard Redmayne (a North East colliery engineer in the 1890s), are quick to pay glowing tribute to the benevolence of Methodism on the miners in their memoirs. But this Methodism was an abstraction, an 'ideal type' influence – when confronted with it in the flesh the response was different; the religious culture of working people is either quaint or humiliating. Redmayne remembers taking tea with a committee of pitmen at Lord Grey's Howick mansion in Northumberland. Aristocracy sipped separately from Redmayne and his miners, so after tea there was time for a stroll in the grounds; our engineer, already snubbed, could not afford another humiliation:

> The grounds were looking their best, the bordering sea a sheet of silver, the air still and hot and jocund with the voices of many birds, a lovely and peaceful scene. I was strolling across the lawn, accompanied by one of the company, Anty Bolam, when all of a sudden he stopped and exclaimed, 'It wad take vary little to mak me gan doon on me knees and offer up a prayer – vary little'. 'Not now and not here, Anty' I begged in consternation, for he had meant what he said, and but for my intervention probably would have offered up a thanksgiving there and then.[64]

Anty Bolam was paying for the sins of his fathers. The spontaneity that was to drop him to his knees was typical of the temperament colliery managers had been trying to crush out of his class for 50 years. In spite of its mahogany pulpits and civic chapels and Liberal members Methodism could not belie its history – ghosts of a wilder past would come to rattle the decorous present.

III. Secular Radicalism

'A combined effort of Methodism and Jacobinism, in itself totally unworthy of the dignity of the House, and a portion of that spirit of intrusiveness which was being exerted in depriving the common people of their few remaining amusements' – and with that dismissal the Bill of 1802 against bull-baiting was thrown out.

As men like Thomas Cooper testify, Methodism was not the only movement in dialectical relationship with popular culture. In 1802 Percival Stockdale had published in Alnwick a tract which identified bull-baiting and slavery as part of the same viciousness that 'tends to petrify the heart of man; and consequently, to deaden his best morality . . . The common, and vulgar kind of pride steels the heart against every tender, amiable, and generous impression'.[65] His opponents saw him as a Jacobin or a Puritan or a Methodist in trying to upset the true English spirit, the Established Church, ancient custom and the Constitution. Certainly, his repugnance to bull-baiting had been the impetus for a Radical view on a standing army – 'it should always be the *regret*, not the pride, of a BRITISH KING, that he has a prodigious army'. The army, bull-baiting and slavery, were all part of one great school of blood, '. . . between the *sport* of *baiting bulls*, and the *trade* of *killing men*, there is a natural and intimate connexion'.

If religious reformers and radicals linked the virus so indiscriminately, then others so linked the professing antidotes. In Stockdale's own town of Alnwick, 33 years later, one Will Hardy was beaten up for venturing to join a feast given by the Duke. Hardy was a radical of known politics whose comrades had opposed the free ale, feast and dance on the grounds that the money could be better given to the poor.[66] Hardy was duly reminded of his radical puritanism. But the problems of persuasion were greater than a bruising; like Methodism, radical politics had to combat the difficulty of holding men not used to systems of adherence after revival had subsided. When the storm had cleared leaders were to learn the difference between enthusiasm and membership and between rebellion and revolution.

In 1819 the Political Protestants of Tyneside could muster 20,000 men to march in protest over Peterloo, 'hand in hand, four abreast, under the direction of their leaders, who carried white rods surmounted with crape . . . The procession halted at the Parade Ground, which being deemed not sufficiently capacious to hold the prodigious numbers that attended, it moved forwards to the Town Moor. The whole body was one hour and a quarter in passing the Barras Bridge at a quick pace . . .'[67] Enaes Mackenzie, who was one of the speakers at the black-draped hustings, tells us that the principles of radicalism spread in the October of 1819 'with all the fervour of a moral or religious feeling' – with all the fervour that in fact enveloped Primitive Methodist preachers two years later. On 25 October, Reverend Charles Thorp of Ryton wrote to the Home Department corroborating this view: 'Such is the organization of the Radicals, which was carried through the coal works of the Tyne, with one or two exceptions, in three days';[68] but Thorp had a tendency to be hysterical; John Buddle, colliery viewer and perceptive observer, lends us a test of accuracy. On the same day we find him, in a very lucid, cool letter, writing to Durham of a revivalist spirit abroad with 'the rapidity of lightning': 'Until within these few weeks, our Colliers . . . never troubled their heads with politics. But within a very short period, their very nature in this respect seems to have been completely changed', Wooler's 'Black Dwarf' is 'to be found in the Hat Crown of almost every pitman you meet'.[69] And yet within two months the movement is clearly waning. A 'mass' meeting at North Shields could only attract 700 on 13 December; and although into 1820 the miners remained sullen, the political element seems to have drained away. Archibald Reed, mayor of Newcastle, could write to Sidmouth in relief on 15 December, '. . . the Radicals are declining . . . the Pitmen in particular are tiring of paying their Pence . . .'[70]

Their pence were subscriptions to the Political Protestants who had formed a society at Newcastle on 3 August 1819. The basic unit of the society was the 'class'; this was the band that strapped the movement together, which, discussing and learning by twenties, sought to discipline the revival. The caucus of organisation, discipline, education and recruitment, the class demanded personal adherence as well as ideological loyalty. Self-education was to be along the lines of Cartwright, Bentham, Ensor, Cobbett, Wooler, Sherwin, and 'The Black Book'; self-control was in the rules:

> V. That the Class-Leader shall enforce order and decorum, and shall, when his Class meets, read or cause to be read, interesting extracts from papers and other political publications . . .
> XIV. Any member guilty of drunkenness, of supporting the Excise unnecessarily, or of trading voluntarily with the supporters and abettors of Tyranny, to be admonished by the Class-Leader,

> and if he does not reform, he is to be expelled, as unworthy of associating with the true hearted friends of the people.[71]

A formula for political 'backsliding', the Tyneside radical class of 1819 combined social salvation and personal reform in the strict style of Methodist economy; and it was natural to do so for although their aims were different, in many ways their problems were the same. 'Their organization is constructed upon the plan of the Methodists, to whom, however, they are hostile and indeed stand in the most deadly opposition.'[72] Mr Wawn, a Newcastle Wesleyan of both Establishments, wrote to Jabez Bunting in October, furious at the plunder of men and ideas: 'It is to me at this time, a subject of painful and depressing concern that two of our local preachers (from North Shields) have attended the tremendous Radical Reform meeting just held here, and one of them spoke at some length, and quite in the spirit of the assembly . . . [the radicals] . . . have adopted almost the whole Methodist economy, the terms of "class leaders", "district meetings", &c. &c., being perfectly current among them . . . if men are to be drilled at missionary and Bible meetings to face a multitude with recollection, and acquired facility of address, and begin to employ the mighty moral weapon thus gained to the endangering of the very existence of the Government of the country, we may certainly begin to tremble for the consequences.'[73] With such horrific potentialities attendant on the instruction of the lower orders, Mr Wawn must have kept a close listening watch on the Sunday School Union of which he was a central figure.

But he need not have worried; October saw the climax of activity, thereafter the movement spluttered into the oblivion of 1820. Most of the classes failed to hold the disaffected, and the auction of politics at one colliery on 19 November is symbolic: '. . . the Pitmen at Percy Main Colliery have broke up their classes, divided their fund, and the furniture in the private Room in which they held their Meetings.'[74]

The fate of radicalism in recession was that, like its religious counterparts, it found itself softened to suit – rather than steeled to win. Political education was humanised away from urgent discussions on Cobbet against gold, to dinners and 'shows' that were about more than mere politics. In 1822 there was a social evening at the Golden Lion in Newcastle to celebrate the release of Henry Hunt 'from the Bastile of Ilchester';[75] abstract argument was replaced by personal identification – it was a night of free born revelry. Apart from a dinner, a cabaret, a sing-song, a drink (two black bottles of ale each) – there was an evening's instruction by nostalgic salute of those things which made them different (saved? pledged? paid-up?) as free-born and of-the-People. Their Saxon forebears, real or imagined, provided identity: had not two kings been reminded by the people that their authority was merely delegated and not absolute? As Saxons they also had a *precedent*, as a speech reminded, 'But the Northern Nations that over-ran Europe at the dissolution of the Roman Empire, introduced a model form of government . . . as far superior to the Greek and Roman commonwealths, as these surpassed the governments of the Medes and Persians'; and *acknowledgement* is important to precedent – Judge Blackstone is a popular reference. So the evening gives a chance for full-blooded trencherman nostalgia: to roar for reform, to recapture ancient dignity, and to rejuvenate one's political soul, singing between quaffs:

> Is this the isolated ground,
> For men of fearless souls renown'd?
> For men who felt as men should feel,
> And boldly grasp'd the avenging steel?
> For men, who, rous'd in Nature's cause,
> Bared the red arm of war, and spurn'd the oppressor's laws?

If it was a night of political revel, it was also a political stage drama. Such meetings had a set form: items were chosen, 'The Sovereignty of the People'. 'Lord Liverpool', freedom fighters and foreign despots; speakers preached and made a toast; and a song was sung by all to a popular tune, all punctuated by cheers and laughter, applause and calls. The report undoubtedly captures the flavour of such a night: '. . . the company finally broke up, and immediately retired from the house, highly gratified, not with drinking wine out of crystal decanters, nor ale out of black bottles, but with "the feast of reason and flow of soul".'

The 'Golden Lion' dinner of 1822, albeit a feast of reason, had the flushed atmosphere of a pub concert on a Saturday night. An 1838 celebration night out at 'The Highlander', Winlaton, in honour of George Julian Harney was more of a Chartist tea party.[76] Again, politics is a socio-cultural activity as well as an ideological one, but this time more in the well-scrubbed atmosphere of a Methodist harvest home. Women from Blaydon as well as Winlaton were there and had been busy: the room was fully decorated with green and crimson hangings on which were portraits of Augustus Beaumont (editor of

Newcastle's *Northern Liberator*), John Frost and other 'distinguished patriots'. 'The patriotic band was of course present.'

The men and women of Winlaton sat down to tea, and with the trays cleared away by seven o'clock, the party could begin. Edward Summerside, the chairman, raised a toast to 'The Sovereign People', and the band swept into 'Rule Britannia'. Another toast of health and long life to George Julian Harney, and the air, 'A man's a man for a' that', followed. George Julian himself then harangued Injustice 'and was loudly cheered throughout', and Mr John Tiddoway struck up 'The Marseillois Hymn'.

As the party waxed livelier, so the toasts grew bolder – 'The patriots, McDonall, Vincent, Collins, Lovett!', 'John Frost, safety and success to him!' – and the songs louder, 'Tyrolese Song of Liberty' and the Primitive Methodist tune-favourite 'Scots wha hae ye'. After John Sybon of Canterbury had preached 'amidst the repeated cheers of his hearers', George Julian rose to respond with a solo song, 'When this old cap was new' – not for nothing had Marx called him 'Citizen Hip Hip Hurrah' with his tilted *bonnet rouge*.

Citizen George Julian Hip Hip Hurrah made the final toast, three times three 'The health and happiness of the cannie Lasses of Winlaton!', and the band broke into a skidding jig 'The Lasses O!' – 'singing and dancing was kept up until a late, or rather an early hour, when the company retired to their respective homes well pleased with the evening's entertainments, having enjoyed with heartfelt pleasure "The feast of reason, and the flow of soul" '.

We have already seen in *Labour Value* how the secular radicalism of the National Miners' Association was skilfully interwoven with the existing culture of the community. And as the *Miners' Advocate* was successful then so did others learn from that success. In 1844 Harriet Martineau was approached by the coalowners with an offer to write a periodical designed to counter the *Advocate*. Although the periodical was never published, Martineau recognised the re-education of the working class in their own culture. On 14 February 1844 she wrote to Commissioner Tremenheere:

> Suppose I were to go back as far in the history of England, as we have clear and procurable records of the modes of life of our middle and working classes, and make stories, presenting the aspects and probable incidents of their lives, – which would show their relation to government and the aristocracy, their position as members of society . . . the series might extend, representing the

> function of every class, profession or ruling influence of any kind – the decline of some orders and the rise of others – the progress of civilization and *comfort* for all, and the essential need that every class has of every other, etc. etc. – I seem to see how in tales as plain as Red Ridinghood, and without a page of preachment or exposition, a knowledge might be conveyed, sound as far as it goes, of the British Constitution, in its philosophy and its history – *Then with what power might we address these readers, thus prepared, on the subjects on which they are now so misled!* I could, but I need not enlarge on this. I am persuaded that the idea is a good one . . . By the time I come down to a Pit Story and Wages, the readers will have seen that their order is not, and never has been, an outcast order, and many other truths which we might now preach to them in vain.[77]

Of course, the uses of the anecdotal style had long been recognised in literature for the working man, and Martineau was its mistress. Trade union dialectic with popular culture of a much more spontaneous sort is represented in George Tutill. Tutill set up his banner making business in London in 1837, and grew as the trade union movement grew. His products dominated the commercial market and his designs became the traditional heraldry of British labour: from the 1880s '. . . with a Tutill banner, a branch *arrived*'.[78] Predictably, the banners' themes were about serious endeavour but the curling scrolls, exotic colours and bold figures of the design are from the fairground side shows where Tutill had been an artist. A painter in the Baroque, Tutill suited the instincts and visions of the unions perfectly. The National Miners' Association accommodated both Cranky and chapel instincts, but its organisation was mainly Methodist and its political principles were mainly Chartist. Reverend J. Miller, vicar of Pittington, had noticed the Methodist-style 'plan' of itinerant lecturers, and the interplay of religious enthusiasm and Chartist principle:

> The Men are wrought into a state of excitement by first holding prayer meetings . . . [then two or three villages meet] . . . where after a repetition of the same excesses they are addressed by a lecturer who is a stranger to them. This new method of combining enthusiasm with the infusion of bad principles may still keep the men from work a little longer.[79]

The Temperance and Teetotal movement was another significant section of working-class secular radicalism. Basing their arguments on city police returns the Newcastle Temperance Society in 1854[80] showed that drink was no affectation but part of the city's economic and social fabric. From writing part evangelic, part investigatory, part statistical, the reader learned that Newcastle spent £130,000 a year on alcoholic beverage. Drink was one demon neither historical nor allegorical to the dry nonconformist of the day – and more insidious still were the flash casinos and musical saloons, the plush lures to the city's young: 'they blend the fascinations of music, with the meretricious decorations of artistic skill, and the pernicious influences of intoxicating liquor'. In other words, such places provided entertainment; the crude bar rooms, existing only to drink, were too vitiated and 'too disgusting to be very dangerous', it was the red velveteen bawdiness 'calculated to deprave the taste, to intoxicate the senses, and stimulate the passions' that the Society took particular exception to.

Teetotalism as a working-class movement had always recognised the cultural problems for the convert: that to sign the pledge meant more than merely refusing drink, a moment's will; it faced the working man with a continuous struggle against the whole spectrum of his former life. Socially, in a society where the pub was all things to all men, teetotal conversion meant the man had to lose his secular life in order to find it. John Dunlop testified to the Select Committee inquiring into Drunkenness in 1834:

> [Temperance this time] . . . asks a great deal more from the working man than the mere disuse of whisky; for the new temperance member must not only refrain from his usual beverage, but, in the course of a week he has perhaps to reverse twenty rules and customs of drinking, as imperative as the maxims of a Turkish *seraglio* . . .

Dunlop was a Scot speaking of Scotsmen; the weight of custom and prevalence of spirits was stronger in Scotland, but his point holds good for England. To give up beer meant the sudden death of a miner's old way of leisure, the anti-drink movement found itself in collision with as much of popular culture as did Methodism or radicalism. The *Northern District Temperance Record* for January 1839 carries an editorial to buck up a flagging morale – their problems, it says, are common to all reform movements:

> These institutions wage war with domestic and social customs

> that have enwreathed themselves into the very texture of our social existence – customs that have linked themselves to some of the finest affections of our nature; and to remove them seems almost violating the felicity of Home.

The movement's reply was to provide an alternative venue for the member's life, but in so doing – like trade unionism, Methodism or radicalism – it had to compromise with the style of life it sought to oppose.[81] A letter to the *Record* in August 1839 illuminated the very same problem Methodism had long known, and the north-east Mechanics' Institute was to know ten years later:

> . . . the inconsistency which Teetotallers display in their zeal . . . on the one hand by meetings and spoken addresses – and the apathy which they shew on the other hand in respect of that species of information which is furnished by periodical publications . . .

The solitary and intellectual pursuit of reading a tract could not compare with the tradition in communication which was social and visual. The temperance movement on Tyneside and in the two counties recognised this fact and used 'the fascination of music' among other things for their own cause. The movement was also in close relationship with Primitive Methodism: men like George Dodds, George Charlton, John Tulip and Robert Archer, prominent teetotallers, were also Primitive local preachers (and among the cadre of the National Miners' Association in 1844); more than that, the organisation, self-concept and missionary tactics of north-east temperance were straight out of a chapel leader's meeting. On 4 June 1838 the Sunderland Temperance Society missioned the colliery communities of Hetton and Easington Lane in Co. Durham. Meeting the Hetton Primitives in the morning, a spectacle was got up and paraded through the black, greasy streets,

> In the front ranks was a banner waving in the air, and on it inscribed 'To Certain Conquest'; then followed about forty juvenile teetotallers with their medals; then the king with a retinue of attendants, then a party of singers, whose pleasing notes bespoke their souls to be engaged in an errand of love.[82]

Arriving at Easington Lane, His Majesty – 'Mr Smirk, the king of the reformed drunkards of Sunderland' – and four other princes of the pledge addressed the crowd. The spectacle then paraded back to Hetton to take tea and preach the word – 'kept up with energy in the midst of a very crowded auditory', 52 miners and their families signed the pledge.

The bright banners and 'pleasing notes' of temperance were raised whenever it seemed temptation might be greatest: the fluttering, singing spectacles were partly to mission the unpledged and partly to hold the faithful in times of trial. Christmas week in 1827 saw the Newcastle Society arranging a feast of meetings, teas and dinners as a show of force and an exhibition of self-improvement: the Sheriff Hill group met at half-past nine in the morning of New Year's Day at Bill Quay on the Tyne, replete with banners and music – the one time in the year when the bass drum could make hangovers ache immorality. The proud, clear-headed procession then marched up the steeps away from the river into Windy Nook and Felling and on to Gateshead, where 200 sat down to dinner at the Zion chapel. For the afternoon 'a high tone of feeling was kept up' and 19 were pledged.[83] Whit Monday was another day in the traditional calendar of drunkenness, and for it, in 1839, the societies of Newcastle, Northumberland and Durham paraded their moral tribune – serried ranks a proof of will in the same style of the Political Protestants in 1819, the NMA in 1844, or the Durham Miners' Association in 1872. They were all soldiers in wars that circumstance had wrought but the organisation had *carried*: against Tyranny, against Lord Firedamp, for the Mines Bill; and this time against Drink, 'Small White Rosettes on the left breast of the coat, and Medals hung with White Ribbon, to be worn by the Members on the occasion'.[84] And if everyone was not a hero of the new republic like Mr Smirk, 'king of the reformed drunkards of Sunderland', then they could think of themselves as Pilgrim, on the Railway of Progress through a muddled and alienated world. As they sang, did not steam power prove water's benevolence? The railway as well as symbolising all that was new, and being the cant term for time and speed, now graced a moral stature:

> He says that the Railway has just been laid down,
> From the land moderation to teetotal town;
> That it runs through a fine healthy country, that grows
> Good teetotal food and new teetotal clothes:
> So Jim was induced, as he held his life dear,
> To venture a trip with the great Engineer.

> The first of the stations is rightly called Health,
> And a little beyond is the station of Wealth;
> Which, when you have pass'd, you may stop if you please,
> At the stations Enjoyment, Long Life, or Heart's Ease.[85]

Temperance in Northumberland and Durham could also talk of sending the lifeboat out to drink-wrecked communities. The movement in the two counties had a strong religious theme; sin, and death by sin, sneaked into the Garden to destroy God's creation. Poisons like alcohol were of sin because they came in death.[86] But in spite of such casuistry, in the practical experience of adherence, the movement offered a secular salvation. The stations, Enjoyment or Long Life, were not on the theological route mapped by Primitive Methodism; and Heart's Ease was blasphemous to a religion offering periodic purges of that ease. Teetotalism had 'conversions' and 'revivals' without the name of God being mentioned, let alone invoked. Social rewards and a ready amelioration gave elasticity to the message; they meant that 'political' and other groups could integrate the theory into their own particular practice without going too far beyond the fringe. For instance, Owenism as a movement in the 1830s, whilst accepting the moral leadership of Robert Owen, grew in spurts, by districts which could have quite distinct differences on the best way to step it into The New Moral World.[87] Lancashire Owenism, in patches, trod with the care of teetotalism. Balls and social evenings *with lecture*, where 'there was ginger beer, lemonade, apples, oranges, tea and coffee, excellent singing and music . . . and as good dancing, and as much decency and propriety in dress and manners as I have seen anywhere'[88] serves to remind us that the forces for amelioration – rationalist or evangelical, personal or collective, or perhaps these categories are useless – all lived out cultural qualities in many-sided dialectical relationships not only with the old hedonism but also with each other.

IV. Liberalism

The fine flower of these years of continuity and change came with the growth of Liberalism as a working-class movement. The 1860s saw the sense of Liberalism quickly appear as a 'community of sentiment'[89] amongst working-class élites. The speed with which Liberalism seemed to take hold is, however, deceptive. That moral sentiment, essentially a Christian dimension, working out a greater civilization, was nurtured and born in the cultural mutations of the previous period. It survived, and found political maturity (though sometimes incongruously), by adoption, through Liberalism.

Consider the *Northern Temperance Advocate*, founded at Newcastle in January 1843. The rest of its title was the *Sunday School Teacher's Manual, and Messenger of Peace*; closely connected to other reforming groups, the Sunday School Union, much of the Primitive Methodist Community and the radical-nonconformist pacifist movement, and selling at 1½d, the newspaper was Advocate, Tribune and Organiser for a wide spectrum of sentiment. Split into three: 'Temperance' information, poetry, songs, reviews, and snippet articles; 'Sunday Schools' advice, knowledge, poetry and information; and 'Peace' anecdotes and propaganda, the style of the newspaper is typical for reform groups of the time. 'Facts' are packaged anecdotally with the authority of a nonconformist pulpit, or in the form of a straight quotation from Royal Commissions, etc., then steered with a moral pointer by the editorial. The *Advocate*'s format is more tract than newspaper: it opens with a long, heavy editorial address; news, views and topical trivia dominating towards the back as the columns get shorter and the titles more eyecatching – from the formal PEACE QUESTION on page three to 'Jealousy, Drunkenness, and Bloodshed!!!' on page eleven.

The *Advocate* straddled two epochs of reform, the cheap tract-by-the-million of the early nineteenth century to the new Liberal provincial press of the 1860s. Its editor would have understood both medium and message of Thomas Wawn's 1818 sunday school pamphlets and the 'marked principles and proselytizing aims'[90] of Joseph Cowen's *Newcastle Chronicle*. The conglomeration that was working-class Liberalism, and the agents that pumped out its mentality, owed more than they would have cared to admit to over sixty years of persuasion:

> Races had their revival in the land, with cock-fights and bear-baiting, hawking and football. 'The king had his own again' and 'cakes and ale' had their swing.

> What more shall be said of the eighteenth century – a century which closed with the erection of a Grand Strand on Newcastle Town Moor?

Both quotes come from the *Monthly Chronicle* of lore and legend for 1889, itself a journal of the Thomas Bruce-*Northern Minstrelsy* type of

Liberal antiquarianism. The drives of industrial capitalism, both personal and impersonal, to destroy popular culture and change the character of its people, became mingled in the Liberal sentiment with a certain view of English history. The Conservative Party, the Church of England and the whole ragbag of patronisers and oppressors who clung to their vestments were identified with the restoration of monarchy and the end of Commonwealth. The political consequences had been tyrannous, the moral consequences appalling, and by some sleight of treachery the English people had sold their birthright for a mess of political pottage. The free-born Englishman was back, though this time with a nonconformist conscience. On 28 March 1854, Garibaldi was presented with a scroll, telescope and sword in the Nelson Street lecture rooms, Newcastle (the same place Joseph Fawcett had recited 'The Miner's Doom' in 1844). His sword of freedom had been bought by public penny subscription, raised by the men who were later to be stalwarts of Newcastle Liberalism including James Watson, Joseph Cowen and George Charlton. On 11 April, the day before Garibaldi – now master of an American clipper – was to sail from the Tyne, a deputation thanked him in the name of Milton. Cowen made the toast, but also present was George Julian Harney, revolutionary Chartist of Winlaton and London and Martin Jude, treasurer of the Newcastle National Miners' Association in 1844 and still active. It says much for the range of Liberalism's 'community of sentiment' that the wealthy Cowen said nothing capable of offending Jude, Harney, or himself –

> General Garibaldi, and may the next time he visits the Tyne be as the citizen of an united Italian Republic . . . And when they who drive out the Austrian build up again a Republican capitol upon the Seven Hills, the heirs of Milton and Cromwell will not be the last to say, even from their deepest heart, God speed your work![91]

But, Liberalism's inheritance was more than ideological. As Vincent makes clear, Victorian provincial politics acted out the drama of the town. In its ceremony, bands, harangues, speeches, colours and seating arrangements the old sense of spectacle lived. This was the hurly-burly of election time; internally, the party worshipped in the style of its nonconformity. As with Methodism (as a movement, staunchly Liberal by late century), the visual spectacle remained, though it was no longer portable – Liberalism inherited the finished article as a piece of static art, whilst its religious precursors had fashioned it by trial and mission. The rally of National Liberal Federations, held at Newcastle in October 1891, listened to Gladstone in a theatre, but the unwitting could be excused for thinking it a chapel. Before the Grand Old Man spoke, political hymns were sung to popular melodies; all the dialectic of old and new is there, sermons, rally rousing, music hall, and planned euphoria when Gladstone finally exhorts and one's soul is refired. 'The Liberal March' is to 'Men of Harlech':

> Shoulder press to shoulder
> Onward march and bolder . . .
> . . . 'Peace, Reform and Liberation'
> Be our true aspiration,
> Till we win them for the nation
> And our land be free.

'On the March' is to 'One more River to Cross':

> Home Rule's our word tonight, my boys:
> There's one more river to cross!
> Old Ireland put to right my boys:
> There's one more river to cross!

And 'The Liberal Flag' to that whore of tunes, 'Auld Lang Syne':

> For Gladstone and the Right my lads
> For auld lang syne,
> We hail him leader of the Rads
> On banks of coaly Tyne.[92]

That 'Delegates will be provided with tea without charge' has a more than familiar ring. Leaders of this remorseless Liberal March of progress are described in a roll call of delegates, the 'Portraits and Sketches' of the programme. They are reminiscent of those *Methodist Magazine* galleries of fathers and mothers in Israel, unforgettable galleries which stand so instructive about Victorian Methodism. The tone is appreciative, encouraging, like a school report, but more fatherly than headmasterly, with just a touch of sales technique for a Liberal personality – the moral personality which will move mountains, and Ireland.

And that personality, as it manifested itself in the miners' élite in Northumberland and Durham, with men like Thomas Burt and John Wilson, was an admirable thing. The late century Liberalism which inherited it was fortunate because it was by then a sleek and influential species of working-class political thought: but the wealth of this patrimony had been made in the cruelty and destruction of earlier years, something easily forgotten by all members of the Liberal family in the 1890s when the old man was dead and industrial capitalism could afford to change its dealings.

However, for all the tracts, classes, societies, rule books, song books, chapels, parades, social evenings, meetings, speeches, libraries and newspapers of the cultural revolution – apart from work and scarcity, the ultimate instructors in political economy – the experience of the intellect remained as flexible for the working man as it was limited. Thomas Burt read Bunyan and Mill more or less as he could get his hands on them, and there he was limited, but he came to them fresh and related them to his own experience and his class without prejudice, and there he was flexible. During the Great War, Jack Common, son of a Newcastle railwayman, remembers as a boy visiting his Uncle Robin – 'crank' of the family, as much because he was a bachelor as because he was an atheist-socialist-vegetarian as well. Common was stunned at the stretchability of this man's mind:

> You'd perhaps expect Jack London and Wells, Blatchford and William Morris, the Rubaiyat and Whitman, Thoreau, Shelley, Kropotkin, Winwood Reade, Haechel, Belfort Bax, any amount of socialist pamphlets and Rationalist Press publications, some of these stalwarts certainly. But all around and overlaying them was a weird assemblage of works on theosophy, transcendentalism, anthroposophy, Spiritualism, Yoga, Flat-earthism, physical culture, the revelations about deadly effect of salt, sugar, meat, feather beds, starch and the alternative advocacy of raw food, grass, or yeast.[93]

Efforts to change the temperament of working people during the first half of the nineteenth century had been by turns vicious and insidious, but they had also been disparate, confused and contradictory. It meant that, for the élite of any pit community, intellectual experience could be as wide, albeit as diffuse, as Uncle Robin's – it bore no trace of the monolith. By late nineteenth century and the introduction of compulsory state 'education' for children we are in different territory.[94]

The role of schools as agents of social control in the pit villages of Northumberland and Durham really began with James Kay's Committee of Council on Education, reporting between 1840-41. He reminded the inspectors that 'no plan of education ought to be encouraged in which intellectual instruction is not subordinate to the regulation of the thoughts and habits of the children', and such was the tone of education in the area for the rest of the century. A system which equated boredom with inadequacy and put discipline before development, effectively blunted not so much the child's mind, but his desire to know it.

The Committee[95] was quick to recognise the uses of music for the task of work discipline: 'Notwithstanding these obvious imperfections, the children and young men and women employed in the manufactories of large towns commonly sing, during the hours of labour, the psalms and hymns which they have learned in the Sunday schools.' It is true that singing is something at the core of working-class life, but the Cranky tradition is 'rather foolish than simple, and fantastic than sprightly' and as such to 'inspire cheerful views of industry'. Schools must propagandise 'Labour Songs' because it is self-evident that: 'One of the chief means of diffusing through the people national sentiments is afforded by songs, which embody and express the hopes of industry and the comforts and contentments of household life.'

When coalowners allowed Methodist preachers land for chapels, they knew that a miner who poached and drank in his leisure would be less than an automaton at work – so did the Committee: 'A nation without innocent amusements is commonly demoralized. Amusements which wean the people from vicious indulgencies are in themselves a great advantage', so the education in hand must 'associate their amusements with their duties'. Stealing popular melodies, as Methodists, Chartists, Teetotallers and others were also doing, not only made the words attractive, but would instil nationalist sentiments sorely lacking in a year twelve months after the Convention, twelve months before the Plug Plot riots. The 'best specimen' of Old English tunes were needed:

> In order that the restoration of this national music may be facilitated, words have been adopted to it, intended to associate it with the customs of the people, and with healthy, moral, and religious sentiments, which may be intelligible and congenial to the minds of the children who are to sing them.

Bob Cranky and his society would have been considered neither intelligible nor congenial. However, Cranky has provided us with a thesis about culture at a crucial time in English social history. Cranky, as we have seen, was met in the nineteenth century by a Cultural Revolution which opposed him but did not and could not ignore him. That opposition had effects which have been considered in Chapters 4 and 5, and which have ultimately led to the state and education. In 1840 the pioneers of state education sought a working man who was 'industrious, brave, loyal, and religious'. By the turn of the century they were to have him. That *Jack Spring* was a story book saint, a fine tenor in a paper chapel, a figment of Liberal-Methodism, may have worried the Committee but it need not worry history because the myth often points to the reality. When industrial capitalism finally began to settle as a *system* after its precarious years from early to mid-nineteenth century, then the disconnected oppositions to Cranky began to merge into an *ideology*. This ideology altered the perception of history itself, and history's perception of the English working class and the response of those who faced conflict and depression during the 1920s and 1930s. As a postscript to Cranky and cultural revolution, Chapter 6 will look at the ideological implications of their exchange and by so doing introduce *Jack Spring* to *Geordie Shieldykes*, and both of them to *Bob Cranky*.

6 POSTSCRIPT

PART ONE: JACK SPRING, 1907

North East coal production increased massively during the second half of the nineteenth century to a 1911 peak of 56.4 million tons achieved by 227,300 men, out of a national output of 271.9 million tons by a national labour force of 1,067,200. The growth of the Coal Industry both reflected and led the consolidation of Britain as an industrial society. By 1914, as the miners assumed their dominant role in the economy, then so did their trade union federations acquire a measure of acceptability and security.

The 'County' developed in the 1850s and 1860s as the essential unit of miners' trade unionism: for the North East, the Northumberland Miners' Mutual Confident Association in 1865, and the Durham Miners' Association in 1869. Both these associations were staffed by men who were Liberals, whose tactics were conciliatory and whose sentiments were Respectable. Two leaders in particular – Thomas Burt of Northumberland (elected MP for Morpett in 1874), and John Wilson of Durham (elected MP for Mid-Durham in 1885) – were among the most paradigmatic of working-class Liberals in the political life of the period.

By the 1880s Primitive and Wesleyan Methodism constituted the established religion in the North East colliery community. Although declining forces in their rate of expansion, the chapels enjoyed an unprecedented phase of institutional respect up to the outbreak of war in 1914.

The local union lodge concentrated the triple forces of trade unionism, Liberalism, and Methodism. These three forces gave the natural generational hierarchy of men who represented them a moral hegemony in the villages. These men in turn succeeded in drawing a consensus on individual and social relationships which pervaded the political perspective of the North East colliery communities.

I. The New Archetype

In an interview in February 1974, just prior to the national miners' strike, Lawrence Daly, general secretary of the National Union of Mineworkers, told a story.[1] It was about a Scottish miner who was caught poaching on an estate, and, when challenged by the laird, the miner asked him how the land originally came to be his. He was told that his noble ancestors had fought for it. 'Well,' said the miner, 'Get your jacket off and *we'll* fight for it.'

This story had appeared as a matter of fiction over 60 years before Lawrence Daly's telling it – only that time the miner was a Durham pitman and not a Scot, the laird an English squire ' "Oh, be gox!" cries Geordie, "I'll soon hev some land o' me aan if that's the way on't. I'll fight tha' for thine", an' he stripped off his coat.'[2]

Goodness knows whether the tale is fiction or fact, whether it was grounded in truth, or boast, or jest, who had garbled it before Guthrie did sixty years before Daly. What remains is that the general secretary of the NUM was making a serious political point at a time of serious political crisis, and in that way does the myth in history point us to the reality. It does not matter if the confrontation had taken place in Scotland or Durham, Lawrence Daly's view of a better society found expression in the *style* of the legend.

By the 1890s and into the Edwardian era, Primitive Methodism had become proud of its successes, and its sons, in the colliery villages of Northumberland and Durham. A much more portly movement now, it created for itself an archetypal style of the pitman it had fought and won, precisely at a time when it was winning him less and less. 'Colliery Village Life', a fictional serial, by W. M. Patterson, appeared in the *Primitive Methodist Magazine* for the whole of 1907 and is typical of a spate of such stories. The author gloats with self-esteem; the reader was to be self-impressed by his own church's camp meeting successes at a time when the camp meeting was all but defunct in the recruiting calendar; throughout, the serial tells of a colliery more quaint than real, of saints and sinners more plaster than flesh and blood. The heroic relationship of Methodism and Mining in the industrial revolution, a legend even today, was a cliché by 1907.

The 'star pitman' of 1907 is Jack Spring, hero of 'Colliery Village Life'. Jack Spring is a converted Bob Cranky: still a proper 'character', Spring is respected by all, possessing all the attributes of traditional lore but now sobered and sanctified by his chapel allegiance. The New Spring, like the Old Cranky, is virile: the previous archetype had been a champion athlete and a bonny singer and could fight with the best of them – the Edwardian archetype had once been those things, but after conversion he had renounced his natural talents for the moral law. Realising the degradation of his connections, 'publican's pet', he severed them; though, make no mistake, the New Spring is no cissy; the whole village of Topton reveres his former artistry. Old Cranky was a man among men, invariably a powerful hewer – Spring retains the manliness as Topton's best hewer, but now flexes mind as well as muscle. To be a man now carries intelligence, the New Spring is self-improving and no dilettante as Cranky was; the company fear his brain but enjoy his hewing and will not dismiss him. Bob Cranky bubbled with zest for the pleasures of life in true Fielding style, but too often these energies were dissipated on the coursing path or at the fair – Jack Spring is similarly an enthusiast, but finds his outlet as an evangelist bringing sinners to their knees, even the district rogue and poacher, Dan Knaggs. Where the Old Cranky had been jovial, the New Spring was a wise counsel: prominent in the Mechanics' Institute; ever a moderate voice at Lodge meetings; a good knight in the town council clearing up corruption of modern proportions. In council meetings Jack found himself in conflict with the chief publican of Topton, for he was a teetotaller and publican's enemy whilst Cranky was a drunkard and publican's slave. All ends well however; the hapless publican is no match for Jack and eventually finds salvation on his knees on the floor of the Council Chamber.

The lassies loved a Cranky, men praised his boldness and laughed at his jokes; for Jack Spring, the saved responsible Cranky, tributes are redirected. With writing sickly sweet – a combination of *Peg's Paper* and *Biggles* – tears flow copiously as men witness his genius, salute his virtue: 'There was admiration in his gaze', 'Jack Spring is the greatest and grandest man aa ever knew'.

The change in the archetypal pitman as a district symbol was not restricted to fiction.[3] The district's definition of a 'character' changed with it; Sir Richard Redmayne, writing in 1942 of the 1890s, presents four pitmen as typical specimens: '. . . "car-act-or" is a word of special application in Northumberland – and I would like to introduce here four of my workmen . . . illustrative of what is understood by the word "character".'[4] Redmayne continues to pay the observer's customary homage to the pitmen. He reckoned there to be a Rabelaisian tenor to their humour (softened, they remain natural comics), but Cranky was dead, and the nearest he gets to explaining this was that 'each was yet racy of the soil'. Homage duly made, the reader is presented with four polite packages of 'character', three of which were fragments of Jack Spring.

The one that is not is Robert Pattison, dandy, *raconteur*, horse-racing fanatic. Of the 1844 union he says W. P. Roberts was merely a demagogue and of Chartism he has little to say – but he can recount every Northumberland Plate winner for forty years! Pattison is lovable rather than respectful, and after all he was born in 1817, a dark age by 1890, so his eccentricities can be forgiven. William Stoker has three hundred books in his cottage and is the self-made intellectual of the group. An expert on English literature, an ardent Liberal, a local preacher, knowledge and virtue had brought him the reward of a full-time directorship of the Co-op. Tommy Cleghorn is the Primitive Methodist evangelist; what is narrow in him is made up for by sincerity; he comes from a race of religious supermen. John Thirlwell 'was then chairman of the local Miner's Lodge, a pale faced, thin, austere-looking man, with black hyacinthine locks, and a black beard'. He had a warm temper but knew his mind, and his job, bearing no grudges.

In fiction, it was the Methodist minister, Rev. C. Bowran, under the pen name of Ramsay Guthrie, who made the greatest single contribution to shifting the measure of the symbolic 'pitman'. Writing at the turn of the century in the indian summer of Methodist influences, he achieved a prolific popularity with such novelettes as, 'On God's Lines', 'Davie Graham, Pitman', 'Black Dyke', 'The Maddisons of Moorlea' and 'The Canny Folks O' Coalvale'. Titles themselves tell us much: he is heavy in regional, family and moral tones, he writes in a robust dialect delicately contrived.[5] As in the old Tyneside songs in the first half of the nineteenth century, the line between fact and fiction is thin: new legends replaced the exploits of brawny Sandgate lads – the scraped message on the tin bottle of a trapped miner, the rise to fame of John Wilson MP, the conciliation of Bishop Westcott during the 1892 strike. Miners as a class are quaint, rather than savage; as individual heroes they have more Spring than Cranky. Village life now has a smug atmosphere, identified to death with its own institutions and incapable of self-examination.[6] What critique does exist is only the token stuff of a sociable religion. The fine qualities of a colliery community, all embedded in collectivism, once defenders and predators of that community to make it survive, are castrated by Guthrie into a carping kind of sociability. Self-complacent, the canny folks o' Guthrie live out an unhealthy dependence on immediate identities – the home, family, or street – they are *homosocial*, forever looking inwards or facing back. Tears, unquestionably Guthrie's literary hallmark, are usually tears of nostalgia, not like the first Methodist tears of hysteria and inspiration. From the stifled 'sob', to the unabashed 'weep', to the selfish little 'sniffle', the colliery village now spills tears as it once spilled defiance.

However, Ramsay Guthrie's novelettes were by no means innocent. They were ideological idylls broadly based on his Methodism and his

Liberal-labourism. *Kitty Fagan: a romance of pit life,*[7] is a story of Blackerton colliery in strike and eviction. Its dominating theme is an individualist morality. Although collective loyalties are recognised, the strike and its consequences are cast in terms of certain work conditions impossible to tolerate, especially union non-recognition; and answers to these problems are matters of individual decision out of conscience. There is no mention of an economic system putting people into specific roles, and how these class roles can influence the 'morality' of individuals in crises. For example, although only nine Blackerton families escape eviction, the decision to evict and the drive to blacklist union men in the first place emanates from the cruelty of one man, the manager Shadrach Reavely, rather than from what was the historical case, a policy decision by the ownership of the industry. The owners, aristocrats in a nearby castle, do make an appearance but only in the angelic figure of their daughter who makes two mercy trips to the evicted; one to take a mother and new baby to the castle, the second with groceries on Christmas Day: 'She neither knew nor wanted to know what it was all about, but to turn poor people into the fields, as though they were tramps and vagrants, was a disgrace to the British Empire' (p. 127). There is some hint of antagonism towards the mother and the daughter's father, Lord Weston: but in Liberal fashion the criticism is not of capitalism, but of a puff-cheeked idle aristocracy living off the labours of a united Coal Trade:

> 'It's that lot that's the root o' all the mischief', Geordie Taylor savagely affirmed. 'I wad like to know what business Lord Weston an' the Lords o' all the other airts, north, sooth, and east, hev wi' their royalty-rents an' way-leaves, an' what not?' (p. 127).

Not that this really matters to the business of life *when you get down to it,* an act of charity can dispel injustice – as when the groceries arrive: 'There was no need for the cordon of police to act as bodyguard. A thousand hearts poured benedictions on the lady from the Castle. The "touch of nature" leaps the chasm of the social cleavage. Love makes the whole world kin' (p. 128).

But if the heart is the source of true justice then the soul is the punisher of injustice. Reaveley, the cruel manager, often felt its grip, 'His soul was a riot.' He at last buckles and sags in his obstinacy when his frail, saintly wife – originally a pit lass just as he was a pit lad – is near to death from heartbreak at the suffering he was creating:

> It intensified his sullenness; it appealed to the latent tenderness. He resolved to be defiant; he was tempted to be gentle. His eyes flashed: his lips twitched; his brow contracted; his cheeks flushed. There was a demon in his soul; there was also an angel (p. 265).

Reavely breaks and gives in – and for Guthrie, when the bowels melt and love's constipation ends, then tears will readily seep. For tears are the physical proof of an individualistic morality: they define a soul's ability *to feel*. The New Jack Spring differs from the Old Bob Cranky not because he is any less game or manly than his counterpart, but because he is a feeling man. In *Kitty Fagan* a body cries, weeps, blows, or flows about once every ten pages; Chapter 6 is called 'Laughter in Tears' – 'Some laughed, some cried, others laughed and cried. There was laughter in the tears, and tears in the laughter.' Throughout the 271 pages, of course, Shadrach Reavely never cries or even hints at it. As late as page 266, and in such circumstances as hearing his dying wife pray 'Oh, my Father! Make him tender, an' soft, an' pitiful, an' forgivin' ', his anguish does not break into wetness. At last, three pages from the end, and with feeling, Reavely relents, yet all he can manage is a 'His eyes were moist with tears', to which 'Mary Reavely cried and laughed, and uttered praises and blessed "her man" '.

Shadrach's show of feeling is the real prize of the story, not the end of the strike; for just as Guthrie admired the arbitration-conciliation policies of the Durham Miners' Association in the late nineteenth century, so he believed strikes to be futile. The last words of the book come from Blackerton's union leader and carry a clear message:

> The gaffer's lost an' won, an' we've lost an' won. Shadrach tired, but he's nivver flinched on the blackleg question. An' so we've lost because he's won, an' the only satisfaction is that we haddent to beg his pardin. An' so, him an' us, the whole bag o' tricks on us, can all cry 'Quits!' (p. 271).

True manliness has also found a new expression. Bill Gibbons is Big Hewer of the pit in traditional style: perfectly athletic, he is celebrated as a working man of 'energy Herculean'. But what was before a virtue, the strength of Old England, is now a sin, a debilitating sin that detracts his manliness – Gibbons is a drinker. In the trials of eviction he finds real character and not the facile heartiness the bar had offered (the publican would not allow him to use his barn for furniture), and in a moral huff the drinker goes teetotal: 'Never nee mair will he be able to say that the champion's in his parlour. I'll turn cadwatter [cold water] an' gi'e me name to the little curate . . .' (p. 166).

If the new Springy Cranky had lost his taste for beer, then he also lost his old lust for life. George Grieveson, when dying, shows an even greater manly courage than Gibbons the teetotaller. The hymn writer of Blackerton – specialising in the Moody and Sankey *genre* where 'the tune were such "roond-aboots" that as likely as not you would be back at the beginning and "givin' her another spell" ' – Grieveson was well prepared for the test. And when death came, before a singing party round his bed George Grieveson showed a strength which made strong men cover their faces:

> 'Here she comes . . . By sartes, an' they're singing "The 'Appy Prospect!" Come on, thoo angel-hinny! I'm waitin' an' watchin'. I'm keen to be within the veil . . . A', I can see them, thoosands upon thoosands, an' they're watchin' the forst foot comin' for me . . . Thoo's welcome hinney', he said, addressing the angel of Death. (p. 196).

Kitty Fagan is soaked in a self-help, answerable-soul morality, and it also makes the odd ideological run for teetotalism and Methodism. Another novelette by Guthrie, *The Old Folks at Home. The Romance of the Aged Miners*, is, by contrast, a piece of sheer ideology. Loosely acted round the then topical aged miners' homes scheme, it is an idyll of retired miners and their wives. All of them are 'characters' in the old, one-dimensional sense, though by now the unrespectable are fewer and less bad, the respectable are more and better than they were. But the 'Aald Men's Scheme', and the 'aald uns' in it are only thin settings for a series of chapter tributes to men and causes that Methodism and working-class Liberalism of the day were anxious to espouse.

The major tribute is to sensible, honest, trade unionism. The Durham Miners' Association emerged in the 1860s as a union which sought arbitration and conciliation rather than class militancy; it was led, in the main, by chapel-respectable, frock-coated and watch-chained, pitmen Liberals, determined to run the DMA on 'sound' business principles. The top hat and velvet collar only came later of course, when the pick had been laid down and leaders like John Wilson took their seat in the House. Wilson's influence in the union was powerful up to his death in 1915: he used that power firmly against 'hotheeds' and 'socialists' whom he saw as unconsciously weakening the class by pushing for isolated and – in his eyes – suicidal colliery strikes. After a union lifetime in conflict with militants and the impetuous, Wilson, by the turn of the century, was taking a buffeting from the ideologically committed and the economically able, potential strikers of Durham's pit rows. And not only them, for Wilson's arch respectability was valid only among certain groups: his own class certainly, the Methodist Society, and that Liberalism outside (and under) the top ten hundred – the middle class were by no means reconciled to trade unionism of any form, and the local establishment, before his death anyway, were happy to take an occasional pot shot at him. In the light of this, Guthrie rushes to his aid; Wilson, John Watson MP in the novelette, is involved in a preposterous piece of fiction to show he is still 'a man o' the people' and not 'above himself': he makes a Westminster-Durham dash to help dig out an old mate he had heard was buried in a roof fall. Watson the MP shows he can still swing a pick. 'He said, "we'll hetta hev Tommy oot", an', MP as he is, he slaved wi' the rest . . . When cheps say nasty things aboot John Watson I feels like committin' morder . . . Man, I like the soond o' his name . . .' (pp. 41-2). Moreover, Guthrie is intent not only on defending the name of Wilson but on defending the stature of his type. The new union headquarters 'haal i' Dor'am', with its flanking statues is a cause for pride: 'Man! I was thinkin' the haall'll look alive noo that the grand aald leaders is to the front for iver an' iver. The sight o' them'll keep the leaders noo-a-days up to the mark an' in fightin' fettle' (p. 156). Or, if the statues cannot manage it, then Guthrie will see to it – one old man is asked what he thinks of the present union leadership, and 'fightin' fettle' is obviously more about slide-rules than militancy: 'Hinney, the breed's the same' Jimmy replied. 'There's hardlies the wild commotions there used to be. Ye see, there's the Conciliation Board an' things is settled wi' figures an' speeches. But there's mighty men i' Dor'am' (p. 161).

And might means moral might; Guthrie's proof is a case of one local preaching (now almost obligatory) union leader who refused the bribe of a warm winter coat. ' "Mister", he says, "there's nowt sae cosy i' winter time as a conscience void o' offence towards God an' man".' As a kind of political descant to moderate trade unionism another chapter sings of the healing grace of Liberal nonconformity. This is where reconciliation between labour and capital can find itself; a dispute is solved when the owner discovers that one trade unionist he had victimised many years before had converted his own son to the Lord.

In Guthrie's ideological mythology, trade unionism and Methodism are almost synonymous. Not surprising then that we find a burst of tributes to the chapel. One chapter salutes Religious Ridicule Refuted, another salutes Miracles, another Conversions That Last, another smugly salutes the Religion of the Working Class steeled hard against 'the infidel controversialist'. The chapter 'Geordie Jacques L.P.' typifies the limits of working-class ambition: converted from a family of drunkards, Geordie rises to the heady heights of the professional ministry – and he does not forget: 'Oh, Mr. Jacques', I cried, 'will you take me in? They are all drunk, mad drunk, and I dare not go near.' 'Come in my canny lad!' he said. 'Come in' and he put his arms around me and let me cry my cry out.'

Where religion is concerned tears may remain the litmus test of goodness. One chapter sheds unashamed tears in relief that the Methodist had seen fit to save the pitmen. A young visitor tells an old man how a 'gaffer', Henry Main, had helped him in an accident. The old man laments that such fine men did not exist in his times, and how this historical neglect had given him a lame arm. ' "Whaat waas the gaffer's name?" the old man stammered, shaking his head and Weeping.' It was *Henry Main*:

> 'Ay gran'fether, he's a local amang the Methydists.'
> 'I thowt as much' the old man observed, still weeping . . . 'I waddent hev had me badly arm if my gaffer had been o' the tribe o' Mister Henry Main' (p. 210).

The village oracle is Dickie Hughes, Liberal Tribune, and to be found in the library. Guthrie devotes three pages to a homely treatise on land policy, where, as in *Kitty Fagan*, the argument is cast in a classic bourgeois mould: 'them' are the Tory gentry, 'us' are the industrial party of worker-entrepreneurs and worker-workers:

> Noo, divvent ye see that the landlaaws waants alterin'? There's a nice little select party o' blood-suckers an' land grabbers, an' they've stolen the land for theirsels. Some on't they keep for deer staalkin' an' fox huntin'. Some o' them hev parks as big as cities. An' when the likes o' us gets the coal an' iron, they claps on royalties an' things o' that sort (p. 179).

The analysis was irrelevant to the industrial and class milieu in which the miners lived, but Guthrie takes no chances, he is not one to provoke any 'extremist' views. Hughes is subsequently slurred; a fine man no doubt, but 'The drink was the Oracle's failing'. Similarly, Guthrie shares too much the traditional middle-class fear of a proletariat of (just above) average idiocy, being swept off their boots by a wilful agitator, to allow the Oracle too much respect. So he warns the reader against any self-righteous demagoguery from this too-clever-by-half political pitman. With a firm cut Hughes's cleverness is put in doubt – he does not really grasp the land problem; asked to explain it, he, like all demagogues, can only bluster: 'Noo, I've said it, an' I'll say nay mair. I once heerd Bradlaugh, an' he was big for the abolishin' o' the law o' promigenitee an' intail an' he was reet. Thaat's what I say!' (p. 182)

Drink was the oracle's failing because in the New Jack Spring fiction of this kind, teetotalism, as religion, is in the mainstream of village consensus. Those who defect are now the eccentric minority. A wife blackmails her drinking husband by reminding him that their dear, dear son, Davie, killed sixteen years before at work, had never drunk a drop, and here *you* are, going out on the anniversary of his death! This was cheap, even by Guthrie's standards; but he really rakes the emotional muck by invoking the scratched message on a tin bottle found beside the body of a victim in the Seaham colliery disaster of 1880 where one hundred and sixty four were killed. Part of the original reads: 'Dear Margaret, There are forty of us all together at 7 a.m. Some was singing hymns but my thoughts was on my little Michael. Be sure and learn the children to pray for me.' Guthrie picks his history, 'He had scratched a message to his parents in the terrible darkness'; but changes its fact, and Davie's message is signed, sickeningly, 'Your dying Davie'. At least in the old legends, when Blind Willie met Billy Scott, and when Captain Starkey, Bullrug, and Nelly Marchy had walked at Bold Archy's wake, the mix-up of fact and fiction was uninhibited, without ulterior motive. Ramsay Guthrie, by contrast, used a matter of genuine grief to wring out his own little bit of journalese morality.

There are other tributes: to Bishop Westcott of Durham, 'the best friend the pitman's had i' my time'; to domestic bliss and a golden wedding; and to the Co-op, saving made easy – but the one that catches the tone of the whole ideological blitz of the novelette comes at the end. The village Methodists needed a new chapel, so they embarked on a praying campaign; in a tribute to Self Help, Nathan prays and shifts himself: 'Nathan was brandishing his hammer and singing the Doxology . . . "Clear the ground! Shift the rubbish! Gi'e the Lord fair play an' then gan on wi' yer prayers" ' (p. 223). Indeed praise God from whom all blessings flow, for with His and Guthrie's help Jack Spring was to usurp Cranky's crown.

II. The New History

A distinct hagiography of Methodist pitmen was building up. By 1909 Bastow Wilson's *A Primitive Methodist Diamond Field. The story of a Northumbrian Mining Circuit*, strolls down memory lane by turns remembering, forgetting and inventing, a new tradition. Before religion the colliers were a dark, brutal crew whose lot had been no better than the ancient serfs; but new heroes had stridden out of religious conversion into social salvation and had suffered terribly for it – as Seaton Delaval's manager put it 'Ah'll whack the Ranter preachers away, they hae tee much gob for me' – and, when evicted, the chapels had provided natural retreat. As well as trade union heroes, there were prize converts to recount, and 'character' preachers like Henry Vogwell from Cramlington; 'in the pulpit he would excitedly pace backwards and forwards, speaking rapidly in a weird, wailing voice, often until he was out of breath', or another, who would regularly fall out of the pulpit such were his exertions. Union heroes, prize converts, larger-than-life preachers were human testimonies surrounded by the trinkets of the hagiography – early struggles with chapel building down to scraped messages of buried hope found with the corpses of colliery disaster.

Of course, in Wesley's own lifetime Methodist literature had flirted with the pit community. Miners in the eighteenth century entered evangelical folk lore as saved wildmen to be hawked around as almost cult heroes. The result was that both the savagery and the mission became exaggerated forces, something from which social history has never quite recovered. But the new hagiography of a hundred years on has different dimensions: if Wesley's men burned only to save souls on the slag-heap, then the new saints carried a social vision – they sought to save lives by the committee room. Bastow Wilson's 1909 romance emphasises the range of Primitive Methodist talent employed in the new institutions of the working class: Tommy Cleghorn, local preacher, remains a character but Bastow Wilson gently chides a single-mindedness that Wesley would have applauded: '. . . he cared to nothing but "the cause"; Miners' Unions, Parish Councils, Co-operative Societies, were nowhere with him; his meat and drink were the property of Zion.'

Thomas Burt MP, 'The First Pitman in Parliament',[8] was the crowning glory to the attributes of the New Jack Spring. By the turn of the nineteenth century the ultimate success for the collier lad was no longer measured by daring and boldness as it had been for Cranky, or hot gospelling, as it had been for early Methodist warriors – but instead by daring, boldness, rhetoric, integrity, honesty, intelligence and self-help shaking down a Liberal seat in the House from the tree of Providence. Burt was the perfect model: from a family of Methodist Rechabites, refugees from victimisation after the 1844 strike; a putter at Murton, to a hewer at Choppington, to MP for Morpeth in 1874; nurtured on Bunyan, Gibbon, Milton and Uncle Tom's Cabin; self-taught in Latin and French; mainstay of the Northumberland Miners' Mutual Confident Association before Parliament beckoned, Burt and Burtism – the product of Methodism giving calibre and gravity to working class pursuits, etc. – was talked into a cliché by Liberal and Methodist reviewers.

Others followed him and opportunities were not lost. *Primitive Methodist Magazine* for 1907 carries an interview, 'From Pit to Parliament', with W. E. Harvey, MP for N. E. Derbyshire: 'Primitive Methodism may well be proud of this pit laddie who has fought his way to a seat in the legislative chamber of a great nation.' All the old-new familiarities are echoed: those fine oratorical skills learned in 34 years of preaching now at the disposal of the country; carried to class meeting in his mother's arms to become a work horse for the circuit. And Liberalism is not forgotten, indeed nonconformity only serves to reinforce it: Harvey hates those relics of patronage still surviving the progressive forces of industry and democracy – education suffers from 'clerical domination', and the House of Lords would be a farce if it were not a tragedy: 'An hereditary chamber is an anachronism in this democratic age. It is a survival of feudalism and must go . . . the bishops, of course must be excluded. There is no justification either in history or in reason for their remaining.' To join the cult it was not necessary to have been a miner, although for certain sociological and demographic reasons they had been the first. Joseph Arch, local preacher and union leader of the agricultural labourers, joins in the atmosphere with self-satisfied relish; elected in 1885:

> I took my place in the Council Chamber of the nation as the representative of the labourer and the Prince of Wales . . . [Sandringham was part of his constituency] . . . Chamberlain was smiling all over his face; if I was smiling it was an inside smile at the thought that my entry marked the triumph of our enfranchisement.[9]

The celebrated track from trapper boy to legislator naturally found complement in popular Methodist fiction. 'Her Bonnie Pit Laddie' by Rev. S. Horton, appeared as a serial in the *Primitive Methodist Magazine* for 1895. This 'Story of Northern Methodism' has young Fred Layard as our archetypal and active reformer. He finally wins respectability (and crowns the dreams of any colliery lad with a serious turn of mind), by becoming colliery manager, marrying the vicar's beautiful niece, being elected Liberal MP, and having a doting son who plays preacher from the armchair.

None of this was achieved however, without struggle. The story has all the contempt of a railway religion's enlightenment for the rustic foolishness that was Anglicanism. The Church of England is identified with farthing candles which only reveal a shady ignorance; a feeble congregation led by Tim Dawson, an ex-farm 'servant' who would mix up his hymn tunes; and greedy, patronising parsons as *gross* as the cause they served. But Providence is double-edged, the same forces 'which destroyed the beauty of the landscape contributed to the making of the Methodist Church'. One bigoted, the other licentious, parson and squire clap the preacher in the stocks 'where he sang and preached to a gaping crowd of rustics till eventide'. The colliery comes and makes these poor rustics miners, the chapel comes and makes them men: the establishment can now no longer rule with a Mogul's whim, '... if he's gannin' tee fight again' the lord and the miners' union at the same time, he'll hev his hands full'.

Miners' unions had lost too many battles to count the Lord among their ranks but how many spirits were tempered by speeches that implied as much, songs of 1844 and 1831 that said as much? In this way the myth can create its own reality, and by the 1890s and after, the Methodist-miners hagiography was doing the same. It was not so much that Burtism and the hall of fame that preceded it was untrue, far from it, for we have witnessed a durable influence in this essay; more that the facts were being enshrined as legend, and the legend bore no respect for balance: pieces were picked out a-historically and put on a plinth as caricatures in a long line which called itself 'history'. The interested were then invited to inspect the gallery of the nineteenth century, and to coo with admiration at the forces of Progress – all the way from eighteenth century rural, superstitious serfdom to present-day industry and democracy, sweetness and light, Methodism and Liberalism. That the Burtist caricature was replacing Cranky as the accepted archetype was surely more a sign of ideological victory than of authentic self-celebration.[10] In the 1820s outside observers made plagiaristic references to the pitman's rough turbulence; by the 1890s, much more likely is the description of him like a regular Jack Spring: 'The pitman, as a rule, is a quiet living, religious, and godly man, who enters with the greatest heartiness into all exercises of the communion, which is generally one of the many Methodist bodies, and *par excellence* the Primitive.'[11] 'As a rule', for the author, is an excuse for the reliance on popular mythology instead of serious study.

When serious study was undertaken, even that did not escape corruption. Welbourne's *The Miners' Unions of Northumberland and Durham* (1923), completely falls for the hall-of-fame interpretation. The chapel brought the colliery gifts from heaven: class consciousness was the bonus – self-management, self-awareness, self-help, self-education, pulpit speaking and the economic arguments of the Sermon on the Mount. And those Burtists who ran the Durham Miners' Association as an élite were everything the *Primitive Methodist Magazine* said they were. William Crawford was such a man, but his successor in 1890 came nowhere near his mark; Patterson 'was a lesser man, possessed of none of Crawford's readiness to shoulder responsibility. He argued where Crawford had ordered: he consulted the men where the founder of the union would more wisely have presented them with an accomplished fact.'[12] In February 1920, Sidney Webb provisionally accepted nomination from a number of miners' lodges in the Seaham division to stand for Labour as their parliamentary candidate. Webb, of course, had won this accolade with his superb defence of the miners' case before the Sankey Commission in the previous year – he was subsequently elected as member of parliament for Seaham in the election of 1922. Between nomination and election, Webb's *The Story of the Durham Miners* was produced by the Labour Publishing Company in 1921. It must have been that Webb the outside academic was over-awed by the men who begged his nomination, because his 'history' is one massive act of tribute to the Methodist penetration. First, he salutes the men who were to be his agents, canvassers, fellow speakers and fund raisers:

> From their [Methodist] ranks have come an astonishingly large proportion of the Trade Union leaders, from checkweighers and lodge chairmen up to county officials and committee men. They swarm on Coop and Friendly Society committees. They furnish today, in the county, most of the working class J.P.s and Members of the House of Commons.[13]

This was largely true in 1921 (though there is not enough mention of other men and other influences), but Webb goes on to make history out of a contemporary natural bureaucracy and popular myth. Those working-class institutions which were thrown up as reactions to nineteenth-century encroachments are cast almost as a suspended species of 'civilizing influence', sovereign and pristine pure. We are told that the miner was sore oppressed because he lacked the very things he himself made: there were no co-operative societies; no miners' halls; no workmen's clubs; no music; no organised recreation; few friendly societies, and, most important of all, no chapels. Apart from being merely wrong on a few points, to say there was no music is laughable; what Webb means is decorous music, soirée-style; and for a socialist to consider colliery schooling in the Victorian period as 'civilising' speaks only of historical ignorance – Webb had swallowed Methodist folklore whole. Pre-history finished, and history began, with the religious revival which Webb puts between 1821 and 1850; what went before was at worst feudal and at best irrelevant. Ignoring any popular tradition in history 'the people' are saved and defended by a religious élite who brought 'civilisation'. This civilisation constitutes the bedrock of the next, which will be evolutionary socialist, but socialism, by paradox, will not come out of history – it will come out of the air:

> What is needed is the power of the Spirit that calls to a higher, more social, and more genuinely civilised life; the power which a hundred years ago was evoked by the religious revival of that time. Who shall today evoke a like spirit among Durham miners?[14]

The Hammonds' *The Town Labourer*[15] had been published four years before Webb's *Durham Miners*, in 1917. It is a magnificent piece of social history well ahead of its time and highly influential even now.[16] But in their determination to enter polemics with nineteenth-century evangelism, and particularly Methodist evangelism among the new proletariat, they unwittingly reinforced the historical myth. The Hammonds believed that Methodism had blunted what 'true' class consciousness might have been had 'it' not lent its pernicious influence:

> It taught men and women to think of themselves, not as members of a society with common interests, common hopes, common wrongs, but as individuals and separate souls, certain to suffer eternal damnation unless they could attain by a sudden spring of the heart a victorious sense of pardon and escape from sin.[17]

The Hammonds' approach is so determined that at times it becomes embarrassingly a-historical. They seem to forget, like Webb, that Methodism was a cultural product itself, that Primitive Methodism at least, *was* the working class and therefore a valid expression of their consciousness: Methodism, we are told, diverted energy from the class struggle 'at a time when wise energy was scarce'; it diverted money from the class struggles 'when money was still scarcer'. The folklore that romanced Methodism as heaven-born, alighting on a troubled society in order to save it, is part taken by the Hammonds to argue that it did not save it. If the preachers arrived in a vacuum so the Hammonds extract them in a vacuum: 'It would be supremely interesting to know what sum was spent on this religion by a class that was thereby diverting its resources from a war for independence.'[18]

The Town Labourer is, however, a better work of history than it is of theory. Later the Hammonds qualify judgements such as these by admitting that the movement was often softened to suit the situation in which it found itself; and of course the whole theme of the work is largely a contradiction of their treatment of Methodism – that class consciousness developed more out of experience than philosophy or theology. What the Hammonds could not qualify, however, was their reinforcement of the legend about the halcyon days of Victorian working-class churchgoing. By setting up Methodism as a 'cross current' to trade unionism and a 'rival flag' to popular radicalism, they undoubtedly stamped academic approval on extravagant claims by Methodist authors of their evangelical successes. Even if we accept, rightly, that the Methodist influence percolated down through the membership to a wider audience, an 1851 Wesleyan-Primitive 13 per cent attendance rate for a legendary stronghold of the chapel is certainly too low to be an effective 'cross current' to popular movements in Co. Durham.[19]

Historically, Methodism could not lose: so profound had been the relationship between Jack Spring ideology, Burtist relevance with the approach of a Labour government, and academic writing, that it was portrayed both as a godly cadre, saviour of the miners, *and* a mass movement, teaching the first rudiments of democratic self-government to a tyrannised third estate.

Thus, charges in the 'opium of the people' vein could be refuted by pointing to popular affections; charges of *populism* – an a-religious workers' social club, freak of industrialisation – could be refuted by pointing to the godly élite. And after Welbourne in 1923, such was to be the tone of Methodist social history for the next 40 years.

PART TWO: GEORDIE SHIELDYKES, 1930

The end of War posed fundamental economic and social questions for British society. The mines had been brought under government control to meet war demands, and in 1919 Lloyd George managed to stall questions about their future control with a Royal Commission under Mr Justice Sankey. The Commission reported in June 1919 and made a majority recommendation for nationalisation. The Prime Minister ultimately rejected this and on 31 March 1921 the mines were officially returned to private ownership. On 1 April 1921 the miners were locked out for refusing to accept proposed wage cuts – they were not assisted by their allies, the transport and railway workers ('Black Friday' 15 April 1921) – and accepted worse terms for a return to work, which they did on 1 July 1921.

The reintroduction of the Gold Standard rate on 28 April 1925 overvalued the pound and threatened exports. More wage cuts were planned but the determination of the miners and the TUC General Council to resist brought government intervention: a subsidy for the industry, and another Royal Commission, this time under Sir Herbert Samuel. The Commission reported on 11 March 1926 and recommended long-term organisational and welfare improvements, and immediate wage cuts. The owners rejected the long term and insisted upon the wage cuts, and longer hours. The miners refused and on 1 May 1926 were locked out again. On 3 May the TUC General Council began the General Strike – the workers' response was magnificent – but conversations with Samuel persuaded the Council that compromise would be possible and they called off the Strike on 12 May 1926.

The miners considered themselves betrayed; would not compromise; and stood alone for six months before accepting terms involving lower wages, longer hours, unequal pay structures and inevitable victimisation.

The inter-war Depression centred on areas which were the traditional sectors of British industry. The North East consequently suffered the poverty and degradation of persistent short time and concentrated unemployment. Jarrow, a shipbuilding town on the River Tyne, symbolises both cause and effect of the 1930s Depression. When 'Palmer's' – a heroic, innovating, Victorian, shipbuilding enterprise in iron and steam – closed its Jarrow yard in 1933, eight out of ten Jarrow workers lost their jobs. 'Jarrow in those days was like a workhouse without a wall round it.' Two hundred Jarrow men marched to London in 1936 to bring attention to their plight.

I. Break-Up

People's savings had dwindled away, and relief had to be sought for women and children. This was obtained on the understanding that any payments made would be recoverable when work resumed. Boots and shoes were wearing out and people had to be fed. Soup kitchens at the Miners' Hall and the Salvation Army provided a mid-day meal of soup and bread for children and people in need. Boots and stockings were given from a boot fund. The wherewithal for these necessities were provided by men and women helpers who foraged around wellwishers for the necessary food and clothing.

But we were losing the battle. By the end of November the men could hold out no longer. Their womenfolk had supported them throughout, but the reports coming in from other coalfields were depressing, and they were bitter and disillusioned. They had been hammered into the ground and could take no more . . .

. . . in such a way did a man of Murton Colliery, Co. Durham remember the 1926 miners' lock-out.[20]

If the Great War had hurried the strange death of Liberal England, then the 1920s were quick to confirm the news to the miners. Lloyd George broke the Government's 1919 promise to carry out, to the letter and in the spirit, the recommendations of Sankey. Sankey's Royal Commission on the mines had compromised on wage and hour demands, but recommended nationalisation: in 1921 Lloyd George decontrolled the mines and handed them back to private enterprise, when wage reductions were immediately announced. Strike followed, but as a prelude of what was to come, it was defeated. 1925 and the economy is lifted back on to the gold standard, further wage cuts are announced, the miners stiffen, the TUC promises, the owners look to a government which dithers its way into the Samuel Commission, which neither side accepts, and on 30 April 1926 the miners find themselves locked out. General Strike! but that folds up by May 12, and the miners stay out till November. Starving, humiliated and down-at-heel, Jack Spring shuffled out of Liberal England and into the twentieth century.

The Coal Industry had been the base of a Victorian economy that consisted of certain staple industries – metallurgy, chemicals, textiles and engineering – which were entrenched by the 1920s in an occupational and regional formation. H.B. Henderson, writing for the *British Association* on 6 November 1926, thought that the 'coal strike' would give a lasting impetus 'to certain profoundly important tendencies' in the economy. These tendencies were the initial pains – and Henderson was quick to see and identify them – of a structural shift in the economy away from reliance on heavy industry, export and brittle occupational and investment patterns. The War had unnaturally expanded the old patterns; the decline in the world trade and the financial crises of 1929-31 were to rush their break-up. The ideological tenets of *laissez-faire*, the geographical concentration, the specialised character of much of the work, and the massive Victorian historical and moral significance attached to the old staple industries blinkered the majority of economists, politicians and businessmen of the inter-war period into believing that the staples represented what the economy was, and would be, in the future. Only the odd prophets like Henderson and Keynes realised that the solution to rising unemployment was a fundamental shift in the nation's economic balance and was not merely a matter of trade cycle patience. As Henderson says in the same article, 'We had become so proud of a Britain whose development was based on an exuberant expansion of export and metallurgy, that we could not bear to think of a Britain developing along other lines.'

Henderson was lucky to be in a position to think of a 'we' in terms of power likely to affect the situation. The miner was not. He suffered isolated strikes, wage cuts and short-time – for him this was the meaning of the 'highly localized character of unemployment'. Moreover, the decline and fall of coal was a lingering affair: the colliery community had rich identifications and were loath to leave the land of their fathers; the large fixed capital infrastructure of mining meant that, in depression, owners were ready to accept orders at any price which would at least contribute to their heavy standing charges, with the result that a long period of unprofitable prices might ensue without the amputation of surplus capacity.

Even so, King Coal slumped from his Edwardian throne quickly enough to show that he was not the man he was. In 1913 the North East had mined 56.4 million tons; in 1933 the figure was down to 40.1 million. Similarly, in 1913 the money value of United Kingdom coal production was £145.5 million; in 1933, £134.6 million. This fall-back was reflected in manpower in the industry: in 1913 the North East had 237,800 mineworkers, in 1933, 151,000; in 1913 the United Kingdom had 1,127,000, by 1933 it had dropped to 789,000.[21] Coal exports are even more pertinent instructors in the context of inter-war economic crises: in 1913 British coalfields had exported 73,400,000 tons; by 1933 and twenty traumatic years later, the figure was down to 39,068,000 tons.[22] In the North East, the south-western part of the Durham coalfield was hit the hardest. A boom area between 1851 and 1881, satisfying an apparently insatiable thirst by the economy for coking coal, between 1921-31 the *whole* district suffered decreases in population of over 10 per cent, and the farthest south-western tips of over 20 per cent. In ten years, for thick clusters of population, this represents a lot of upheaval and suffering.

Sudden upheaval and suffering had not been generally acceptable to the social vision of pre-1914 Britain. Poverty might continue to ache but it was possible to extract it, and upheaval was unthinkable – our heavy industries were inviolable and after Orwell, God would always be in His heaven, battleships would always be in the Channel and the pound worth a Pound. Those nonconformist Gladstonian Liberals, Burtists and popular ideologists, who had helped create sentiments of capital-labour co-operation and everlasting Progress with God and Free Trade, found either themselves or their ideas floundering in the mud of Passchendale. 1926 and Depression was to seal the sense of their incredibility. The cheery optimism of Jack Spring, the sober integrity of Fred Layard, had been dramatic symbols for the old sentiment. They had stood for ambitions to live out lives grounded in values which by right would command for the miner happiness, prosperity, civic freedom and social cohesion. Then, there was War, and General Strike, and lock-out, and Depression, to brutally re-assert the facts of economic power and cause the individualist, Burtist ideologies to look at best the moral luxuries of a relatively stable bygone age, to look, at worst, capitalist lies spun to deceive. Fred Layard's son, who played preacher from the armchair whilst his MP father reformed the world, would find in later years that he trod Daddy's footsteps at the peril of his own anonymity – for Daddy had failed and the world was a different place.

For areas like the North East, Scotland, Lancashire and South Wales, the 1930s were to have a profound influence on the worker's view of himself – an influence which casts a long shadow on the minds of that generation even today. In some quarters the Jarrow Crusade is talked of as a 'victory'; a moral victory perhaps, but the sight of those gaunt faces looking even more pinched beneath wide-brimmed caps, tramping in step to mouth-organs to beg for work, should forever be a reminder of defeat. Where workers' banners, in a flap of crimsons, emeralds and golden tassels had once really proclaimed 'crusade', the Jarrow banner was a plain statement of appeasement. For the miner, the Cranky cockiness was an impossibility and the Jack Spring hope a shattered myth. Bored and frightened, those who had been unemployed for a long while only wanted work, and just what that might mean rested in confusion. Some looked to war:

> I don't know, war is horrible and a waste, but you get something to do and usually enough to eat, and you have friends with you and you feel you are of some use – but you're a bloody fool, really, because they don't really want you, and they don't really think you're a hero or they would not let you go on the scrap heap when it's all over.[23]

To the outsider this loss of confidence from a man traditionally celebrated appeared as a nullity. In 1936, John Newsom, desperately sympathetic to a once proud class, talks glowingly of the 'Surrey Appeal for Jarrow' and the Hertfordshire Appeal for Durham County', and in his eagerness to help, nullifies the very self-celebration that had enabled the miner to endure:

> No longer does the South countryman regard the miner in the words of an eighteenth-century writer as 'a rude, bold savage, apparently cut off from his fellow-men in his interests and feelings', or to quote a more recent author, 'a wild, drunken fellow with a whippet dog at his heels; a man who is a "hero" in a pit disaster and a coarse brute at all other times; a mischief maker, always on strike and against authority'. He has found that they are, in fact, men very like himself . . .[24]

Newsom was intent on drawing a contrast and naturally omits the Methodist romance; he was, nevertheless, wrong – as far as a single society can produce two different men, the London civil servant and the Durham miner were different. The 'South countryman' may indeed have dispelled his belief in the old descriptions, but for the miner, as we have seen, the image could reflect itself in the reality. Newsom's humanitarianism however, demands respect, even if his appeal plays fast and loose with reality. Ironically, what cannot be respected are those efforts during the period to portray the miner in the 'marxist' frame of 'social realism'.

II. Social Realism

> Geordie Shieldykes was the last of the shift to stagger home tonight. He swore all the way to keep his spirits up. The door of his house closed with a bang. That was how he wakened his dozing wife every night, for he made her serve him hand and foot whatever time it was . . .
>
> Great bleeding gashes glared on his arms and knees where the sharp fanged rocks had bitten and torn . . .
>
> She left him to soak while she poured out the tea . . . the pit of his stomach wallowed and he vomited between his knees into the tub.

This is how Geordie Shieldykes, on page ten of J.C. Grant's 1930 tale, *The Back-to-Backs*, makes his ideological bow on to the stage of pit mythology. Cranky and Spring had been artefacts it is true, but they had also found warrant, although unevenly, from some of the community they purported to typify. Shieldykes on the other hand was a monster spawned out of ignorance, and a pity for the working class that had soured into revulsion rather than matured into comradeship. It was a monster in which only the intellectual middle-class left could believe. If Cranky's workers were a bawdy bunch of cartoons, and Spring's – in Shaw's words – 'vaguely imagined as a huge crowd of tramplike saints', then Shieldykes's working class were hardly better than animals breeding in a capitalist 'jungle'.

> [at the coal-face] One could scarcely call it water because it was a compound of innumerable chemicals and human filth. Yet pitmen were grateful for it often enough when the heat became unbearable . . . Then they would drink the liquid out of their hands, or, if working on their bellies, suck it up with their lips. It was delicious, then (p. 88).

Grant's *Back-to-Backs* is worth closer study not because it is typical of left-wing views of the worker in the 1930s, but because it is the most extreme of the 'social realism' *genre* I have read, and thereby shows up facets of those views particularly pertinent to this essay. Moreover, it is worth investigation because it was accepted at the time by critics and labour politicians as a serious effort to describe the miner realistically, as he was. That they could do so speaks only of their ignorance; and their ignorance will reaffirm the role of myth and ideology in the history of the pitmen.

So, with the words of Liam O'Flaherty's Introduction in our ears, let us look at Geordie Shieldykes's colliery village of Haggar: 'But alas! it smells terribly of truth. It is the truth. It seems that every honest man, taking up a pen to write, must now tell in brutal fashion of the brutality of our economic governance. D. H. Lawrence, T.F. Powys, Rhys Davies, James Hanley . . .'

The social realistic world of Haggar is mapped for us, 'Is it to be wondered at that the lads from the banks of the sacred Wear called the place Haggar le Hell?' (p. 72). A hell-hole indeed; the main street runs from pit-head to graveyard and is forever shrouded in a dank mist; the first shift staggers home horizontally against a shrieking wind clinging from lamp post to lamp post. As they cling, rats leap from the gutters to sniff offal from their pockets – behind the rows looms the slag heap, moated by a swamp useful for the odd dead whippet or bastard child. Dante, the chip shopkeeper for instance 'had often been seen going to the swamps with a sack on his shoulder'. There was a railway, built for coal, out of Haggar to the Durham coast, but no one was sure where the passenger line was, and its use was mainly restricted to suicides. Death and accident defy happiness in Haggar: Geordie's conversation with his wife Jane is no brighter than, 'Ah well, it's something not to be dead. Maybe my turn will come. It was poor Mike Thompson's tonight'. And if death did not get you then accident or senility did. In the summer, when the sun shone:

> People she had never heard of or seen before were dragged out of dim corners and sheds for the duration of the sun's brief visit, blinking, white, often hideous creatures, to be packed away again for weeks, maybe months, maybe years . . . Witless no doubt, but she was often astounded to hear how relatively young some of them were. They did not speak or move; just sat there gazing at the gutter, helpless, childish, disgusting. Yes, men and women of the pit became old and rotten so quickly . . . How it drained the women! The shifts, the worry, the children seem to have taken everything except the bones with their covering of hard creased skin. Even the hair had gone . . . (pp. 201-2).

Miners' wives are grey waddling barrels of suffering:

> . . . a type of womanhood common to every pitman's hovel in Haggar. The pit stamped them all alike, like pennies at the Mint. Only when they were little children could one notice any difference between them . . . but soon enough they married and had bairns, and became more and more alike as time went on (p. 164).

'Permanent prostitutes', some of them knuckled under until widowhood and senility arrived, others behaved true to their social role and then the children suffered. Every night sobbing children stalked the neon lighting of Haggar's public house, waiting:

> . . . perhaps they knew how their drunken parents would kick them and beat them later on, for nothing. There were silent children too – thin, little, white faced creatures – crouching in the shadows of the walls, their eyes, like sheep's, full of bewilderment, sadness, terror (p. 48).

Geordie Shieldykes's family is an awful parody of Lawrence's Morels. Tom, the son, bears the same emotional-umbilical relationship with his mother, Jane, as Paul did for Gertrude, 'he loved her as passionately as he detested his father'. Tom is a quiet, sensitive lad, so unlike his brother Willie who shares a murderous relationship with father, but at least they recognise each other as father and son. Tom, by contrast, burns away any human acknowledgement – he looks at his father: 'His eyes and features took on a sort of animal ferocity. Then he turned towards his mother and, as he did so, it seemed as if he had torn an ugly mask from his face, for his countenance now suddenly beamed with infinite tenderness and affection' (p. 77). Jane and Geordie vulgarise Lawrence to the grotesque; is this an unhappy working-class marriage? 'And if her husband were actually dead, if he was removed out of her life altogether, she would miss him, but not as much as the crockery' (p. 84).

The men of Haggar do not love, they go into heat. Sex floats in the air like a disease; it strikes; the bowels tremble and chill, the legs go hot, the body flushes blood and soil, and in an instant relief must be sought: 'Tonight when I left the club I felt as if my whole body was burning. I often feel that way . . . Then I see women, and I've got to swallow hard and run for it. It's a mercy for me there's such a place as the heaps' (p. 173).

The heaps are the slag heaps which ply a nightly trade of prostitution and abortion; 'Why! I've only had half a dozen lassies, fat with bastards, during the last two weeks', speaks the consultant abortionist whose surgery is a shed, and who also has a side-line in pornography. The prostitutes are clown-painted fourteen-year-olds; 'If the Devil had explored the most vicious corners of Hell, he could not have discovered anything to compare with the vices and fornications practised nightly on the heaps of Haggar' (p. 272). A tempestuous virility is not only the pleasure of working-class men; the women, presumably before marriage shackles the storm, also share its cravings. Ailie, family friend of the Shieldykes, knows Willie to be savage, but the sight of his trunk-like thighs stepping out of the bath tub makes him a noble savage. He goes to the heaps, and that squalid knowledge excites Ailie into following him:

> Then a curious thing happened. Ailie got up from her seat slowly . . . Her appearance resembled a sleep walker's. She seemed to be acting unconsciously, as though under the influence of some unknown spiritual power . . . Something shone before her eyes – huge, violent, passionate, ecstatic, heaving with immense vitality, blinding her with its fiery whiteness. It flung itself fiercely about her like a sheet of pure white flame, scorching her with delicious agony. It seemed to suck up her blood with its terrible heat . . . her chastity, sexual tendencies, unmentionable cravings: the pure white flame absorbed them all and her separate existence ceased (p. 77).

Parallel with a natural virility, Grant retains the colliery ethic of manliness; an ethic that swelled the pitman's pride in the first half of the nineteenth century, the patriotic base to his radicalism, and the chorus line to his songs; an ethic which developed in Victorian England into self-help for collective amelioration: by 1930 manliness is back to horny-handed muscle again, but the Burtist intelligence has gone, so has the Cranky humour and the man is a brute. Grant's Willie Shieldykes is the old caricature Big Hewer warped by the new. His father says of him:

> He's going fast to the dogs is Willie. The best lad in the place, bar none, at hewing, football, quoits, or anything you like. I've done all I could to save him. Ay, kissed him, begged him on my knees, cursed him. Even fought him in the yard yonder till he nigh bashed my old face to pulp and I was on the ground with my arms round

> his shins begging him to give up the drink. But he just kicked me in the guts and left me lying half-dead till the missus found me moaning and bubbling like a bairn. Never mind, I loved him just the same (p. 73).

The Back-to-Backs is an appalling novel; it carries little story; it is more a ruthless panorama of ugliness and deformity with Tentergarth, the Nietzschean intellectual, significantly the only one with insight into its *raison d'être.* The author must have had artistic ambitions that transcended the mere recounting of fact, so twisted is that fact, but the point is that the dust jacket remarks hail the novel as a documentary piece and not an artist's impression. H.E. Bates thought that 'its fidelity to truth is implacable'; Philip Snowden, then Chancellor of the Exchequer, previously chairman of the Independent Labour Party, and author of books on socialism, thought the writer had 'undoubted genius'; Gordon MacDonald MP thought it 'a splendid work' and hoped 'it will have a large circulation, more especially among the non-mining community, where the need for such a book is evidently great'; and Charles Dukes MP thought it a testament to social realism:

> This book is fit to rank with Zola's *Germinal.* Its realism will no doubt shock the smug responsibility of those who think only of the working classes when industrial disputes arise. The book should be widely read of all who are interested in the improvement of the conditions under which workers live.

Sanity is thankfully restored with the remarks of Wright, MP for Rutherglen since 1922, and a pit lad at the age of twelve: 'Having read every novel dealing with mining I could obtain, I unhesitatingly vote this one the worst of all, and had I any responsibility I should destroy it. It is a filthy, false, and prejudiced book, a libel upon a fine body of men and women.'

Rather than destroy it one must try to understand it, and the kind of literary marxism in the thirties that spoke of dehumanisation and the end of culture at the hands of a decadent capitalism. By 1930 the cultural revolution which society had suffered during the nineteenth century had lost its impatience and its tenseness. The generations of workers whose turbulence had so upset bourgeois economic rationale had gone, the new generations were by then culturally – if not ideologically – attuned to the disciplines and mores of industrial capitalism. The working class, it may be remembered, are a phenomenon of capitalism and not socialism. Raymond Williams,[25] from a passage in D.H. Lawrence's *Nottingham and the Mining Country,* seizes on Lawrence's thesis that the 'din-din-dinning' of the new industrial culture had won his own generation to its material ways of thought. Williams takes this to understand the consequent mentality of the thirties: 'It thus became possible for men in such a position to believe, and with a show of reason to argue, that the residual majority, the "masses" had, essentially, got the way of life they wanted, or even, the way of life they deserved – the way "best fitted" for them.' Now, it is true that the victors write the history: that industrial capitalism came as a 'foreign' force, at first precarious, but then gaining economic and class strength enough to exterminate a popular culture, could never have happened, to read most late Victorian historians – and indeed, many afterwards. As Marx observed in volume I of *Capital,* the bourgeois 'begins *post festum,* with the results of the process of development ready to hand before him. The characters . . . have already acquired the stability of natural self-understood forms of social life, before man seeks to decipher not their historical character (for in his eyes they are immutable) but their meaning.' But in some way, to fully accept Lawrence's thesis of 'the whole material prosperity above all things' – and then to pose its opposite, workers who are not materialistic, brings us back to the sickly atmosphere of Jack Spring, workers 'vaguely imagined as a huge crowd of tramplike saints'. History does not allow us the prerogative to pick and choose its actors in such a manner; a working class that was not materialistic, that had not undergone 'din-din-dinning' would not be a working class. There is nothing 'natural' about history: to attempt to change it *is* history, and our right, but to merely wish it were something else is unrealistic.

The Back-to-Backs does neither. To call the people of Haggar 'beaten down' and materialistic is too kind: a brutal, rapacious capitalism has had the effect of making its miners as brutal and rapacious as itself. Geordie Shieldykes is not a man who, if history makes him – then he makes history; he is rather a waxen, *post festum* dummy in the hands of his environment. Grant uses the bourgeois apologetic, that the 'masses' had got what they deserved (as animals, a jungle), in the same a-historical way – but *inverts* that apologetic, and exaggerates the situation, in order to generate sympathy for them. Not surprisingly, politicians and authors with no knowledge of the mining community or its social history, responded with a sympathy essentially bourgeois because it patronised the worker as a pitiful creature who must be helped – just as observers a century previous had pitied him as a savage creature who must be feared. Out of the fear of government commissioners and coalowners had come the help, but later, by 1930 the plea was that if this is what uncontrolled capitalism does to men then it must be bad, the hideousness of Haggar serves the indictment. The Labour Party is assumed to be an immutable organisation that exists to bestow political philanthropy and help the working class; not an organisation that historically and ideologically, in its idea of social relationship, developed out of that class to help itself. Philip Snowden might have remembered that as he praised an author who libelled the very people who had funded his political career.

Ignorance before history, if not the law, can be a valid excuse; what is less excusable is the position of writers and critics to the left of Snowden who used his kind of interpretation to point in a different direction. Writing such as *The Back-to-Backs* supports Raymond Williams's view that 'marxist' intellectuals during the thirties displayed a barren disposition to history and the working class when, given their theoretical affiliations, they should have known better. Of course, the rubber truncheon threat of Fascism (a nightmare thread through Orwell's writings) in combination with unemployment and poverty was a sapid reminder of what might happen – but this fear was at once accentuated *and* the battle against it positively weakened by a dogma which stated that 'the history of all countries shows that the working class, exclusively by its own effort, is able to develop only trade union consciousness'. Carefully considered, Lenin's dictum is only marginally more optimistic than Grant's brutalised world of Haggar. The intelligence and nuance of Cranky as *Social Fool* is impossible amidst the collective crudity of the Shieldykes' mob. We are back to *the masses* who can only react and not think. Fear is accentuated because Fascism now equals Communism as a spectre haunting Europe; in crisis the masses will be fought for as if they are a bone lying prone between two dogs, and winner take all. The battle against Fascism is weakened because socialism is not so much regarded as primarily subject to the position and experience of the working class, but more as an objective force which transcends that experience to be brought to the class from outside. The depression in England was local; the high levels of unemployment were regionalised by geography and industry among heavy working groups regarded in more buoyant days as the classic proletariat, heirs to revolution. The effect was concentrated, so the English response to poverty and unemployment was essentially placid; socialism in its above form came in such circumstances as an intellectual proposition doomed to failure: as whole areas were laid bare, so the struggle was cut off and isolated and then the fight seemed elsewhere – factories were closing and even the owners seemed common victims of natural disorder; it was difficult to hate the young man from the means-test too much because he was only doing a distasteful job to avoid the queues of the unemployed. If there was a fight, then it seemed to be won or lost away from home, it certainly did not seem to be in debates about dialectical abstractions.

Fearful of the apparent nullity, the intellectual left only exaggerated it in their own minds, and worsened it as far as it existed, by marxist theories of a working class only capable, by their own experience, of 'economism'. As Williams observes, men then become masses to be captured – objects rather than subjects of power.[26]

And what power! its location may be by the trail of dehumanisation past the back-to-back squalor of Haggar and places like it, but this is where history has told us to look and look we must. Liam O'Flaherty's Introduction to Grant might warn us to pinch our noses against the stink of barbarity as we pass Haggar, but the smell is at least 'manly', of sweat, and the promise is that its barbarians – merely by accident of economic fate – hold the key to a greater civilisation:

> . . . the vitality of this modern world has fled the cottage, the villa and the boudoir. Power is in the shrieking, smoking, machine. It is a rough power, gaunt, raucous, bellowing, a spitting, swearing, violent power, but even so, it is more admirable in spite of its barbaric violence than the languid homosexuality and lesbianism which is the sole stock in trade of its alternatives.

III. Two Other Portraits

Not all the popular fiction of mining communities during the 1930s followed the ideology of social realism, though it remained the distinctive trend. A.J. Cronin's *The Stars Look Down* was first published in 1935 and had gone through eight impressions, including cheap editions, by 1939. Cronin does not entertain sentiment at the expense of a good story, but his characters are firmly grounded in the Liberal virtues and vices of high Victorian-Edwardian society. David Fenwick is the hero: a self-taught Northumberland miner, full of integrity with just a touch of passion, David becomes Labour MP for his coastal pit town of Sleescale. There are two villains: Richard Barras and Joe Gowlan – Barras declines as Gowlan rises, such are the times. Owner of Sleescale's Neptune Colliery, Barras had been a capable engineer and heroic entrepreneur during the hey-day of the 1880s. Enterprise muffled the engineering though, and his desperate pursuit of a dangerous seam ends in flooding and burial for a whole shift. A latent guilt festers on Barras's soul, and with the coming of War this once worthy man turns from a sleek, proud, ostentatious puritan into a hot-flushed and flag-waving patriot craving the sex he never had and the victory he fights at home. His tormented soul drives an ever more reckless course until his heart fails, a stroke ensues, and Victorian capitalism pays for the hypocrisy it always was. Gowlan, by contrast, drags himself up from the gutters of Sleescale. Unprincipled, deceitful, treacherous, Gowlan will create and seize the opportunity to 'get on' by any means he can. Impersonating a limp, Gowlan wheedles his way to a commanding position at Millington's armaments factory while other men (including the boy-scoutish owner) fight a war. A war profiteer by 1920, Gowlan goes on to be a Tyneside tycoon by 1930. He is a man of means, any means: the moral for the times is set when Gowlan buys out Barras's hapless but well-meaning son and takes control of the Neptune; David Fenwick loses his seat in Parliament and returns to hew, for Gowlan, at the colliery. The working-class hero has nothing but his honour; the cheapjack city slicker, out for quick profit and asset stripping, is the face behind the mask of the new capitalism. One can have no doubt of Cronin's message – thou shalt not covet Mammon from whence cometh our ills – when the novel ends as Gowlan becomes the Conservative MP for Sleescale:

> He was a king, he was divine, power illimitable was his. He was only beginning. He would go on, on. The fools beneath his feet would help him. He would mount to the heights . . . Peace and War answered his call. Money belonged to him. Money, money, money . . . and the slaves of money (p. 503).

One of those fools beneath his feet spits at David:

> 'You're beat, damn you', gloated Ramage. 'You've lost. You've lost everything.'
>
> 'Not everything', David answered in a low voice (p. 503).

The moral victory was Fenwick's, power belonged to Gowlan, but the reader is left in no doubt about whose will be the ultimate success. Empires founded on war profiteering and financial rackets will surely fall because, morally, they are rotten to the core; Gowlan must get his come-uppance; the fruit of victory so luscious to behold, will turn to ashes in his mouth. Cronin has witnessed the Depression, so he cannot share the Edwardian beliefs in progress, of society getting more enlightened and more prosperous in a decent sort of way for ever and ever. Richard Barras's stroke and eventual madness register Cronin's view of old-style capitalism, always latently schizophrenic, meeting its final crisis in the thirties; Joe Gowlan is the decadent cad who has replaced him; David Fenwick, in his honesty, represents the final synthesis. It is Cronin's moral persistence, his underlying deployment of individual behaviour at the base of the social condition, that grounds him in pre-war sensibilities. He is neither pessimistic nor callous. Progress still exists and it is soon to have its rightful inheritors.

Richard Llewellyn's *How Green Was My Valley*, first published in 1939 and running to thirty impressions in nine years, is the major mining novel to come out of the 1930s. It is about South Wales, not Northumberland and Durham, and writes of different traditions and different miners to those considered here. Its popularity however demands some historical perspective. As literature *How Green Was My Valley* is a hymn: a rich rolling language flooding across emotional hill and dale – as one reads one imagines knowing now of Welshness itself. Whilst Cronin is the story teller, Llewellyn is the poet: any page could be spoken as social poetry. The novel stands as a rebuff to the hard genre of its time. Llewellyn unashamedly wallows in nostalgia for a world before War and Strikes and Depression, for a lost world when men were noble, for a lost valley that once was green. He is in sorrow for the thirties, cannot face them, and ducks out to tell the tale of Huw Morgan who peers back over the brow of 1914 and down, down into the valley of his youth. Huw Morgan, like his creator, is aware, but unrepentant, of his failure to make sense of the new age; contemptuous of it, it is never mentioned; only memories of what have gone before make it bearable:

> Thirty years ago, but as fresh, and as near as Now.
>
> No bitterness is in me, to think of my time like this. Huw Morgan I am, and happy inside myself, but sorry for what is outside, for there I have failed to leave my mark, though not

> alone, indeed!
>
> An age of goodness I knew, and badness too, mind, but more of good than bad, I will swear. At least we knew good food, and good work, and goodness in men and women.
>
> But you have gone now, all of you, that were so beautiful when you were quick with life. Yet not gone, for you are still a living truth inside my mind.[27]

These words come at the end, but Llewellyn's first words declare, with a sadness that chokes, Morgan's intention to retreat from a place he once loved but which has since changed. The Valley he knows, as opposed to the Valley he remembers *is* the 1930s, and his decision to leave it is one man's response to the new nullity that seems to confront him: 'I am going to pack my two shirts with my other socks and my best suit in the little blue cloth my mother used to tie round her hair when she did the house, and I am going from the Valley.'

Shieldykes, Fenwick, Morgan; three miners of the inter-war years; creations and creators of three ideological mythologies – left realism, Liberalism grown-up, halcyon days before. That Shieldykes finally strangles himself; that Fenwick gathers up his honour in defeat; that Morgan slips away with his best suit and memories bundled together in the little blue cloth, are endings which, in their tragedy, tell us that the miner in image had come of age since the careless nascent days of Cranky, the Panglossian days of Spring. By 1939 no one is grinning, few are cocky, and the nonconformist romance is over; Morgan's mother mourns the death of her husband:

> 'God could have had him a hundred ways', she said, and tears burning white in her eyes, 'but He had to have him like that. A beetle under the foot . . .'
>
> 'If I set foot in Chapel again, it will be in my box, and knowing nothing of it. O, Gwil, Gwil, there is empty I am without you, my little one. Sweet love of my heart, there is empty.
>
> Well.'

IV. Kiddar's Luck and Kiddar's History

For the unborn miner of course, it was all a matter of luck. Born in Benwell in the year of Trafalgar he would suck his milk in the house of an élite group of workmen. He would grow up in a subculture that celebrated him as a 'character', that nurtured him as born to be a pitman – nothing else would do. Seizing his manhood with the pick in

1826, one year after trade unions were legalised, he was to know vast upheavals in his status and culture, but it was unlikely that the old Bob Cranky hedonism would ever leave his all-too-fleshy lips. Many would try to wipe them clean but their efforts can be best measured by generations. If those to come were not to know his privations, neither would they know his mettle.

Born in Murton, one of the new East Durham collieries, in the year of the Exhibition (1851 was also, significantly, Religious Census year), the babe would live to know a more stable age than his grandfather. By the time he was a hewer, class lines were entrenched, society's bourgeois-industrial future was guaranteed, and forces that had once been seen as ideological hucksters or worse were now developing institutional respectability. The cultural revolution was not yet finished, but Forster's 1870 Education Act had sealed its success, and indeed, most colliery communities in the two counties had known serious 'education' since the 1850s. This miner was no longer part of an élite; massive expansion in a labour-intensive industry had drained away much of the former notoriety and sense of exclusiveness. Jack Spring's respectable promise however, beckoned hopes of a new élitism – self-help towards water pipes, gas pipes and piety.

The grandson of this Murton collier, according to his luck could well have been born in 1892, year of the famous Durham lock-out. A portent of his future he would be hewing by Triple Alliance whispers only to be swept away by greater alliances into French fields. A world fit for heroes greeted this Durham lad with wage cuts and strike in 1921, seven months' lock-out in 1926, with only unemployment and poverty to follow. If he had taken Spring's promise, and lived to see 1933, then surely he must have considered it broken. Though never a Shieldykes, and only by fits a Morgan, his self-image was confused in the way a worker's without work must be – probably Orwell's impression of the fatigue and apathy in the Lancashire coalfield of 1936 is as good an impression as we have. And from this, in fear of its prospects do we get Grant's Haggar and Llewellyn's Valley.

Cranky was a celebration, Spring was an ideological hero and Shieldykes was an ideological freak but all of them lend insight into three epochs in English social history. Cranky and Spring were strong images and had *historical impact* as suspensory atmospheres in the divide between class and class. If class is an economic and social relationship, then class consciousness is born of that relationship. The popular songs of Tyneside were set in styles by men who were not pitmen or keelers but whose image of what it meant to be a pitman or a keelman was, in the main, embraced by them as – if not the truth – then as lending a suitable atmosphere to the truth. Manliness as a self concept was a lot more sordid in 'the truth' than the popular fantasy of it, but when radicalism harnessed it to Paine and made it a *responsible* brawn, then miners like Hepburn were on their way to a class consciousness capable of transcending both the brutalised 'truth', the popular fantasy *and* political abstractions to find personal repercussions in an altogether nobler sense of his own manhood. As we have seen, the National Miners' Association in 1844 similarly took traditional manly-mythology and sought to turn it into a reality more responsible and enlightened. Radicalism's gambit had been the ancient one according to free-born Englishmen; the NMA centred their re-education round the traditional importance of the coal trade – originally popularised in squabbles between the London rich and the Newcastle rich over the latter's monopoly tendencies. The union caught the rebound to propagate an early notion of labour value, self-pride as workers indispensable to the economy, as men without whom fashionable Barts and effete ladies would shiver. That the 'Son o' the Tyne' myth was mixed in with consciousness, giving a regional rather than a class dimension, probably blinded the local leadership to the facts of an industry rapidly expanding nationally, leading them to overestimate the North East's position. Indeed, the following year, in 1845, the coalowners implied their recognition of this by abandoning the monopolistic Vend after a chequered career of 135 years.

The NMA systematising identities that were already there – born out of former relationships – and giving them a new turn to meet new economic realities. Methodism, on the other hand, came breathing blood and fire against the old values, created its own myths, and, *a priori* tried to form a new consciousness. Partly sincere, and partly to polish the haloes of its own saints, Methodism presented a lurid atmosphere of savage pitmen and their ways. This atmosphere was conceived by the tramping preachers in a religious relationship, but they were the unwitting apostles of what was to become the mores of working class 'respectability' – a social relationship. Reading the directories, traveller's descriptions, 'histories', government reports and colliery managers' evidences of the 1830s onwards, one can see just how far the Methodist myths had penetrated: the pitmen are an unruly bunch indulgent in a vicious way of life and efforts must be made to 'ameliorate'. Methodism is universally praised, not for its religious gut, which is often sneered at, but for its 'moral' work in making the miners a more sober and orderly class – bringing them into a right relationship with society rather than with Jesus. Of course, the ameliorators had their own sincerities, but the atmosphere originally conceived as the divide between God and Man became a constituent of the divide (and therefore the relationship) between class and class. For the local-preacher pitman, respectable in his poverty, this atmosphere nursed his feelings of superiority over his fellow workers, but it also sharpened his class sensibilities towards, in his eyes, a decadent and filching ruling class. If drunken pitmen were immensely wicked then so were the aristocrats who made no pretence at sobriety: the similarity between the lumpenproletariat and the high aristocracy is a long-lived observation in the English labour movement. The bourgeois view of things was to set up Parliamentary commissions and statistical enquiries to get the facts, and then act on those facts in the light of their own neuroses about rape and violence, and the legend of the pitman as a dangerous, uncivilised *enragé*: the facts could be fair but the atmospherics of class relationship dictated how they were to be read.

By the turn of the nineteenth century Methodism had added some new trinkets to its rosary. The old gaudy ones were still there, but men like Thomas Burt, Joseph Arch and John Wilson were fine new ones of considerable taste. Reading Wilson's autobiography, one cannot help but wonder to what extent the old man confused his life story with Bunyan and Jack Spring. He trod a stout road though, too stout in fact, for what was a minority career became emblazoned in Methodist ideology as, to greater and lesser degrees, a general one. The pit boy to politics hall of fame, forever upwards and in linear progression, signified a continuity in the mythology winning consensus enough to deceive serious historians by 1917. Sidney Webb in 1921, Welbourne in 1923 and Wearmouth in 1937, writing of the miners, must be tempered by an appreciation that they too casually accepted the atmospherics of class rather than the substance (though they are themselves 'realities' and a part of that substance). 1930 penury, depression, disillusion and the Shieldykes' impact has, I hope, been given some meaning in this chapter.

History only exists in the writer's pen: it is not a sovereign quantity somehow trailing out behind us like a great winding-away into the distance. The past has been but it lives only as much as society is aware of it. Society itself is created by crises of power, class and economically defined; but what style crisis takes, and how society emerges afterwards depends on how men, and classes, see themselves –

and *that* is an *historical feature*, stemming from the writer's pen, the singer's voice, the preacher's exhortation. Fact, myth and image, are grit to the oyster; and when the shell is broken, consciousness is the pearl, or the stone. If this is true of the past then it is also true of the future: there is no future but what we make it.

It was said earlier that for the unborn miner, whether he became Cranky or Spring was only a matter of luck. And so it was, but he might have been other things, and that was not luck but class structure – and *there* is the history and the future:

There were plenty of golden opportunities going that night. In palace and mansion flat, in hall and manor and new central-heated 'cottage', the wealthy, talented and beautiful lay coupled – welcome wombs were ten-a-penny, must have been. What do you think I picked on, me and my genes, that is? Missing lush Sussex, the Surrey soft spots, affluent Mayfair and gold-filled Golder's Green, fat Norfolk rectories, the Dukeries, and many a solid Yorkshire village, to name only some obvious marks, I came upon the frost-rimed roofs of a working-class suburb in Newcastle-upon-Tyne, and in the back bedroom of an upstairs flat in a street parallel with the railway line, on which a halted engine whistled to be let through the junction, I chose my future parents. There, it was done. By the time that engine took its rightaway and rolled into the blue glare of the junction arcs, another kiddar was started, an event, one might add, of no novelty in that quarter and momentous only to me.[28]

That is, only to him and to us.

REFERENCES

CHAPTER ONE

1. Raymond Williams, *Culture and Society*, Pelican, 1968, pp. 99-119. In social history there were always marvellous (and honorary) exceptions to my general observation: particularly E. P. Thompson's *The Making of the English Working Class*, London, 1963, meant a lot to me and my 'generation' of students – a brilliant work which moves with a pace and a low thunder which has shifted the whole balance of English social history. As I write, things are changing very quickly indeed towards a 'people-based' history. Ruskin College History Workshops and their regional co-operatives have been crucial here, and Raphael Samuel must have earned himself journeyman's status with his superb ' "Quarryroughs": life and labour in Headington Quarry, 1860-1920. An essay in oral History', *Village Life & Labour*, London, 1975.
2. Sir Richard A. S. Redmayne, *Men, Mines, and Memories*, London, 1942, p. 8.
3. George Parkinson, *True Stories of Durham Pit Life*, London, 1912.
4. For a detailed and perceptive look at this kind of difficulty see: Stephen Yeo, 'On the Uses of "Apathy" ', *European Journal of Sociology*, No. XV, 1974, pp. 279-311.
5. B. Trinder, 'Religious Tracts as Sources of Local History: Some West Midlands Examples', in the *Local Historian*, vol. 10, no. 3, 1972, suggests another similar source both in its virtues and vices.
6. C. J. Sharp, *English Folk Song, Some Conclusions*, London, 1965, p. 20 (first edition 1907). I am indebted to the introduction by M. Karpeles.
7. A. L. Lloyd, *Folk Song in England*, Panther, 1969, (first edition London, 1967). A heroic, *tour de force* of a book; essential reading for anyone.
8. A. L. Lloyd, p. 318.
9. This would be anathema to Sharp! In his campaign to introduce folk songs into schools he saw them as vanguard in the fight against popular music – people 'will instinctively detect the poverty stricken tunes of the music hall and refuse to be captivated and deluded by their superficial attractiveness', C. J. Sharp, p. 173.
10. John Bell, *Rhymes of Northern Bards*, Newcastle, 1812.
11. Sir Cuthbert Sharp, *The Bishoprick Garland, or a collection of legends, songs, ballads &tc. belonging to the county of Durham*, London, 1834.
12. Cuthbert Sharp, preface. Cuthbert Sharp collected many of his songs orally, and it is as well to remember A. L. Lloyd's warnings that the methods and devices of such men were a long way from the sophistication of Cecil Sharp's.
13. Newcastle Society of Antiquaries, *Northumberland Minstrelsy*, Newcastle, 1882.
14. David Harker, *Introduction*, in John Bell's *Rhymes of Northern Bards*, Newcastle, 1971, reprint.
15. Cuthbert Sharp, op. cit.
16. John Bell, 1971 reprint, p. 106.
17. David Harker, 1971 reprint, p. xliii.

18. David Harker, 1971 reprint, p. xliv.
19. David Harker, p. liii. Bobby Nunn, 1808-53, was a Newcastle slater forced like so many into part time entertaining after a bad accident. He toured concerts, benefit clubs and ladies' boxes by evening and worked as a labourer during the day. Ranking with Corvan, Ridley and Wilson in popularity, he was the first.

    Edward Corvan, 1830-65, was a Liverpool Irishman whose home was Newcastle. He was the first known artist of the area to combine the writing and singing of local songs into a full time profession.

CHAPTER TWO

1. Unless stated otherwise, the songs quoted are from John Bell's *Rhymes.*
2. William Mitford, *The Budget*, 1816.
3. John Selkirk, 'Bob Crankey's 'Size Sunday', in John Marshall's *Northern Minstrel*, part 2, 1807.
4. *Tyne Mercury*, 1 June 1814.
5. From *Allan's illustrated edition of Tyneside Songs*, Newcastle, 1891, Newcastle 1972 reprint with introduction by D. Harker, p. 187. The Amphitrite was one of the more famous of the river's brigs, two hundred and twenty one tons, she was built in 1776 at Shields.
6. From *Allan's* (1891 edition), p. 155. Allan's 1872 edition notes the author as anonymous, but reckons the song a pay-night classic from Wrekenton pitmen of 1820s.
7. *Allan's*, p. 256.
8. HO/28/9. Petition of seamen in Admiralty correspondence, January-March 1793.
9. G. A. Williams, *Artisans and Sans Culottes*, 1968, p. 105.
10. James Morrison, in *Marshall's Chap-Book*, 1823.
11. James Morrison, The Newcastle Noodles, in *Marshall's Collection*, 1827. 'Archy' refers to Archibald Reed, then Mayor of Newcastle.
12. Anonymous, in *Marshall's Collection,* 1827. Purported to have been written during the trial of Queen Caroline in 1820.
13. In *Allan's Tyneside Sons.* Unless otherwise stated all the songs quoted henceforth are from this collection. First published in 1862, *Allan's* collection ran to six editions with amendments by 1891. The work made a deep scoop of Tyneside songs for the whole century, though most of the songs I use here are from 1840s to 1860s. *Allan's* was reprinted in 1972 with a good introduction by David Harker.
14. Thomas Wilson, 'A Glance at Polly Technic', 1843. Robert Emery, 'Baggy Nanny; or, the Pitman's Frolic', 1842.
15. Amazingly, two popular amateurs were still entertaining with such stuff in the 1880s. George Barron's 'Bill Smith at the Battle of Waterloo', and J. A. Stephenson's 'Hawk's Men at Waterloo'.
16. John Lee, *Wrestling in the North Country*, Consett, 1953, p. 88.
17. *Monthly Chronicle of North-Country Lore and Legend*, Newcastle, 1890, vol. 4., pp. 110-14.
18. *Monthly Chronicle*, 1888, vol. 2., p. 80.
19. *Monthly Chronicle*, 1890, vol. 4., pp. 100-14.
20. Quoted from J. L. & B. Hammond, *The Skilled Labourer*, London, 1919, p. 19.
21. Anonymous, 'The Pits and the Pitmen', n.d., p. 20.
22. Quoted from A. L. Lloyd, *Folk Song in England*, Panther, 1968, p. 379.

23. A. L. Lloyd, p. 364.
24. Sir Richard Redmayne, *Men, Mines, and Memories*, London, 1942, p. 18.
25. There is a wealth of evidence on this. Suffice to recommend a look at the 1842 *Children's Employment Commission*, Evidence and reports of Leifchild and Mitchell; and a listen to *The Big Hewer*, a *Radio Ballad* by Ewan MacColl and Peggy Seeger, Argo Record Company, RG538. mono. Also A. L. Lloyd, op. cit., pp. 317-412.
26. David Douglass, *Pit Life in Co. Durham*, 1972, History Workshop Pamphlets, Number 10.
27. William Whellan, *History, Topography, and Directory of Northumberland*, Manchester, 1855, p. 133.
28. Eneas Mackenzie, *An historical, topographical, and descriptive View of the county of Northumberland*, Newcastle, 1825, vol. 1, pp. 208, 209.
29. *The Report of the Newcastle Religious Tract Society for the year 1817*, p. 24.
30. J. R. Leifchild, *Children's Employment Commission*, 1842, part 1, p. 514.
31. William Whellan, *History, Topography, and Directory of the County Palatine of Durham*, Manchester, 1856, p. 83.
32. Assize Records at the Public Record Office: ASSI/45/38. Coal Trade Committee Minute Books: letter, Potter to Buddle, 8 June 1812.
33. *Miners' Advocate*, 27 January 1844. There were tumultuous strikes in the area in 1831 and 1844. The owners made a deliberate point of publishing how well the blacklegs, many formerly agricultural labourers, did at hewing. They also smirked on how all the old talk about being bred to pitwork was so much myth. This is very doubtful as to accuracy, but the fact remains that the owners were aiming at the core of solidarity, and they knew it.

CHAPTER THREE

1. *Children's Employment Commission*, 1842, part 1., pp. 503, 671.
2. *Miners' Advocate*, 23 March 1844.
3. Darlington Primitive Methodist Circuit, *Account of monies and members*, 1837-48.
4. Edward Chicken, 'The Collier's Wedding; A Poem', Newcastle, 1778 (5th edition).
5. Thomas Wilson, 'The Pitman's Pay; or a night's discharge to care', 1830, Gateshead edition.
6. Bridal favours, p. 111; Bridesmaids, p. 113; Nosegays, p. 118; Saluting, p. 140; Winning the Kail, p. 153; Bride Ale and feasting, pp. 149-50; Wedding pipes, p. 160; 'Throwing the Stocking', p. 171; Eating Sack Posset, p. 174; vol. II, 1849 edition.
7. *Newcastle Magazine*, 13 September 1826. Chicken's poem appeared as a chapbook, Wilson's firstly in instalments in the *Magazine*, and then in all manner of cheap publications. Wilson's remark is interesting in view of the welter of pitmen songs then in existence. Wilson was an authentic self-help hero; he had started life as a trapper boy and ultimately became a wealthy and respected merchant.
8. These were customary reasons for celebration and taking the day off work, e.g. first cuckoo heard; a gaudy day would be called to celebrate a fellow miner's engagement.
9. *Monthly Chronicle of North-Country Lore and Legend*, Newcastle, 1889, vol. 3., p. 445.
10. Rev. R. Warner, *A Tour through the Northern Counties of England and the Borders of Scotland*, London, 1802, 2 volumes, p. 305.

11. Eneas Mackenzie, *An historical, topographical, and descriptive View of the county of Northumberland*, Newcastle, 1825, volume 1, p. 203.
12. Mackenzie, p. 202.
13. Mackenzie, p. 204.
14. R. Wilson, *The Coal Miners of Durham and Northumberland: their Habits and Diseases, a paper read before the British Association for the Advancement of Science, at Newcastle, September, 1863*, pp. 7-8.
15. John Sykes, *Local Records; or, Historical Register of Remarkable Events,* 1833, Newcastle (1865 edition), vol. 2, p. 166. The parade had taken place in 1823.
16. *Monthly Chronicle*, 1887, vol. 1, p. 43.
17. *The Diaries and Correspondence of James Losh*, vol. 1, Diary 1811-1823. Edward Hughes (ed.), The Surtees Society, vol. CLXXI, 1962.
18. The account is a compound of the newspaper reports of: *Tyne Mercury*, 24 July 1821; *Newcastle Courant*, 21 July 1821, *Newcastle Chronicle*, 21 July 1821. Quotes used are from the *Tyne Mercury.*
19. *A Complete Collection of original Newcastle Coronation Songs,* published by John Marshall, 1822, Newcastle.
20. *Tyne Mercury*, 24 July 1821.
21. *Newcastle Courant*, 21 July 1821.
22. *Newcastle Chronicle*, 21 July 1821.
23. It may have only been a minor incident, but the ideological interpretation of the day's events remained an issue for nearly twenty years. In 1838 Thomas Hepburn, the great radical and miners' leader, told an estimated 70,000 at a suffrage meeting in Newcastle that 'When George the Fourth was crowned, the men of Newcastle were to be seen feasting on beer and beef, provided for them by the tyrants. Now they were met for another purpose – a purpose that would make the tyrants tremble with fear.' *Northern Liberator*, 30 June 1838.

    Notice the shift in the radical position: by 1838 it accepts that the multitude *had been* swinish – but of course this was not the case *nowadays!*
24. Thomas Oliver, *A New Picture of Newcastle Upon Tyne*, Newcastle, 1831.
25. HO/42/22. (October-November 1792). Cochrane to Dundas, 20 Nov. 1792.
26. HO/42/22. (October-November 1792). Rowland Burdon to H. D., 20 Nov. 1792.
27. *Second Report from the Select Committee on Accidents in Coal Mines: with the Minutes of Evidence taken before them.* 1854. James Mather, 1652, p. 99.
28. *Primitive Methodist Magazine*, 1879, pp. 243-4.
29. Rev. James Everett, *The Walls End Miner: or a memoir of William Crister*, Halifax, London, 1835, p. 78.
30. John Wilson, *Memories of a Labour Leader: The autobiography of John Wilson J.P., M.P.,* London, 1910, p. 201.
31. Taken from Clowes's Journal, in Rev. H. B. Kendall, *The Origin and History of the Primitive Methodist Church*, London, 1905, vol. 1, p. 54.
32. J. W. Fawcett, *Memorials of Early Primitive Methodism in the County of Durham, 1820-29*, Durham, 1908, p. 34.
33. Rev. John Petty, *The History of the Primitive Methodist Connexion from its origin to the Conference of 1859*, London, 1860, p. 341.
34. Rev. H. B. Kendall, op. cit., p. 371.
35. *Primitive Methodist Magazine*, 1883, p. 496.
36. ibid., 1849, p. 698.
37. ibid., 1847, p. 457.

38. ibid., 1841, pp. 310-11.
39. ibid., 1841, pp. 464-5.
40. George Parkinson, *True Stories of Durham Pit Life*, London, 1912, p. 10. Parkinson was an eminent Wesleyan, talking here of the 1850s.
41. Obituary of Edward Thompson, in *Primitive Methodist Magazine*, 1834, p. 32.
42. Rev. W. Walters, *The History of the Newcastle On Tyne Sunday School Union: from its formation, to the close of its fiftieth year*, London, 1869, p. 124.
43. Walters, pp. 3-4.
44. Walters, p. 5.
45. *Primitive Methodist Magazine*, 1847, pp. 257-8.
46. This edition published at Alnwick in 1840. A very thin, poor quality, chapbook price 2d. Songs are interspersed with tiny and serious-minded woodcuts illustrative of the verse.
47. This style is still, in literal form, being preached in some Methodist sunday schools. The author recently attended one at Wigan Independent Methodist Sunday School Anniversary, where the guest speaker actually used puppets to illustrate his talk to the children sitting up before the congregation.
48. Walters, op. cit., p. 86. 1818 Report.
49. Walters, op. cit., p. 231. 1833 Report.
50. Walters, op. cit., p. 110. 1820 Report; p. 185. 1828 Report; p. 188. 1828 Report; p. 248. 1835 Report.
51. Walters, op. cit., pp. 104-5.
52. *A Plan for establishing a Repository of Cheap Publications on Religious and Moral Subjects*, Manchester, 21 March 1795.
53. *The Report of the Newcastle Religious Tract Society for the year 1817*, Newcastle, 1817, p. 17.
54. *Report*, p. 13.
55. R. G. Bouyer, *A collection of Papers relative to the Northumberland Lending Library for the Poor*, Durham, 1823.
56. E. Mackenzie, *A descriptive and historical account of the town and county of Newcastle Upon Tyne including the Borough of Gateshead*, Newcastle, 1827, vol. 2, p. 573.
57. *Report of the Commissioner* appointed, under the provisions of the act 5 and Vict. c. 99, *to Inquire into the Operation of that Act, and into the State of the Population in the Mining Districts*, 1850, p. 52.
58. From, *Report of the Commissioner* appointed . . . *in The Mining Districts*, 1847.
59. From, *Report of the Commissioner* appointed . . . *in The Mining Districts*, 1851.
60. HO/44/18. Wm. Coxon to Peel at Home Department, 2 May 1828.
61. Richard Carlile, *A Respectful address to the inhabitants of Newcastle Upon Tyne and its vicinity*, Newcastle, 1834.
62. Evidence of Francis Place, from *Report from the Select Committee on Education in England and Wales; together with the Minutes of Evidence*, Appendix, and Index. 1835, p. 70. 804; p. 69. 791; p. 70. 800.
63. *Children's Employment Commission* 1842, part 1, p. 518.

CHAPTER FOUR

1. *Miners' Advocate*, 13 July 1844.
2. *Report of the Commissioner* appointed . . . *in The Mining Districts*, 1846, p.8.

Dr Wearmouth's books are the fullest accounts of the Methodist role: *Methodism and the Working-Class Movements of England 1800-50*, London, 1937. *Some Working Class Movements of the Nineteenth Century*, London, 1948.

Sydney Webb's *The Story of the Durham Miners*, 1921 (Labour Publishing Co. Ltd.) pays an extraordinary act of homage, past and present, to the Methodists in Durham civic life. Webb himself became a county MP for Seaham soon after – it may have affected his sense of objectivity, but at least he was in a position to know.

3. *Wilful Murder of M. Pearson, at Castle Eden*, 3 February 1843. A broadside, extracted from a newspaper.
4. *Copy of Verses on the Castle Eden Tragedy*, 1843, (Sunderland).
5. *Report of the Commissioner* appointed . . . *in the Mining Districts*, 1847, p. 9.
6. ibid., p. 8.
7. Evidence of William Willis, age 15, driver of South Hetton: *Childrens Employment Commission*, part I, p. 163.
8. *Primitive Methodist Magazine*, 1857, pp. 394-5.
9. George Parkinson, *True Stories of Durham Pit Life*, pp. 10, 14.
10. Percival Stockdale, *A Remonstrance against inhumanity to animals*, Alnwick, 1802.
11. A. Watson, *A Great Labour Leader; the life of Thomas Burt, M.P.*, London, 1908, p. 71. The speaker is Thomas Burt of Northumberland.
12. 'Incumbent in the Diocese of Durham', *A Few brief Observations, Illustrations, and Anecdotes respecting pitmen in a northern colliery village*, Sunderland, 1862, p. 13.
13. P. E. H. Hair, *The Social History of British Coalminers 1800-1850*, p. 290 (unpublished Oxford Ph.D. thesis, 1955).
14. Morris Smith, 'Victorian Music Hall Entertainment in the Lancashire Cotton Towns' in *The Local Historian*, 1971, vol. 9 no. 8.
15. HO/45/644. From depositions of the victims.
16. *Miners' Advocate*, 24 February 1844.
17. *Newcastle Journal*, 20 April 1844.
18. ASSI/45/63. Depositions taken for the Northumberland Lent Assizes, 1833.
19. When Lord Londonderry evicted his workmen, two thirds of the Durham Primitive Methodist circuit became homeless. See E. J. Hobsbawm, *Labouring Men*, London, 1968, p. 26.

    Also, from Darlington Primitive Methodist Circuit; Account of monies and members for 1844: 'The above number had tickets left, but a vast number of them had not met of a considerable time, but lest they should complain that we had taken advantage of dismembering them during the pitmen's strike we kept them in to give them an opportunity of continuing'. (the Methodist 'ticket' showed current class membership).
20. See 'Literature as Propaganda: The Coal Miners' Unions, 1825-1845', in, Martha Vicinus, *The Industrial Muse: A Study of Nineteenth Century British Working-Class Literature*, Croom Helm, 1974. Professor Vicinus' literary study usefully touches on many of the general themes of this work.
21. Unless otherwise stated, all the songs quoted are from a collection in Wigan Public Library.
22. This was clearly resurrected from a song of 1831, 'Dialogue between Peter Fearless and Dick Freeman'.

    A. L. Lloyd reckons the tradition of Dialogue in order to explain was inherited from old folk balladry. His chapter on Industrial Songs in his

Folk Song in England is an invaluable contribution from a man both musician and historian. Probably the most famous of the crop of explanatory dialogue songs from 1844 is William Hornsby of Shotton Moor's 'The coal-owner and the pitman's wife . . .', 'Good morning, Lord Firedamp', this woman she said'.

23. *Miners' Advocate*, 27 January 1844.
24. *Miners' Advocate,* 24 August, 1844. 'The Miners' Doom' was written by Henderson Fawcett, a miner of South Wingate. It could be sung to the tune of 'Misletoe Bough'.

CHAPTER FIVE

1. HO/40/30/2. Letter, Bouverie to Phillips, 12 April 1932.
2. Anon. 'The Pits and the Pitmen', n.d., p. 29.
3. See J. U. Nef, *The Rise of the British Coal Industry*, London, 1934, vol. 1.
4. This has by no means gone today. A novel of 1946, *The Earth Beneath* by Harold Heslop follows the tradition of historical novels about mining by casting 'womenfolk' as grey, colourless creatures only occasionally putting a word of 'feeling' in between the long rough gorges of men's conversations. Women are mere incidentals to a life for Men, and Jenny, after her last rebuke, can only summon an – ' "All right, all right," she said softly, wiping a tear from her eye with the corner of her apron.' (p. 107).

   John Newsom's *Out of the Pit. A challenge to the comfortable*, Oxford, 1936, quotes a twenty-three year old SW Durham miner, unemployed since 1932, as feeling an awful sloth in his uselessness, 'Lots of us need hardening, physically and underneath we'd like to feel we were of some importance.' There is just a hint of what this lost pride in his physical strength and social significance could lead to: 'I read a book the other day about the way Hitler has dealt with the unemployed. I think there's something in it.' (p. 25).
5. HO/42/7. The writer is anonymous.
6. J. R. Boyle, *The County of Durham*, London, 1892, p. 111.
7. *The Report of the South Shields Committee appointed to investigate the Causes of Accidents in Coal Mines* . . . 1842. Appendix no. 4 to Report from the Select Committee on Coal Mines; together with the Proceedings, etc., 1852, p. 160.
8. *Report from the Select Committee of the House of Lords appointed to inquire into the best means of preventing the Occurrence of Dangerous Accidents in Coal Mines* . . . 1849, p. 159. 1521.
9. G. A. Cooke, *Topographical and Statistical Description of the County of Durham*, London, 1824, p. 54.
10. *Childrens Employment Commission*, 1842, part 1, p. 667.
11. George Parkinson, *True Stories of Durham Pit Life*, London, 1912, p. 16.
12. Jack Lawson, *A Man's Life,* London, 1949, pp. 46-7.
13. Robert Edington, *An Essay on the Coal Trade with strictures upon the various abuses now existing,* London, 1803, p. 7.
14. HO/65/2. Circular of 20 May 1818.

    Norman McCord ('The Seaman's strike of 1815 in N. E. England', *Economic History Review*, 1968, second series xxi.1), found this popular gratitude very strong among all classes but shipowners on Tyneside in 1815.
15. William Whellan, *History, Topography, and Directory of Northumberland*, London, 1855, p. 136.
16. Alexander Barrass, *The Pitman's Social Neet*, Consett, 1897, p. 30.

17. *Miners' Advocate*, 9 March 1844.
18. *Durham Chronicle*, 10 March 1832.
19. *Miners' Advocate*, 24 February 1844. Letter from LATE TRAPPER BOY, whose letters were welcomed and given wide coverage by the editorship.
20. A leaflet, *To Irish Blacklegs*, reprinted from the *Northern Star*, 1 June 1844.
21. *Miners' Advocate*, 21 September 1844.
22. *Miners' Advocate*, 13 January 1844.
23. HO/40/42. Reported speech of George Binns.
24. Shadon's Hill report, the *Miners' Advocate*, 20 April 1844. Black Fell report, *Newcastle Journal.*
25. *Miners' Advocate*, 4 May 1844.
26. ibid.
27. A broadside address, *A Few Friendly Words to the Pitmen of Durham and Northumberland by one who is well acquainted with them*, 1844.
28. From Sydney Webb, *The Story of the Durham Miners*, 1921, (Labour Publishing Co. Ltd.), p. 47.
29. Robert Forbes, *An Essay on the Abridgement of the Hours of Labour in Mines, Pits, &c.* Holytown Miners' Prize Essay (Coatbridge), 1844, pp. 14-15.
30. From Rev. James Everett, *The Walls End Miner: or a memoir of William Crister*, Halifax, London, first edition 1835, p. 31.
31. Rev. H. B. Kendall, *The Origin and History of the Primitive Methodist Church*, London, 1905, vol. 1, pp. 220-21.
32. *Primitive Methodist Magazine*, 1825, pp. 213-15. Journal of Nathaniel West.
33. From Sam Smith, *Anecdotes and Facts of Primitive Methodism,* 1872, in H. B. Kendall, p. 222.
34. Thomas Cooper, *The Life of Thomas Cooper, written by himself*, London, 1872, p. 174.
35. Rev. Joseph Parker, *A Preacher's Life, an autobiography and an album,* London, 1899, pp. 55-6.
36. HO/40/9/5. Letter, 22 March 1817 to Sidmouth.
37. Rev. John Petty, *The History of the Primitive Methodist Connexion from its origin to The Conference of 1859*, London, 1860, p. 62.
38. Petty, p. 215.
39. HO/42/105.
40. Jacob Ralph Featherstone, *Weardale Men and Manners*, Durham, 1840, p. 45.
41. Joseph Ritson, *The Romance of Primitive Methodism*, London, 1909, p. 268.
42. *Primitive Methodist Magazine*, 1857, p. 445.
43. From, Rev. H. B. Kendall, vol. 1, pp. 222-3.
44. From, Rev. H. B. Kendall, vol. 1, pp. 32-3.
45. *Primitive Methodist Magazine,* 1870, pp. 423-7; 1894, pp. 391-2.
46. *Report from the Select Committee on Inquiry into Drunkenness, with minutes of evidence and appendix,* 1834, pp. 53, 571.
47. *The Primitive Methodist Hymnal compiled by a committee appointed by the Conference of 1882.* In the author's possession 1,052 hymns from the 'Christian Life' to 'The Future State' for young Eastwood to follow its dedication: 'I will sing with the spirit, and I will sing with the understanding also', (1 Cor. XIV. 15).
48. From, Rev. H. B. Kendall, vol. 1, p. 371.
49. Rev. James Everett, *The Walls End Miner*, 1835, p. 133.
50. Robert Southey, *The Life of Wesley and the Rise and Progress of Methodism,* London, 1820, – for a supremely intelligent description of this and

other features of Methodism to a contemporary.
51. Rev. W. Walters, *History of Newcastle Sunday School Union,* 1869, p. 155. From SSU Reports for 1818-20.
52. E. Mackenzie, *An historical . . . view of the county of Northumberland,* 1825, pp. 205-6.
53. William Andrews, editor, *Bygone Durham*, London, 1898, p. 261.
54. J. R. Featherstone, *Weardale Men and Manners,* pp. 47-8.
55. *Primitive Methodist Magazine*, 1824, pp. 58-61. Report of Thomas Batty.
56. *Primitive Methodist Magazine*, 1870, pp. 246-8; 1849, p. 641; 1870 pp. 423-7.
57. Rev. James Everett, p. 27.
58. Everett, p. 66.
59. Rev. W. Brown, *Centenary of Primitive Methodism in Hetton Circuit,* Durham, 1923; Rev. J. Broadbent, *A Sermon, embracing Counsels to Converts, street singing, theatre preaching, Total Abstinence, and male and female evangelists*, Sunderland, 19 April 1868.
60. Rev. Joseph Dawson, *Peter Mackenzie. His Life and Labours*, London, 1896, pp. 58, 269.
61. Dawson, pp. 321-2.
62. Dawson, p. 330.
63. Dawson, p. 321.
64. Sir R. A. S. Redmayne, *Men, Mines and Memories,* London, 1942, p. 29.
65. Percival Stockdale, *A Remonstrance against inhumanity to animals, and particularly against the savage practice of Bull Baiting,* Alnwick, 1802, p. 24.
66. *Monthly Chronicle of North-County Lore and Legend*, Newcastle, 1889, vol. 3, p. 55. The feast was in celebration of the Duke of Northumberland's successful exclusion of Alnwick from the Municipal Reform Act. A course which the town radicals had opposed.
67. E. Mackenzie, *A descriptive and historical account of . . . Newcastle Upon Tyne*, Newcastle, 1827, vol. 2, p. 82.
68. HO/42/197. Letter, Chas. Thorp to Phillips. 25 Oct. 1819.
69. HO/42/197. Letter. John Buddle to Rev. H. Phillpotts, 25 Oct. 1819.
70. HO/42/201. Letter, Reed to Sidmouth, 15 December 1819.
71. HO/42/197. *Declaration and Rules.*
72. James Losh to Lord Grey, 19 November 1819, in Edward Hughes, *The Diaries and Correspondence of James Losh,* vol. 1. (The Publications of the Surtees Society, 1962-3).
73. Thomas Percival Bunting, *The Life of Jabez Bunting*, London, 1859, vol. 2, p. 167.
74. HO/42/199. Letter, Reed to Sidmouth, 20 November 1819.
75. *The Northern Reformer's Monthly Magazine, and Political Register,* January 1823, vol. 1, no. 1.
76. *Northern Liberator*, 6 December 1839. Winlaton's iron men had an awesome reputation for 'physical force' radicalism stretching as far back as 1816.
77. From R. K. Webb, *The British Working Class Reader 1790-1848,* London, 1955, p. 96.
78. G. A. Williams, introduction, *Banner Bright*, editor J. Gorman, London, 1974, p. 7.
79. A *Plan* of itinerant NMA lecturers for January 1844 exists at Wigan Public Library, 'Pitman's Strike Collection'.
80. Newcastle Temperance Society committee, *Newcastle as it is; reviewed in its Moral Aspects, Social State, and Sanitary Condition,* Newcastle, 1854.
81. 'Probably the most famous temperance activity of the coalowners (including

Lord Londonderry, the Earl of Durham, the Bearpark Coal Co., Love and Pease) was the attempt to start the British Workmen's Public Houses. These would offer "all the advantages of drink taverns without the drink". The Shakespeare British Workman was inaugurated in Durham North Road ... in March 1874.' R. Moore, *Pit-men, Preachers, and Politics*, Cambridge, 1974, p. 83. Moore's work represents an important contribution to the history and sociology of community.

82. *Northern District Temperance Record,* July 1838.
83. *Record,* February 1838.
84. *Record,* May 1839.
85. *The Northern Temperance & Rechabite Almanack . . . 1843 . . . being the Seventh Year of the Reign of her present Majesty; the Eighth of Rechabitism; and Ninth Year of Teetotalism,* Newcastle, 1844.
86. *Northern Temperance Advocate,* July 1843. Arguments favoured at a Nottinghamshire Primitive Methodist meeting on the question.
87. There is a discussion of Owenism in its working-class context by Eileen Yeo, 'Robert Owen and Radical Culture', in S. Pollard and J. Salt (eds.), *Robert Owen; Prophet of the Poor*, London, 1971, pp. 84-114.
88. *Report from the Select Committee on Inquiry into Drunkenness, with minutes of evidence and appendix*, 1834, p. 321. 3817, evidence of John Finch.
89. The phrase is Prof. John Vincent's – see his *The Formation of the British Liberal Party 1857-68,* Pelican, 1972. His work opens out some challenging and original channels of thought.
90. Vincent, p. 101.
91. *Monthly Chronicle of North-Country Lore and Legend,* Newcastle, 1889, vol. 3, p. 131.
92. Programme, National Liberal Federations, *Annual Meetings held at Newcastle Upon Tyne,* 30 September – 2 October 1891.
93. Jack Common, *Kiddar's Luck,* 1951, (1971 reprint), pp. 189-91.
94. For a fuller discussion of this see my forthcoming article in *Past and Present,* ' "Oh Happy English Children" Coal, Class, and Education in the North East', November 1976, No. 73.
95. *Prefatory Minute of the Committee of Council on Education relating to a manual of Vocal Music,* 1840-41.

CHAPTER SIX

1. *The Guardian,* 4 February 1974.
2. Ramsay Guthrie, *The Old Folks at Home. The Romance of the Aged Miners,* n.d., London, p. 181 (1919).
3. An eloquent account of the general ideological shift in attitudes towards the English northern working class from the 1870s onwards is given in, G. Stedman-Jones, *Outcast London. A study in the relationship between classes in Victorian Society,* Oxford, 1971, pp. 1-16: '. . . when Chartism declined the industrial north assumed a more genial countenance. For it was in the north that working-class institutions embodying self-help, sobriety, and religious dissent developed to their greatest extent in the the period after 1840. When Victorian writers and politicians began to extol the growing morality of the working class, they drew their mental imagery from the small towns of Lancashire and the West Riding.' p. 11.
4. R. A. S. Redmayne, *Men, Mines, and Memories,* London, 1942, p. 30.
5. For the domination of late century working class *Dialect Writing by* domestic subject-matters, see: M. Vicinus, *The Industrial Muse*, Croom Helm,

1974, pp. 208-25.

6. I am grateful here to Sid Chaplin's superb essay 'The Plush-Lined Ghetto', in *A Tree with Rosy Apples,* Newcastle, 1973.
7. Ramsay Guthrie, *Kitty Fagan: a romance of pit life,* London (1901).
8. *Wesleyan Methodist Magazine,* 1908, pp. 864-9.
9. *Primitive Methodist Magazine,* 1921, pp. 252-6.
10. Cranky as an authentic self-celebration, and the Cultural Revolution which opposed it, represented a real dialogue between cultures and classes. Chapter 6 is only a general survey after the initial engagement – it does not continue the close dialogue for the late nineteenth and twentieth centuries. To test the authenticity of the Burtist archetype and the validity of its dialogue, twentieth-century forms of working-class associational life need continued study and interpretation: some suggested areas for observing the effect of capitalist conditions on culture would be the Home, the Cinema, the School and Sport – particularly Association Football and Rugby League. Trade unions and public houses (although probably without the intimacy of their forbears), remain important areas, chapel and religion do not, and the Seaside Holiday would be an important new area.
11. Rev. J. Christie, *Northumberland: its History, its Features, and its people,* Carlisle, Newcastle, London, 1904, p. 110.

    It is worth remembering that the Cranky image took a long time to fade away. A full-blooded example of the bourgeois myth was during Thomas Burt's evidence to the select committee in 1866: asked how miners spent their 'Pay Saturday' Burt replied that some liked to drink –

    They do not drink champagne in your district on that Saturday?

    No, they are not champagne men. (*Report from the Select Committee on Mines*. 1866, p. 13).
12. E. Welbourne, *The Miner's Unions of Northumberland and Durham,* Cambridge University Press, 1921, p. 256.
13. S. Webb, *The Story of the Durham Miners,* 1921, Labour Publishing Co. Ltd., p. 24.
14. S. Webb, p. 145.
15. J. L. and B. Hammond, *The Town Labourer 1760-1832,* London, 1917.
16. Edward Thompson's *The Making of the English Working Class,* London, 1963, in its general conceptualisation of English social history draws heavily on the Hammonds.
17. Hammonds, p. 284.
18. Hammonds, p. 285.
19. R. F. Wearmouth puts the combined Methodist influence in 1850 at two million people (*Methodism and the Working-Class Movements of England 1800-1850,* 1937, p. 16). But K. S. Inglis balances this figure somewhat by pointing out that two million was a tenth of the total population, and the largest Methodist body, the Wesleyans, had the lowest proportion of working-class adherents. (*Churches and the Working Classes in Victorian England,* 1963).
20. Sam Emery, from a talk given by him at Murton, in November 1973.
21. B. R. Mitchell and P. Deane, *Abstract of British Historical Statistics,* Cambridge, 1962, pp. 115-19.
22. Mitchell and Deane, p. 121.
23. Interview with a S. W. Durham miner, from John Newsom, *Out of the Pit. A challenge to the comfortable,* Oxford, 1936, p. 66.
24. John Newsom, pp. 83-4.
25. Raymond Williams, *Culture and Society 1780-1950,* Pelican, 1968, pp. 202-3.
26. Raymond Williams, p. 275.

27. Richard Llewellyn, *How Green Was My Valley*, London, first published in 1939 (1967 edn.), p. 376. For a view of Richard Llewellyn as an essentially reactionary writer see: David Smith, 'Return to the Natives', in 'Miners and the Coal Culture', *New Edinburgh Review*, no. 32, March 1976: 'I suppose if something big had been written once, then something bigger it has to be when you do it again, for good old boys they were, those that read my book, and are gone. All gone.

'And green they were, yes, but please Thee, Lord God, green, greener they may be now.'

Thomas Hepburn (1796-1864) was leader of Northumberland and Durham miners during strikes of 1831-2. A convinced radical, he was prominent in the Newcastle Chartism of 1837-9.

28. Jack Common, *Kiddar's Luck*, 1951 (1971 reprint), p. 7.

INDEX

C3